G000230473

verticaleditions.com

A PROPER FOOTBALL EDUCATION

To Brian

Enjoy the read

White Army

[signatures]

MARK PATTERSON

WITH KEVIN O'HARA

VERTICAL
editions

First published in the United Kingdom in 2021 by Vertical
Editions, Unit 41 Regency Court, Sheffield, S35 9ZQ

VERTICAL
editions

www.verticaleditions.com

Follow us on Twitter:
@VerticalEds

Cover design by Sam Turner

ISBN 9781908847256

A CIP catalogue record for this book is
available from the British Library

Printed and bound by Jellyfish Print
Solutions, Swanmore, Hants

CONTENTS

Mark Patterson, born and bred in Darwen; a local boy who set off on his career at Blackburn as a feisty and skilful player, and was no shrinking violet! He gained the admiration of senior players and management in his early days and he could not only make and score a goal with his footballing ability, he could also look after himself for a diminutive five-foot-six wide player.

On many occasions down at Pleasington playing fields, where we trained in those days, we had to separate him from his opposite full-back as Paddy had given as much as he'd got, and sometimes a little bit more, when trying to win the ball back. It was probably something we secretly admired, even though it was against his teammates and they often ended up needing to be separated. Paddy had a fine career - not quite getting a full house in trying to play for all the Lancashire town teams, but not far off.

Derek Fazackerley, ex-Blackburn Rovers

When apprentices were real apprentices, every job within the football club was assigned to them - from sweeping the terraces after a home game to cleaning every pair of pro's boots. These modern-day scholars don't even lift a finger when it comes to kit, boots or changing-room cleanliness. There are staff to do it all for them. The world has gone mad when it comes to instilling discipline, respect and professionalism in the modern game. I still believe the old values are the best values. They certainly stood me in good stead.

David Lee, ex-Bolton Wanderers

Paddsta was a great teammate and you could always guarantee one thing with him – you would always get 110 per cent. He worked his bollocks off in training and never slacked in games either, even at times I might have had to help him with his pints!

Don Hutchinson was at Sheffield United at the time as well and was always throwing around nicknames; and poor Paddy got some terrible stick about his ears. We used to say he could hear everything that was being said with ears like those! But the banter we had between us lot of players was different class and it was always in a great manner. Paddy stayed at my place a few times after we all used to get out together and it saved him driving home. I can only sit here and smile and laugh to myself about those, but it's all laughs and giggles!

A top bloke and a top teammate, who was always there for you if you needed anything, and a great professional. He was a hard-working midfielder who worked his socks off in the middle of the park, and we had a great laugh together. All I can say is, some stories can never be told.

Dougie Hodgson, ex-Sheffield United

PROLOGUE

HE'S DEAD

August 17, 2002

The charity golf competition at Worsley Marriott Golf Club had been a great success, and also a welcome break from all the shit that was going on in my life. I had a real thirst on and was more than ready for a few beers after my round. I'd left my phone in the car so, as I came off the 18th, I headed to the car park to retrieve it.

I was keen to check whether any of the lads had left messages to see if I would be going out later on. *Is the Pope fucking Catholic?* It would be a no-brainer anyway. By this point, my main escapism from my mounting financial debts was to go to the pub. Me and Lindsey had been split up for a few months so when I checked my phone and saw that I had around 20 missed calls from her, I knew that it must be something serious. Instinctively, I thought something must have either happened to our daughter Jade, who was 15, or 13-year-old son, Scott. Every parent's nightmare.

Lindsey seemed to take ages to answer when I called her back. More time for me to be thinking the worst. *What's happened? Please nothing serious.* Me and Lindsey may have gone our separate ways, but I still adored my two kids. "Mark?" she eventually answered.

"Yeah, what's happened?" I asked. Everythin' all right?" I knew, deep down, that it couldn't be.

"No, it's your dad. He's had a heart attack..."

"What?!"

My dad had just had his 60th birthday 10 days earlier, but he was still as fit as a fiddle and working a few shifts for my younger brother, Sean, after recently retiring from his warehouse job.

Lindsey wasn't sure of his condition, but told me he had been rushed to Bolton Royal Infirmary. So I chucked my clubs and golf shoes in the boot of the car and set off to the hospital. I hoped I'd get there and see him sat up in bed, having been given a scare. Surely it could only be a scare? I couldn't contemplate anything worse. Dad had been there for all of us through thick and thin, working his arse off to put money on the table every week. He was now enjoying himself, working with our Sean; doing a bit of building work, kitchen fitting and joinery. All the things he liked to do in his spare time anyway.

On the way to the hospital I tried to call Sean and my older brother, Tony. Both were permanently engaged. "Come on, come on," I said to myself. "Get off your fuckin' phones and ring me. Tell me dad's going to be ok." My mind was working overtime.

I put my foot down. I haven't a clue what speed I was doing; I just wanted to get there and see my dad, and make sure my mum was okay as well. God, what must she be thinking? They'd been together 40-odd years. Then, my phone rang. It was Lindsey.

"Mark?"

"Yeah," I said.

"He's dead."

"What?"

"I'm sorry, your dad's dead."

All I could do was repeat the question. "What?" Then silence. I couldn't take in what she had just told me. Dead? Numbness. *Dead?* I couldn't muster a reply. My head was in bits. How I didn't run up the arse of the car in front of me, I'll never know. After flying up the M61, no doubt smashing the speed limit, I was suddenly crawling along in the inevitable traffic jam coming off the junction. Me and Lindsey spoke some more, but I can't remember anything else we said.

The phone rang again and this time, it was Jade on the other end. She was heartbroken, struggling to understand what had happened to her grandad. I was trying to be the strong one, attempting to console her, like any father would to his daughter, but it was no good.

The tears were flooding down my face and I could barely get a word out. I remember the traffic trickling past and people gawping at me.

God knows what they were thinking, but it really didn't matter. I was trying to calm Jade down, with the few words I could muster. He wasn't just a brilliant dad; he had also been a brilliant grandad as well.

I made it to the hospital car park and quickly abandoned my car. As I was running towards A&E, our Sean walked out in front of me. "He's gone, Mark," he said. "He's gone."

We hugged, then he walked me to the room where my dad was, explaining on the way what had happened. Sean and dad had been working on a new build and my old fella had started to feel a bit short of breath. He'd gone outside, quickly followed by Sean and sat down, holding his chest. Dad then fell forward. Sean had run across to him, but he reckoned dad was dead before he hit the floor. A neighbour with a bit of first aid knowledge had tried to resuscitate him, but couldn't bring him back.

When I walked into the room, dad was still lying on the resuscitation table, looking like he was having one of his 40 winks following a hard day's graft. This time, though, he wasn't going to wake up and have one of my mum's brews. The man who I had looked up to as a little kid, who had been there all through my career, good times and bad, was right in front of me. But now I would never get the chance to thank him for everything he had done for me.

This amazing man, along with my mum, had brought us up to have respect and good manners. He'd got up between four and five in the morning, day-in and day-out, year after year, to go out and do long distance lorry driving before finishing off working in the warehouse. He looked after me, my brothers, and his wife, who he adored, so well. But now he was dead.

After his funeral, I went off the rails with the booze even more. I was earning a crust playing at semi-pro level and in the process of gaining my UEFA coaching badges. I really wanted to stay in the game as I really didn't have anything concrete to fall back on.

I had a little bit of experience in landscape gardening, after setting up a business while I was at Bolton Wanderers, and was also attempting to build up my property portfolio. It was going to be my backup should my managerial career fail. For the following few years, I continued playing, bought and sold a couple of houses, coached, and managed a couple of non-league clubs.

I also worked for my mate, Ash Reece, in the building trade for a while. Ash really came to my aid when I was out of work, giving me a job and allowing me to rent the flat above the office for a nominal amount. It was also supposed to be a deterrent to any burglars but if anyone had broken in, I don't think I'd have been in any fit shape to do anything about it.

This is when my boozing hit the peak. Following another piss-up I staggered through the door, fell into the bathroom, and sat on the side of the bath. I knew I was in trouble, financially and mentally. My boozing was just covering the cracks and I knew it had to stop. I was at my lowest ebb that night. I had a good talk with dad in heaven, and vowed to sort my life out. I was getting deeper into debt and by 2007 I finally had to declare myself bankrupt.

How the hell had I ended up where I was? In 1995 I had achieved every schoolboy's dream and made it to the pinnacle of English football, playing in the Premiership for Bolton. I'd played against Blackburn Rovers, my boyhood team who gave me my professional debut, and beat them, even though they were the reigning Premiership winners and had Alan Shearer. I had captained Bolton. I had scored in the top-flight against Liverpool at Anfield. I moved to Sheffield United, under the great Howard Kendall, and was on over £100,000 a year, plus win bonuses. That's a great enough salary these days, so imagine what it was worth 25 years ago.

Now though, I didn't even have my own pot to piss in.

I have managed to turn my life back around now and wanted to write this book both for my mum, who kept us in line and brought us up at times in circumstances that would drive any normal person mad, and in memory of my dad. Also, for my family and friends, and anyone who fancies having a look into the ups and downs of an old school professional footballer.

Dad, I hope you read this from above with that big smile on your face!

1

WHERE IT ALL BEGAN

1965 to 1975

I was born and bred in Darwen, a little mill town near Blackburn that is just about as Lancashire as it gets. Think whippets, flat caps, massive mill chimneys billowing out thick grey smoke and narrow cobbled streets, and you have a picture of how Darwen was pre-war. And for a while, post war too.

By the early 1970s most of the mills were closed and the chimneys became redundant. One by one they would be painstakingly demolished. I remember the steeplejacks scaling these monsters and, brick by brick, smashing them down. Fair play to them, it wasn't a job I could have done. I was definitely no Fred Dibnah. I still get a twitch in my balls when I look out of my bedroom window now, as I've never been one for heights.

So how did I get to the stage where, by the age of 15, I was good enough to represent Lancashire under-19s, play for Blackburn Rovers A team regularly on Saturday mornings, get the shit kicked out of me playing for a men's team in the afternoon and even make my debut for Rovers' reserves?

My mum and dad were always unbelievably supportive, providing the boots and balls and running me all over Lancashire every Saturday and Sunday. My childhood mates and my great training partner that lived straight across the road from me, a large mill wall that thankfully still hadn't been knocked down, were all a big influence on my career.

Ever since I was a little boy, I'd had a football at my feet. When I was five, I got an orange and black 'Striker' football for Christmas. It was as light as a balloon and would move all over the place when you kicked it. On the first day back at school following the Christmas holidays, I sneaked the ball into school in my school bag. Don't ask me how, but I did!

As soon as the bell rang for playtime, I was out in the playground with my ball. Straight away, it was like bees around a honey pot. There were 30-plus kids chasing the ball around the yard until Mrs. Houghton, my class teacher, stormed out and confiscated my favourite Christmas present, giving me a right bollocking at the same time.

You couldn't take footballs to school in the infants and now I knew why. There were casualties everywhere, grazed elbows and knees. Mrs. Houghton had my prized possession, and I didn't think I would get it back. I didn't care for her very much at the time but at the end of the day, she returned my ball to me. Not before giving me a lecture, though. *"Yes, Mrs. Houghton..."*

There may have been no footballs allowed in the infants, but that didn't stop me playing every single day. I was brought up in Lloyd Street, a long row of terraced houses running off Blackburn Road. Our side of the road was known as the rough side, and still is. But what it did have was that large mill, right opposite my house, which was perfect for my early football education. When me and my brothers got fed up with playing games or fighting each other, I would grab my ball, trot out the front door and instantly become my boyhood hero Peter Barnes, the great Manchester City left winger. I'd stay out, hitting the ball against the mill wall, for hours on end, either until mum shouted me in for tea or it went dark.

I'm a lot thinner on top now, to say the least, but back then I had long blond hair like my hero. I tried to emulate his style and even used to dream that I was him. Knowing how much I was obsessed with football, compared to my brothers, my mum and dad would let me come back downstairs at night and watch the football on *Sportsnight,* hosted by the late, great David Coleman.

Mum and dad sent us to bed every night and normally we would piss about for 10 minutes or so and get the usual bollocking off my mum, who told us to get to sleep or we would have no TV for a week. As soon as Tony and Sean nodded off, if footy was on I was allowed to creep downstairs and watch it. Unfortunately, if either of them couldn't get to sleep I had to stay in bed. I can honestly say there were times I cried my eyes out if I missed a game; such was my love for football.

Over the next few years, I honed my skills against that big, ugly mill wall, striking it with the laces, inside of the foot, outside of the foot, using the rusting dark blue drainpipe as a target. I would miss it more often than not, but it was never going to get the better of me. I would also practise chipping the ball on to the kerb on the other side of the road as well, controlling the successful ones that popped up to me on my chest or knee. Or, more often than not, retrieve the unsuccessful ones.

Hundreds of times a day, bang, bang, bang, bang, I hit that mill wall. Kathleen and John from the next door up were okay with it and didn't mind the constant thuds. They had older kids themselves, which I think helped. But the miserable bastard next door down was a right moaning old fart. "Piss off" were his favourite words. In fact, come to think of it, I think they were the only words he ever said to me.

I remember one day, for some reason, he was out of order with my mum. When my dad came home from work and found out what had happened, he went out, quick as a flash, banging the grumpy bugger's door down. The neighbour answered and before my dad had a chance to grab him, he pulled a blade out. Dad came back pretty shook up and we kept our distance from him after that. He definitely wasn't a full shilling.

By the age of eight I had progressed to playing footy in the back alleys; one-v-one or three-v-three or 'three goals and you're in the nets', depending on who turned up. It was soon apparent that the practicing against the wall had paid off. I could hold my own with all the older lads, on the back alleys around Preston Street, Snape Street and Greenway Street which became our stomping ground for years.

By now I was in the juniors at Avondale Primary School, where we could play footy during the breaks, and my talent was soon spotted by Mr. Crowther, the sports teacher. Not just because all I did outside the classroom was play football, but also because my mum got the weekly food shopping from his parents' grocery store.

Old Mr. Crowther would drop the groceries off to our house every Friday night and from time to time it would be his son. He saw me banging the ball against the mill wall and would comment on my dedication. When I got into the primary school team two years younger than the rest of the boys, it wasn't because of favouritism. The fact I had been playing football most days since I was five probably helped, and I can remember my debut for the school team like it was yesterday. I was a substitute against St Francis Primary School from Blackburn, and Mr. Crowther put me on in the second half. I was eight, playing against 10-year-olds, but I held my own and started every single game after that.

I loved it. The only thing that I felt a bit uncomfortable with was how girls, even then, would flock around the older boys after a football game. I was a bit shy to start with, but I soon got used to it! But it was an early lesson in how being good at football would get the girls going after you, even if you weren't blessed with film star looks, although later in my career I would be likened to a few film stars: Gizmo from the *Gremlins,* Yoda from *Star Wars*, Galen from *Planet of the Apes* and Gollum from *Lord of the Rings.* Yes, I took some shit, but it was all part of the dressing room banter.

Another added bonus of making the school team was getting to play on grass alongside Steve Eggleston, my teammate from the streets. Eggy, as he's known around the Blackburn and Darwen area, went on to play over 1,000 games in the local men's leagues on Saturdays and Sundays and was a fiery little bugger on the field, who could mix it with anyone when he needed to. You didn't play that many times in the Blackburn Combination without having something about you and we have a great laugh now talking about our football escapades. No matter what level of football you play, there's always a story. And Eggy has loads of them!

On one occasion, he didn't use his head. Or rather he did, which ended up with a visit to the dentist for the unfortunate opponent and a big dentist's bill for Eggy. His missus, Gill, was well pissed off. And when she got pissed off, you kept well away. In fact, you still do. But he was always there for me when I needed him, and still is, through the good times and, more importantly, the bad.

Back in the day, though, all we were bothered about was playing football together, either in the school yard, school team or in the back alleys. Eggy's younger brother Mick, who tragically took his own life in his early 20s, would join us every night and weekend to pick sides and play in the alleys. I'm still friends with another lad who came along, Andy Young, and the games were always very competitive and aggressive. Many a time you'd be unceremoniously smashed into a neighbour's back door, but then you knew your turn would come and the revenge would be sweet. There were times when there would be a bit of handbags, dummies would be spat out and you might take your ball home the odd time. But we always returned for more the next day.

Totally different from today. We'd been let out every night and weekends from before we were old enough to go to school. As long as we kept to the local back streets, we were fine. Can you imagine that now? By the time I was 10, the reins were loosened a little and I was allowed a bit further afield. Still, Avondale playing fields, on the other side of the busy Blackburn Road, were supposed to be out of bounds because there had been a number of accidents in the past; one where our Tony had had a lucky escape, but also a more tragic accident where a young child had been killed. If my mum knew we played there all the time, I'm sure I would have been given a clout and not been allowed out for a long, long time.

Mum also watched me play every home game. By the time I was in year five I was already the best player in the school, and the Darwen area, for above my age, and she was very supportive and encouraged me no end. By this time, my dad still hadn't had the chance to watch me play in a game. He was a lorry driver, which meant he would work for up to 10 hours a day and sometimes longer and although he may not have been able to watch me during the week, he more than made up for it at the weekend; especially every other Saturday when he would take me down to Ewood Park to watch our beloved Blackburn Rovers.

I have so many fond memories of standing on the Nuttall Street enclosure with my dad. The 1974/75 promotion season from the Third Division stands out, especially the game against our promotion rivals Plymouth in the February of that season. The manager was Gordon Lee and my favourite player, Ken 'Beamo' Beamish, was our centre-forward. Plymouth, our main rivals for the title, had recently beaten us at Home Park, so it was a massive game. They brought 5,000 fans all the way up north and when they went 2-0 up, the noise from the away end was unbelievable.

I was just a few months short of my 10th birthday but remember what happened next like it was yesterday. The mood in the crowd was sombre and when Don Martin blazed a penalty over the bar, everyone thought that was that. Plymouth fans had already been goading Rovers' supporters anyway, and the penalty miss made it even worse. Fighting broke out all over the place.

It was nothing new, and I had seen it loads of times before. Back then, fans of either side just paid at any turnstiles and you would often get a group of opposing fans deliberately paying to get in a home team's section of the ground, looking for a fight. This was no different, and skirmishes were breaking out all over the ground.

On the pitch, Beamo scored a header just before half-time to change the mood and give us a bit of a chance. I don't think anyone could have predicted what happened next and the second half is still the best 45 minutes I have ever seen at Ewood Park as we scored four more goals to win 5-2. The roar as the goals went in was unbelievable and the record shows that there were just under 15,000 fans in attendance. What a game and what a season as we went on to become champions and make it to the Second Division. More importantly, I had memories forever with my old man.

The first time he watched me play for Avondale, I was really excited and wanted to show him how good I was. Watching me dribble past two, three, four players and scoring a goal really did surprise him. Me? I was just being Peter Barnes.

***

In my last year at Avondale, I was chosen to represent Blackburn and

Darwen junior schools and met a lad from Blackburn who was a real player. Being honest, I was a bit jealous because he took a bit of my limelight. He was as good as me, if not better, and I didn't like it. My competitive streak was already coming out by now. It was a lad called Ian Walsh, known as Tank because of his physique.

He was a big boned central midfield player, with a sweet left foot and great in the tackle. Put both of us together, with his attributes and my agility and trickery, and you would have had a top player on your hands.

Both Tank and Eggy were also superb players, and both could have been professionals. But despite all their talent, neither made it. Tank was taken on by Bolton as an apprentice, but was advised to lose a few pounds by his manager. Probably due to the pressure and fear of not making it, he went too far the other way and became anorexic, which cost him any chance of a future as a professional. He was more than good enough to have had a great career, too.

One Blackburn lad that did have everything as a footballer was Mark Brennan, who was a year younger than us, but as strong as an ox. He played with us in the Blackburn and Darwen town team and signed apprentice forms for the great Bobby Robson at Ipswich, playing over 200 games in midfield for them. Mark went on to play for amongst others, Middleborough, Manchester City and Oldham.

What was the difference between me and them? It may have been natural ability but without doubt my parents' support, that mill wall and my willingness to practise, practise, practise, against it and my friends played a massive part in me fulfilling my dream to play professional football for my hometown team. Only a few years later, at Cold Blow Lane, did I encounter another Millwall – which wasn't quite so welcoming!

2

SCHOOLBOY FOOTBALL

1976 to 1979

Now 11 years old and in secondary school, after one of the hottest summers on record, I was playing more football in a month than some overpaid, injury-prone Premier League players now play in a season. Morning, noon and night, seven days a week, I was either practising, playing with my mates, or playing for a team. When I wasn't playing, I would be on the Rovers with my dad and mates.

Me and Tank were selected for trials for the Blackburn and Darwen town team, the next step up for us both against over 40 lads from other secondary schools in the area. I was really keen to show how good I was but as we were getting changed, I realised I was going to have a problem. I'd forgotten my bloody boots. As usual in Blackburn, it was pouring it down and the surface was unbelievably slippery. But I was determined to get selected, so slipped my pumps on.

It didn't affect me. The first time I got the ball, I ran past four or five players and smashed it into the net, before skidding to a halt and heading back to the centre circle. One of the coaches noticed my footwear. "Where's your boots?" he shouted to me. I thought I was in trouble. "Sorry sir, I forgot them," I replied. He started laughing. "Well, I don't think you need them, do you?"

Me and Tank both made the cut and played together for the district team all through school. I had also started playing every Saturday for a local side, Park Lane Rangers, after my mum saw an advert in the newspaper from the manager, Keith Whiteside, who was looking for new players. My dad took me down, I absolutely loved it and by the time I was 11, I was holding my own in the under-14s side. Looking back, playing against older boys from such an early age definitely helped my development as I was getting kicked and knocked about, and had to learn how to deal with that. I was only knee high to a grasshopper, but my speed of thought and tenacity started coming through from an early age.

At that time, it was probably every little boy's dream to play for his hometown team and I wanted to make my dad proud. Luckily for me, all that practising against the mill wall, and man of the match performances for the school and representing Blackburn and Darwen under 11s, had got me noticed. During the six-week holidays I went to visit my mum's sister, Aunty Jean and cousin Michael, who lived in the Cotswolds. Whilst I was down there a letter had dropped through our door, addressed to Mr. and Mrs. Patterson, with a Blackburn Rovers stamp. When I returned home, my mum had a grin as big as a Cheshire cat on her face.

"Mark, there's a letter for you here," she said. I didn't suss that she knew where it was from. A letter for me? I was just hoping I wasn't in the shit and it wasn't a letter from school, as I wasn't always the best behaved. I looked at mum, who looked at me, then I looked at dad. "Go on, open it then son."

I looked at the front of the envelope and spotted the Blackburn Rovers Football and Athletic Club stamp on it. I quickly ripped it open and started to read. It was an invitation to attend trials at the training ground, at Brockhall. I looked back up at mum and dad. I'll never forget the proud look on their faces. "Well done son," dad said. "You might end up playing for the first team one day."

It was a dream come true. To get selected for trials at a professional club in those days really meant something; much more than it does now. Nowadays all the professional clubs are taking on little boys from four years upwards and then keeping hold of them until they think they aren't going to make it. Then they spit them out, leaving their parents to explain to them that they'd been let go. Let go at seven, maybe eight years old! What's that all about? Signing kids up to an 'elite' academy, stopping them from playing with their mates and then killing their dreams? It's a bit sad, really.

It was a big deal and as one of the youngest players at the trials, at 12, I remember feeling a bit nervous at the start. One of the watching coaches must have noticed, and pulled me to the side. "Listen lad, just enjoy yourself," he said. "Go and play as you do with your mates and you'll be fine." It was great advice for a nervy young lad, and I was soon buzzing around the pitch. I got selected. Within weeks I was training with the Rovers twice a week and absolutely loved it. The youth team coach was Alan Bradshaw, who was previously a teacher and had also played professionally for Rovers, Crewe and Macclesfield. It was pure and simple training, nothing fancy and certainly none of the tactics young kids get fed now. It was a case of turning up, getting on with it and enjoying it, and I did just that. I absolutely loved it.

It was all I thought about between playing football at school. I'd get home from school really excited, wolf my tea down and get to training. It was the biggest buzz ever, telling your mates at school the next morning. It was the best time of my life; eating and sleeping football, with not a care in the world.

Every so often the first-team manager, John Pickering, would come and watch the training sessions, giving me even more kudos at school where all the lads, and some of the girls, were Rovers-mad. Football became my focus all through school, at the expense of my education, and by 15 I was playing for Rovers' youth and A-team. Tank had been picked up by Bolton as well and had to leave a school game one Saturday morning at half-time, to go and play for the Wanderers' youth team. Imagine that now!

I starred in the second half, scoring a cracking goal, and had a brilliant game. At the end of the game, and out of the blue, our PE teacher Jeff Clarke told me I was the best player the school had had since he had been teaching there. And he had been there a long, long time! It was a pivotal moment for me, and I'll never forget it. His words made a real difference and from that day onwards, I had a real belief in myself. That one sentence meant so much to me and made me feel like a world beater.

I was soon brought back down to earth, though. By the following season I was playing in a men's team every Saturday afternoon, despite only being a fifth-year at school, and routinely got kicked from pillar to post by some pisspots. It was a great way to keep my feet firmly on the ground. Unless I was jumping over the two-footed tackles, anyway!

3

FROM BOY TO MAN (WELL, NEARLY!)

1980

By the time I was 15, I was still on the books of my beloved Rovers and also playing against fully-grown blokes every Saturday and for an under-16 team on a Sunday morning. My dad thought it would toughen me up, playing in a proper men's league, and boy was he right. It started with a visit from Bill Stemp, the manager of Darwen Amateur League side Darwen Olympic, and it was the next step in my football education. It was definitely an experience which stood me in good stead.

I would play Saturday mornings for Rovers' A team, or my school team Darwen Vale, and then for Darwen Olympic in the afternoon. The games were usually on the usual local council playing fields at Blacksnape, on a plateau on top of a steep hill in Darwen, and it was cold and windy at the best of times up there. The pitches were shit, and most of the time covered in it.

They were either bone dry and bobbly or an absolute bog and loved by dog walkers or strays. The smell of dog shit was always in the air and often stuck to your boots. If you were especially unlucky, you would slide through it in a tackle when someone hadn't moved it before the game kicked off.

None of that stopped the lads donning their boots, slapping on the Deep Heat or Fiery Jack and working up a thirst for their Saturday night piss-up that lay ahead. Being so young, the first thing I had to do was get used to the changing facilities and the adult sense of humour. The two teams set to do battle shared the same changing and shower areas and the smell of 20-odd hairy-arsed blokes in a confined space, some smoking and most still stinking of ale from the night before, is one to never be forgotten.

After overcoming the initial shock of their banter – what they had been up to the night before, how much they had drunk, any ladies lucky enough to experience their sexual skills and what they were getting up to after the game – I began to really enjoy it. Andy Young, my street-mate, had also started playing for Darwen Olympic, so that helped me settle in a bit more as well.

By this time I was about five foot tall and nine stone wet through, but what I did have was bags of confidence. I could beat opponents my age with ease, and it didn't take me long to adapt to playing with and against blokes too. I learned to jump, for one, or I'd get smashed. It was a men's league and everyone was treated as one. If you didn't jump high enough, it was tough shit.

I had a great first season, getting stronger and stronger and better and better as it wore on, and by the end of it I was winning man-of-the-match awards regularly and we were in the running to win the league. That was when we came up against a team called Greenfield. As a team, they had a bit of everything but mostly, they were a group of hard, dirty bastards and I was about to be taught a footballing lesson.

Greenfield had two key players in their side, the Donaldson brothers. Jimmy and John were both quite small, but aggressive. John had the more natural ability, Jimmy was the hatchet man. It was more than just any other game, as a potential title decider, and so called for some intimidation tactics. I was getting changed next to a bloke called Derek McDonnell, who was about 22 at the time and had been playing in the league for a few years. Derek was a bit of a fanny but, on his day, could be quite an effective player.

By now most of our players had left the changing rooms and were on the pitch, going through their pre-match routine of having a fag and a brew. I was always one of the last out, being a bit shy of getting changed with all my hairy-arsed teammates, and I was just pulling my shorts up when I heard someone growl: "Hey, are you that fuckin' Patterson kid?"

I turned round to see a smallish bloke, with a bearded face, flashing me a dirty look. "Yeah you," he said again. "You little cunt. If you go past me today, I'll break your fuckin' legs. You'll never play again."

I wasn't sure if he was taking the piss, but I didn't bother to ask. I turned to Derek, looking for a bit of back up, but he had tactically bent down tying his laces. When Jimmy Donaldson walked out of the dressing room Derek stood up, smiled at me, and just said: "All the best son" before trotting off. Fuck me, I thought. Welcome to the real world.

I spent the whole of the first half avoiding leg breakers and jumping over two-footed lunges, with no protection from the ref and not much back up from my teammates. The one decision the ref did give me led to me getting cracked in the ribs from one of the brothers. I was just about to take the free kick I had just won, but got smashed with an elbow from the side which bloody hurt. Bill Stemp probably saved my career by taking me off at half-time. We were already getting hammered and ended up losing 5 or 6-1, but to be honest, looking back, we were beaten before we had got on the pitch. It was a football lesson learned.

My other childhood mate, Eggy, was playing for his works team Conver Foam by now, so when that fixture came around, I knew it was going to be a bit juicy. Best mates or not, there were bragging rights at stake. Sure enough, as soon as the game had kicked off, I was on the wrong end of one of Eggy's lunges. I remember my mum watching the game and shouting on the pitch to him that if he did it again, he would never have kids!

At the end of the season, I got another lesson about the harshness of football that would follow me into the professional game. This time, I was on the receiving end of one of Bill's poorer decisions when we played a team called Corinthians in the League Cup final. I had played in every round of the competition and had even got a bit more involved in the changing room banter, becoming one of the lads.

As I arrived for the match, my confidence was sky high. I was really looking forward to pitting my wits against a lad I knew called Jimmy Khan, who was only a year older than me. It felt like the first time on the big stage and I was eager to play and show everyone what I could do. Confidence was definitely not what I was lacking.

So, imagine how I felt when Bill pulled me to one side before the game and told me I wasn't in the starting 11. My reward for having a great season, and being on the verge of signing as an apprentice for Blackburn Rovers, was to be told that I was on the bench for the biggest game of my young life. Bill wanted to make sure that all the older lads got a game because cup finals didn't come around very often. Cheers, Bill.

Jimmy Khan ran the game and we got beat 1-0. He went on to play World Cup qualifiers for Pakistan, but I still reckon it would have been a different scoreline if I'd have been playing. I still tell Jimmy that now. These things stick in your mind. But unfortunately for me, and for various reasons, this wasn't going to be the last big game I would miss out on during my career.

Fortunately that night I was able to drown my sorrows at the trophy presentation at the under-16 team I played for. One of the lads who had signed schoolboy forms at Rovers, Mickey Bell, asked me to play for his local team Leyland Mayfield, in the Chorley and District Sunday League. Not content with playing twice on a Saturday I really enjoyed it, probably because by that time I was really standing out against players my age.

The cup final defeat coincided with the club's end-of-season presentation and I soon forgot about not getting selected earlier in the day as I picked up several different trophies for my performances over the season. I celebrated by downing five pints of beer over the duration of the night. The only problem was that I was 15 and had never drunk that many in my life. By the end of the night, I was bolloxed.

Mickey's mum had kindly volunteered to give me a lift back to Darwen along with my stash of trophies and I very quickly had to politely ask her to pull over for a pit stop outside Leyland Town

Hall. I threw up, all over the Town Hall steps and I can remember the rest of the journey home as if it was yesterday, farting and burping all the way. Mickey's mum definitely wasn't as happy as I was.

When I staggered through my front door with my loot my mum and dad could tell I was pissed and just started laughing. I plonked the trophies down and staggered upstairs and fell into my bed. Come on, we've all been there … happy days!

4

THE BALLS ARE OUT

February 1981

I can honestly say that if I hadn't made it as a professional footballer, I haven't got a clue what I would have ended up doing after leaving school. I lived and breathed football and in my young
head, I was certain that one day I would be running out at the
hallowed turf of Ewood Park as a first-team player.

Maybe it was schoolboy naivety or maybe it was what every young
sportsman needed: total self-belief, probably helped by being told I
was the best player my school had ever had. Although for every motivating teacher like Mr. Clarke, I'm sure everyone will have come
across a negative one as well. I was cocksure that I was going to make
it as a professional footballer but Mrs. Horsfield, my fifth-year history teacher, was adamant that I was delusional.

It probably didn't help that, in her classes, I was always either dick-
ing about at the back, reading my *Shoot!* magazine or daydreaming
out of the window, not taking the slightest bit of notice of her. So
I was never going to be one of her favourites and, week after week,
she'd give me the same motivational talk. "Patterson, you need to
keep your feet on the ground and concentrate on your classwork.
You'll never be a professional footballer."

I'll never forget the look on her face one cold winter morning, during double history just before lunch, when the sports teacher Mike
Hodkinson came in and told her he was taking me out of the class,
because I had been chosen to play for Blackburn Rovers' first team

that night! It was a friendly up in the north east and Howard Kendall, then Rovers' player-manager and an Everton legend, wanted to have a closer look at one of his youth players. Rovers' first-team were riding high in the second tier of English football at the time. I didn't smirk at Mrs. Horsfield as I walked out of the classroom.

Honest.

Even at 15, I was playing regularly for Rovers' youth team and the older age group with Lancashire schoolboys and although playing for the first team was totally the next level, mixing it in the adults league probably helped my cause. Before I had time to really take everything in Mr. Hodkinson took me home to pick up my boots, via the Co-op where my mum worked so I could get a key.

When she saw me walking through the shop door, in school time and with my teacher, my mum's face crumpled. She must have thought that I was in bother. Once we explained what was happening, she burst into a big smile and after a club lunch, of a pie, I was on the team coach heading to County Durham for a friendly against Crook Town.

The gaffer had sorted it as a bit of a thank you to the non-league side, as Rovers had signed a player from them, and suddenly I was on the team coach with some of my heroes who I had watched as a fan at Ewood Park. I was as quiet as a mouse.

It was even more surreal in the changing room as the big kit skip came out and the strips started getting handed round. As I expected, I was to start on the bench. No worries. Even if I only got a few minutes at the end of the game, I'd be the happiest schoolboy in the world, putting on a Rovers senior shirt for the first time and getting on the pitch. As long as I didn't embarrass myself, that's all that mattered.

I was still a bit wary of getting undressed in front of grown men. At Darwen Olympic I had grown in confidence on and off the pitch, but these were some of my heroes. So I turned to face the wall, whipped my school pants and undies off and quickly slipped my footy shorts on, covering them with some tracksuit bottoms that had been thrown at me. I then put a Rovers first team top on for the first time. It absolutely drowned me, but that didn't matter. What a feeling!

By the time we'd got on the pitch to warm up it was snowing, and the wind was blowing it straight into our faces. I spent the first half sat on the bench, absolutely freezing my young nuts off, and loving every minute of it. I was living the dream. I kept taking in the glare of the floodlights, the swearing from the bench and Howard Kendall barking out his orders every now and then.

It was brilliant.

Then, in the changing room at half-time, Howard walked in and looked at me. "Right son," he said. "Get stripped, you're going on for the second half."

Then he came over to me and put his hand on my shoulder. "Don't be afraid," he said. "Get on there and play as if you are playing with your mates. Every time you get the ball, take 'em on, do whatever you want. Just enjoy it."

Before I knew it, after a few pats on the back and good luck comments and the removal of my tracksuit bottoms and top, I was on the pitch, in the left-wing position and ready to give it the best 45 minutes of my life. It was still snowing lightly and the wind had really got up. As the second half began, I knew I was going to have a little problem. In my pre-match nervousness, I'd forgotten to put the jockstrap on that was thrown to me. I thought I might look a bit stupid in it, as I'd never worn one before.

As I started making runs up and down the wing, the wind kept blowing up my XXL shorts and exposing my private parts. It was fucking freezing, so hopefully nobody would have seen too much to be offended by, but I kept having to hold my shorts down with one hand and run at the same time. Howard had started the second half watching from up in the stand, where it may have been a bit warmer. After noticing my weird running style, he came down to the side of the pitch and when the ball went over to the opposite wing, he shouted me over.

"Paddy, what the fuck's wrong?" he asked me. "Have you pulled your groin, son?"

"No gaffer," I replied. "I've no jockstrap on and me cock and balls are all over the shop."

I bet it was the first time Howard Kendall, part of the famous Everton holy trinity midfield trio of Kendall, Ball and Harvey in the 60s, had heard anything like it. The lads in the dugout were pissing themselves laughing at this point.

"For fuck's sake," he said. "Why haven't you put your jockstrap on?" I didn't have time to admit that I thought it would look stupid before he ordered one of the subs to give me theirs. I managed somehow to slip the sweaty jock on and trotted back on to the field. It held everything in place for the rest of the game and I went on to have a great second half, dancing past the full-back a few times and putting some decent crosses into the box.

It was a day never to forget. I had hopefully started to prove Mrs. Horsfield wrong, and exposed my talent (the footballing one) to Rovers' first-team manager. What a man he was, by the way. A great man-manager, too, who I would join forces with once again later in my career. Howard was eventually entered into English football's Hall of Fame after leaving Rovers to return to Everton, after we had narrowly missed out on promotion to the First Division on goal difference. He couldn't turn down the chance to return to his beloved Everton, this time as their manager, and Bobby Saxton took over. He certainly had some big shoes to fill.

STREET RIOTS TO THE RIOT ACT

July 1981 onwards

By the age of 16, when I left school, I had been training regularly with Rovers, after school and in every school holiday, for almost five years. I was playing regularly with the youth team and A team, and got more and more reserve-team experience as well. I was pretty confident that I was going to get an apprenticeship, but there was still a little doubt in the back of my mind.

What was I going to do if I did get knocked back? I was by no means the brain of Britain and I had no plan B whatsoever. I totally disregarded my exams. I think I only turned up for four and tossed them all off. I don't think I ever actually knew what grades I did get.

So, when the letter and the offer of a Rovers apprenticeship came through our front door, I think my mum and dad were more chuffed than me. But I was definitely relieved! It was the next stage on the journey to becoming a professional footballer, a step closer to playing in the league for Blackburn Rovers. But looking back now, I realise how lucky I was to get the opportunity. There were so many other lads that I played with in the Lancashire schoolboy teams, and a lot of talented players right up to reserve level, who were never really seen or heard of again. My blind confidence at that time meant that I was oblivious to the reality that I had no God-given right to be taken on.

When I talk to people about players who didn't make it, I hear a lot that you need a bit of luck to become a professional. When I was young and naïve, I would have disagreed totally. I had the ability, confidence, and self-belief that I would become a footballer. In my eyes, I was always going to make it. But I found out later that I actually did have a very lucky break when I was a rebellious teenager, expecting to become an apprentice. In fact, I was taken on as a second choice.

There was a lad from Bolton called Gary Mather, who also played left wing and was bigger and quicker than me. He was offered an apprenticeship before me, which would have meant I would have been overlooked. Fortunately for me, his dad made him continue his education, sending Gary to college. I thought I was good enough to have made it at another club should he have been taken on, but I'm glad I never had to actually go down that route.

Instead, in July 1981 – against the backdrop of a red-hot summer and riots going on across the country, and with my other former schoolmates waiting to go to college, start work or take up apprenticeships in construction – I started the next part of my Rovers football education, hopping on the bus to Ewood Park every morning for my apprentice duties.

On one of those first journeys, I started to get 'bumpy bus syndrome'. It wasn't travel sickness! It was probably more to do with my adolescent age and hormones, and did affect me every day for a little while before I managed to get it under control. Remember that song by *The Beatles, A Day in the Life*, that spoke about 4,000 holes in Blackburn, Lancashire? Well, I don't know whether it was those potholes in the road, or just because I was at that age, but on the bus on the way from Darwen to Blackburn, the inevitable would happen and I'd feel the rise, let's say, in my tracksuit bottoms. Anyone watching me get off the bus every day opposite Ewood Park must have thought I was training to be a break dancer rather than a footballer, as I tried to hide it. Some things just stay with you forever!

***

It was early on in my apprentice days when I realised how lucky I had been to be chosen. Only around six apprentices were taken on and there were lads at Rovers from all over the country. It was a bit dog-eat-dog, really, as you tried to impress the coaches to ensure you were either taken on for another year, or be lucky enough to be offered a professional contract at the end of your apprenticeship. You had no choice but to grow up quickly in that sort of environment and although it was a brilliant time, it also wasn't a cushy number like it is for most 16 and 17-year-olds at professional clubs now.

Alan Bradshaw was still the youth team coach. He kept me in line knowing that I was a local lad and a bit of a bugger. My school escapades included setting off the fire alarm, playing truant and having a quiet word, let's say, with two lads from another school who I caught kicking my jumper around the changing rooms. That saw me banned from all school sports for a month – and Alan knew all about it, because my old sports teacher, Mr. Hodkinson, was a close friend of his.

So he knew he had to keep me disciplined. Like the other apprentices, that meant daily chores and I had to make sure kit was put out for the senior staff before 9.15am. Afterwards we did some actual training, the changing rooms then had to be brushed and mopped and the toilets and bath were to be gleaming before I caught the bumpy bus home at 4pm, choosing a seat on the top deck to have a crafty fag on the journey.

I hated the chores but some matchday ones saw me meet a legend of football. In November 1981 Rovers made it to the third round of the League Cup and landed a plum home tie against Nottingham Forest, at the time still one of the best teams in European football and recent twice European champions. They were managed by the great man himself, Brian Clough, and I was on evening duties of cleaning the away changing room after the game. Before the game I was given a ball that needed signing by both sets of players for the sponsors. I took it to the visitors' dressing room and knocked on the door. It flung open straight away. "Yes, young man, what can I do for you?" It was the man himself.

"Excuse me, Mr. Clough, please could your players sign this ball for our match sponsors?"

"Of course, young man," Cloughy replied. "Come in but be quick." As I was entering the dressing room Mickey Bell, my drinking partner, who had also been taken on as an apprentice, walked past me and asked abruptly: "Can I get this shirt signed?"

"No, piss off," was Cloughy's reply as he showed Mickey the door.

Obviously my good manners had done the trick. I quickly whipped round some of the most famous footballers in England at that time before Clough asked: "Finished?" I nodded, and he added: "Good lad, now get out of my changing room or I'll set this big black man on you."

Justin Fashanu, towering over me, gave me a smile. No way did Brian Clough mean it in any way other than in fun, and I can honestly say that I never saw any racism internally at any clubs I played for. From the terraces I think we all know that it was a totally different matter and I think the goings on after the Euros in 2021 have shown that, 40 years on, we still have a long way to go.

Fashanu scored the only goal of the game to win it for Forest and afterwards I was stood in the corridor, mop in hand, waiting for the Forest team to leave so I could do my chores and get home. Brian Clough came down the corridor, chatting to Bobby Saxton and as he went past me he stopped, turned to me and said: "Young man, good luck in your career. Your parents should be proud of you." Well, I was gobsmacked and I think Saxo was too. He knew I could be a bit of a cheeky bugger and sure enough a month or two later, I went from accolades from Mr. Clough to a bollocking from Mr. Saxton.

At 16 I was the smallest apprentice at the club and one day, a labourer working on the new stand collared me to give me a bit of Lancashire advice. "Eh, Darwen lad," he said. "Look at yer. Five foot nothing and nine stone piss wet through. We need to get some meat on yer." He was a big bodybuilder, built like a brick shithouse, and having seen him in Darwen walking his dogs, I thought it would be wise not to ignore him. So I took him up on the offer and he took the time to put me through my paces in the multi-gym under the stand at lunchtimes.

I started to enjoy it, as he showed me exercises to build up my upper-body strength, and I started to bulk up in all the right places. I became harder to knock off the ball in training and it gave me even more confidence to get stuck in, if I needed to. I don't know if it was because I was a local lad, or if it was just bravado because I was so small, but I was a proper cocky sod throughout my first year. I wasn't there to make friends and looking back, I wasn't the easiest person to get along with. My confidence and focus meant I often overstepped the line, getting me in trouble with the senior staff, and there was one particular apprentice that I and some of the other lads didn't get on with.

He was a lad called Paul, from Manchester, and was in his second year. He thought he was top dog; he was a big lad, and the general feeling was that you didn't argue back to him. On one particular day, though, he was being a pain in the arse with me and I'd had enough. As I was walking into the home team dressing room, with him following, I slammed the door straight in his face.

As soon as I did it, I thought: "Oh fuck, I'm in for a pasting here". He was nearly a foot taller and a couple of stone heavier than me, and I started to realise that I had possibly bitten off more than I could chew here. Quick as a flash, he had opened the door and pinned me against the wall before giving me a smack in the chops. It definitely took me by surprise and I was in a bit of shock as he let go, backed off and started giving me some verbals.

The other lads looked as stunned as I was, but I knew I had to do something or I would lose face and look soft. So I kicked him in the bollocks and started windmilling him. He fought back but I somehow managed to get him in a headlock which prevented him from giving me a good kicking, and luckily my weight training kicked in. He was much bigger than me, but he couldn't get the better of me when the wrestling began.

Our physio, Tony Long, witnessed the last bit of the action and wasn't happy, sending us both to the manager's office. Back then, that consisted of two terraced houses on Nuttall Street, next to the ground. Paul was walking in front of me and as we passed the new stand building site, I heard a shout from up on the scaffolding: "Eh up, Darwen lad, have you done that to him?!" A nod from me had my weight training instructor laughing out loud. "Fuckin' brilliant. Good lad!"

Paul had now lost face, as well as having his own covered in blood, and as he reached the top of the steps leading to the 'office' he turned and tried to volley me in the head. Luckily I was expecting it, and took evasive action. He then walked into Bobby Saxton's office, slowly followed by me. The gaffer looked up from behind his desk. He looked at me, barely five-foot something and now about nine and a half stone after my weight training sessions, and then Paul, who was knocking on six foot and a few stone heavier. I must admit that by this time I was shitting myself, thinking I could be kicked out of the club; my dream of being a professional footballer could be over.

"What the fuck's been going on?" he asked. "Paddy, have you done this to him?"

"Err, yes boss," I meekly replied.

Bobby started shaking his head. My mind was racing. "Please don't get rid of me," I was praying, silently, in my head. "Please don't get rid of me..."

The gaffer pointed to me. "For fuck's sake," he growled in his gravelly Yorkshire accent. "Get out of my office, you little..."

Bobby then turned to Paul, who was holding his nose together and probably waiting for some comforting words. "And you..." he said. "You get out as well, and get yourself a set of bollocks, for fuck's sake. You're a centre-half!"

Later in life I found out that the big labourer who had taken me under his wing was a guy called John Garner. The Garners were a tough family, well known around Blackburn, and went on to run bodybuilding gyms, with John being one of the main men in the Blackburn area. Each time I saw him around after that he would still call me "Darwen boy" and although he had a reputation, I'll always be grateful that he took the time to give me a bit of advice. It stayed with me for the rest of my career.

6

BEER, FIGHTING AND
THE SAVIOUR

1982

I continued to be a bit of a lad as I entered my second year as an apprentice and, looking back, you could see why I wasn't far off getting kicked out of the club. Essentially I was just a daft lad from Darwen, who used to hang about with all the other daft young lads from Darwen. I'd started smoking by 15 and by 17, I'd got a real taste for beer. Women also started to come into the equation and all three usually came together on Saturday nights, when we'd end up in the local nightclub, Bogart's.

I mated around with all the Rovers fans and one in particular, Sam Stone, was a bit of a nutter, to say the least. He was originally called Paul Marsden, before changing his name to Sam Marsden before eventually settling on Sam Stone and although he was a great lad, he was a bit troubled – which usually came out when he'd had a few beers. It nearly always ended up with him fighting, and the rest of us jumping in if anyone else joined the fun.

Things were very parochial at that time and coaches full of equally testosterone-filled lads and lassies would arrive at Bogart's from many of the other Lancashire towns. The result was that either inside the club itself or outside at throwing out time, things would always kick off with our visitors from Blackburn, Burnley, Bolton and Accrington.

I know it wasn't big or clever, but with no social media around then there wasn't the same level of exposure on young footballers as there is now and you could get away with a lot without the club finding out. I was always on the periphery, but when you went out with a group of lads there was always a chance you would get dragged into it and, to be fair, there was quite a thrill to it. It didn't matter whether we were in Darwen or on a night out of town; in the madness of the early 1980s, we always seemed to end up in a brawl.

I remember my first coach outing to the Bierkeller in Manchester where, as the night wore on and groups of lads started to get more and more rowdy, glasses stupidly started to get thrown about. Those litre steins are not the smallest or lightest things to be whizzing past your head and it carried on outside with a group of Manchester lads, who regrouped across the road. This was a time when football hooliganism was rife and lads from different football towns and cities stuck together … even if you were on the verge of becoming a professional footballer.

On our way back to the coach, one of our lads got knocked over by a Triumph TR7 and the driver just sped off. It was probably for the best, from his point of view, as Sam would have probably lamped him as well. Another time, when we somehow ended up on the piss in Morecambe, Sam ended up scrapping with some Geordies. In typical fashion, he walked on to the stage where they were gathered, found the biggest one and headbutted him.

"Fuck's sake, here we go again," everyone thought. Before you knew it, the Geordies were chasing us down the pier along with their blades. Luckily we got out of that one, and fortunately – and probably only because of the lack of CCTV in the 1980s – Sam didn't get himself into too much trouble through fighting. The club never found out about my Saturday night excursions, and I didn't end up in any real bother either. Result. Sam is still a good mate now, a great lad who runs his own business.

My first real girlfriend then came along and helped me to put me on the straight and narrow. Lindsey worked in the office at Conver Foam, the same company Eggy worked for. One Sunday afternoon Lindsey and her friend came into the George pub in Darwen, where me and Eggy were playing pool. We challenged them to a doubles match and although we beat them easily the banter was great. I took a liking to Lindsey. Over the following weeks those feelings became stronger and a few months later we started going out together. That curtailed my drinking exploits and the chance of getting into trouble as I started to go out with the lads less and less.

Back then, pubs closed at 2pm and reopened at 7pm, which meant we had to find somewhere else to crack on. Often, we would nip to the off-licence, buy a few cans and walk over the road into Sunny-hurst Wood. There we would set up a small makeshift pitch and try to play footy, half-pissed and on the wrong end of a bollocking from people who would be out for a Sunday stroll with their families.

Such excessive Sunday drinking was actually the norm at most football clubs in the early 1980s. Maybe not to the extent that I was throwing them back, granted, but a Monday training session was all about sweating the Saturday and Sunday night beer off. How things have changed!

7

SIGN HERE, SON!

May 24, 1983

By the end of the 1982-83 season, I was well established in the reserve team and felt really comfortable in and around all the professionals at the club. Possibly too comfortable. I was doing well on the pitch but off it, I was a bit of a pain in the arse for the Rovers coaching staff. The football part I loved but, in those days, we trained until midday or half-12 at the latest and then had some dinner, either from the Chinese chippy over the road or the legendary Leaver's pie shop. The steak pies were to die for, and still are.

Once the stodge had digested and the pros had either gone down the bookies, to play golf or snooker or even to the boozer, we would crack on with the daily chores – cleaning their boots, scrubbing out the changing rooms, including the shit houses and baths, and sweeping the stands. It was the worst part of being an apprentice footballer and I hated it, especially on a Monday after running off my hangover. "What's the point of this," I used to think to myself. I was there to be a professional footballer, not a cleaner. Either way, my wages were nowhere near high enough for the work I was doing.

I moaned all the time that I would be better off financially on the dole. It was actually slave labour, but that was the norm back then. As much as I disliked the chores at the time, I know now that it was about discipline and learning the work ethic. Looking back it obviously did me no harm whatsoever. Things looked up on my 18th birthday, when Bobby Saxton pulled me into his office. For once, I was hoping for some good news rather than another bollocking. Bobby was a stocky fella, but had not been the tallest for a centre-half. He had a nose that told you he liked heading the back of centre-forwards' heads. He was a proper man's man who didn't take any shit, but was fair and had the respect of all the players and staff. He set off talking in his gruff Yorkshire accent.

"Right son," he said. "We're going to give you a two-year contract. You've done okay but you've still got a lot of hard work to do. You've got big balls [thanks, Bobby] which you need, but you need to change your attitude. We'll give you £90 a week and if you are doing well in 12 months, we'll put it up to £120 a week. I'm also going to give you a £1,000 signing on fee so that'll be £2,000 over two years. You okay wi that?"

Okay with that? *Okay with that?* Fucking hell. I thought I'd won the Pools. "Yes boss, that's great, thanks."

Notice anything strange? Not an agent in sight. Just me being told how much I was going to earn from my first-ever professional contract. I was a local lad living a few miles from the ground, so I'd already been doing all right off my £40 a week apprentice wages. I was at home with my mum, dad and two brothers in a two-up-two-down terrace, giving them £10 a week board money. Compared to the apprentices on the same wage who had to pay at least £20 for their digs, I thought I was doing okay – especially with an extra tenner to spend on fags, beer and the bandit in the pub. Now my wage increase took it to another level.

My mum and dad were over the proverbial moon. By this time, my dad was doing less hours on the road and was getting to as many of the games I played in as possible, encouraging me all the time. So, when I told them both the news that I had signed a professional contract they were both really proud. I'll never forget the smile on my dad's face.

I had done it. I was officially a professional footballer. I should have been absolutely ecstatic – and I was chuffed to bits, don't get me wrong – but to me, it was the natural next stage before I would make my debut for the first team. Looking back I must admit I was naïve.

But I also think that that streak in me, that determination and belief that I was going to succeed, really helped me. It was just like going to work, albeit in the best job in the world.

Getting on that bus, having conquered bumpy-bus syndrome, and then playing football for a few hours and earning a few quid. I was living the dream. When the next season started, I would be in the first-team squad. And I wouldn't have to do those bastard chores anymore!

8

PRE-SEASON – IT'S A DOG'S LIFE

July 1983

Blackburn Rovers now have a multi-million-pound indoor and outdoor complex on the outskirts of the town. On their return for pre-season, the players will have access to a wide range of sports professionals to help support them and get them back to peak condition. Fitness coaches, nutritionists, sports masseurs and so on. They may even have also been given a light training schedule to keep them ticking over on their holidays.

In the 1980s, we would train on the council-owned Pleasington playing fields in Blackburn, sharing them with dog walkers and everything that came with that. After about eight weeks off, which most of us spent smoking and drinking too much, we were given a certain date to report for training and maybe got some new training kit, if we were lucky. Money was tight at Rovers in those days and it wasn't unheard of to get thrown some hand-me-downs instead. How times have changed!

From the first day, I loved being in and around the first-team environment. I joined a really tight-knit and established group of players that included goalkeeper Terry Gennoe, defenders Jim Branagan, Mick Rathbone, captain and eventually record appearance holder Derek Fazackerley, and fans' favourite Glenn 'Kill 'em' Keeley. We also had a left winger, Noel Brotherston, who was a Northern Ireland international and an all-round brilliant guy. Rovers' main man at the time was striker Simon Garner, who had scored 22 league goals the season before and to this day remains the club's all-time record scorer.

I was joined as a first-year professional by two local lads in Simon Barker and David Byrom, and the banter and camaraderie were fantastic. Another Blackburn lad, Peter Devine, had recently signed for his hometown team from Bristol City and was a proper character from Mill Hill, which wasn't one of the posher parts of the town. He had started off playing in the United States for Vancouver Whitecaps and on his first day at Blackburn he walked through the home team dressing room door wearing a shirt that was open to his belly button and a big gold chain nearly touching his navel.

Mick Rathbone was on to him straight away. "Fucking hell," he said. "We've signed the Mayor of Mill Hill!" The name stuck throughout his time at Ewood. Peter is also one of a small number of players to play for both Rovers and Burnley, but he's most famous – or infamous – on YouTube for missing a penalty in 1991, playing for Lancaster City in a Northern Premier League Cup final against Whitley Bay. It's had over a million views and made *Nick Hancock's Football Nightmares.*

My first pre-season with the first team finished with a trip and a few games on the Isle of Man, which was a great craic. I can honestly say, that looking back, the next few years training and playing under Bobby Saxton, and his new assistant, Tony Parkes – who had just hung up his boots after 350 league appearances for the club – were absolutely brilliant. Yes, there were ups and downs, but what a great start of my football education as a professional.

Pre-season always began with a weigh-in, with the results compared to before our pre-season breaks. The lads would crowd round as players jumped on the scales, and those who had overindulged over the summer got a great amount of stick before we'd dust off the cobwebs with the obligatory cross-country run.

The circular run was over a big bridge, through the scenic Witton Park, back up the road, through the crematorium and then back over the bridge, finishing outside the pavilion. Most of us would be blowing out of our arses by then, with only the odd exception. Our left-back Mick Rathbone – or Basil, as everyone knew him, after the famous actor who played Sherlock Holmes – was the fittest man in the world. Or certainly the fittest man at Rovers. A fantastic man, and still a good friend, he would win every cross-country run and fitness test at the Rovers and my first one was no different.

From the first pre-season session to the last cross-country run of the season, Basil would always be first back followed by the rest of us. By the time the stragglers had got back, Basil had already got his Alsatian dog, Max, out of his car and was playing with him. Generally I would finish in the top five – as I knew I should, being one of the young lads – and as expected, the full-backs and midfielders would generally be towards the front. In my first session, Simon Garner came plodding in last, shouting at a perplexed Bobby Saxton: "You'll never get to the bottom of me, gaffer." Even Terry Gennoe and the centre halves would finish before him.

Garns was as mad as a box of frogs and smoked a minimum of 20 fags a day. Loads of us enjoyed a sneaky fag in those days, and some were more blatant with it than others. Simon, though, absolutely kicked the arse out of it. But Bobby was a terrific man-manager with a great sense of humour, and didn't mind Garns coming in last on the cross-country as long as he was still banging the goals in. The fact that he was still regularly scoring 15 to 20 goals a season, despite his nicotine habit, helped his cause!

Bobby was another who brought his dog to work with him, a little old white Scotty dog called Skip. It was as blind as a bat but was never usually a problem. Whenever he wandered off, Saxo would give it a whistle and back Skip would scamper. One morning though Skip wandered off and there was a bit of a commotion on one of the distant pitches over the bridge. We heard a yelping noise and saw the manager's dog being attacked by two greyhounds, who must have had dodgy eyesight as well and mistaken Skip for a rabbit.

As a few of us ran towards the bridge, we could see that the dogs' owner was struggling to get them off the poor little thing. Basil, the top professional who would never go over the top of a fellow player, was also a big dog lover and was having none of it. He charged over and jumped in with a two-footed lunge, sending the greyhounds flying and yelping. On the pitch, it would have been a double red card offence, but it did the trick.

The gaffer's dog wasn't white anymore, with a chunk missing out of its neck and a bit of claret showing. But after a trip to the vets, it was back with us a few days later, with one of those funnels around its neck. You really couldn't make it up! Can you imagine a Championship manager taking his dog to training? I'd go on to witness some very funny moments on training pitches in my career and Baz's two-footed lunge is up there. But it would be hard for anything to beat Bobby Saxton's plunge into the River Darwen.

I've no doubt that if Skip had ever wandered off and fallen into the river which ran through the middle of the Pleasington playing fields, Bobby would have been in to rescue it. What you wouldn't expect, until you knew how tight money was at the Rovers at that time, was that he would fall in and nearly drown trying to save one of the training balls! In those days we started with about 20 of them, the old Mitre Multiplex, and that was it for the season. The budget was so tight that if we lost any, or they popped, we just had to make do. We were always fishing balls out of the river.

On a particularly horrible day, when it had been pissing down for a few days, the river was really swollen. The gaffer was wrapped up with his big bright orange cagoule on, hood up, marshalling the troops. You could just about see his round face and flat nose sneaking out. It was nearing the end of the season, and the ball count was low. So, when one of them went into the swirling river, the gaffer went to try and fish it out, but leant too far over the edge and toppled in. In an instant, he was in and had gone under.

We all ran forward, worried for him, but the current had swept him away and he came up 30 yards down the river. Then he went under again, before bobbing up and down for another 50 yards. I really did fear for the gaffer's life, as did the other lads, but there was nothing we could do. He was heading towards the bridge, which was his last chance to haul himself out; otherwise he was a goner. Miraculously he managed to get out, piss-wet through and in a state of shock. "Fucking hell," he said. "It's going to kill me, that river."

In the meantime, though, Paul Comstive, who had the nickname 'Pie Man' due to his love of pies – he used to have two every day for his lunch – saw that the ball was still bobbling along down the river and ran alongside before shouting "I'll get it." He dived in, Tarzan-style, and came out the other side, wet through but with the ball under his arm. Paul was a great lad, who went on to play for a number of north-west clubs before sadly passing away far too early in 2013.

The club may have had no money, but the banter and camaraderie was superb for team bonding and really helped me become a fixture and fitting of the Rovers' first-team squad. It's fair to say that first pre-season training went well and when the season started, I was champing at the bit to make my first-team debut – something I had dreamed about since I was a little lad up against that mill wall.

9

FIRST SEASON ECSTASY TO SECOND SEASON WOES

1983-85

In the early-to-mid-1980s, like most other teams, Blackburn Rovers only had around 16 full-time professionals, so I knew I would get a chance if a few regulars got injured. I was a newly-crowned professional footballer and had played a number of games in the reserves, so had high hopes of breaking into the first team. I didn't have to wait too long, as I was told I would be travelling up to Carlisle for our second match of the season. We had drawn our first, 2-2 with Huddersfield Town, and had a few injuries to regular first-teamers, so I was named on the bench. I made sure I remembered to take my jockstrap.

We won 1-0 and although I was itching to get on, I didn't. The game was tight and there were no injuries. I was gutted, but I knew it was only a matter of time. My disappointment didn't last too long. On the coach back home I was told that, because I had travelled and been in the squad, I would get a £120 win bonus. *Holy shit!* I really was living the dream and Colin Randall's winner suddenly felt more important. Even if he hadn't scored, I'd have got a £60 bonus for the draw anyway. Happy days!

With players coming back I went back to reserve team duties, before I was called up to the squad to play Manchester City away. It was unbelievable for me – as I mentioned earlier, Peter Barnes was my boyhood hero, and Man City were my boyhood 'big team'. Watching

Match of the Day and *The Big Match* on TV, I dreamed about playing at Maine Road in a proper match. I had played there for the reserves, but this would be in front of a proper crowd.

I was 18 and we were going up against one of the favourites for the Second Division, but I did not think for a minute that I would bottle it if I got a chance to play. I was desperate to get on and when we walked out of the tunnel at 2.55pm on that Saturday afternoon, it was as if all my wishes had come true. I'd made it as a professional footballer.

We went into the match with our tails up after Simon Garner had unbelievably managed to score all FIVE goals in the previous week's 5-1 thrashing of Derby County and I sat on the bench before the game, trying to take everything in. A couple of thousand Rovers fans had made the short journey, helping to take the crowd to over 25,000 as we pitted our wits against the title contenders. With 15 minutes to go, we were 6-0 down.

The great Derek Parlane, once dubbed the King of Ibrox in his Rangers days, was running riot and banged in a hat-trick. Without a few missed opportunities he'd have matched Garner's five the week before. We were lucky to be nil; we were that bad and they were that good. Despite the scoreline I was loving the whole atmosphere, but Bobby Saxton wasn't quite as happy. He'd been huffing and puffing and effing and jeffing most of the game, before, with fifteen minutes to go, he turned to me to signal the start of my professional career with those immortal words that I will never forget: "Go and get warmed up. I don't care who the fuck it is, but the next person to give the ball away is fuckin' coming off and you're going on!"

I was 18 and making my senior professional debut, against one of the biggest teams in the country. It really didn't matter to me what the score was. I was just in awe. To be fair, City had taken their foot off the pedal by that point and luckily, we didn't concede any more. I cleared a goalbound header off the line and then decided to take on Paul Power, the Man City legend. I didn't get past him, and he smashed me. It's nearly 40 years ago now, but I still remember thinking: "Fuck me, I've just been tackled by Paul Power!"

The Saturday after the mauling at Maine Road we were due to play the previous season's FA Cup finalists, Brighton and Hove Albion, who a few months earlier had nearly beaten Manchester United at Wembley. We had such a small squad that I knew I'd have a chance of making my full debut, especially considering Noel Brotherston had been out injured for a few weeks and Colin Randall was still limping around with a sore ankle.

So, with his options limited, Bobby Saxton gave me the nod to make my first-team debut at the ripe young age of 18 years and 4 months. The crowd was 5,054, a far cry from the 25,000-plus I'd played in front of the previous week, but it didn't matter one bit. I was about to make my first-team full debut at Ewood Park. It doesn't get any better than that! I suppose I should have been a bit nervous. But possibly through the exuberance of youth I couldn't wait for the kick-off. Knowing that my mum and dad and a load of friends and family were in the ground made me even more determined to do well.

When the game actually did kick off, I was glad that through playing for Darwen Olympic as a young lad I'd learned to jump high when the tackles started flying in. Boy, did they fly in. I soon realised that hardened professional footballers don't make concessions for young lads making their debut. Brighton may have lost the FA Cup final replay soundly and also been relegated the previous season, but they still had a good side which included Tony Grealish, Steve Gatting and Jimmy Case, the ex-Liverpool star. All were hardened pros who were soon mixing it and took no prisoners right from the start of the game, which soon became a very bad-tempered affair.

I was even more impressed that Joe Corrigan, the ex-Man City legend and former England international, was between the sticks for Brighton. He was nearing the end of his career and had just returned from a short spell in America, playing for Seattle Sounders. I was at the other end of my career, fulfilling my boyhood dream mainly by skipping over tackles from Jimmy Case. It was a real baptism of fire, and Jimmy was quickly booked for a crunching tackle which would have been a red card today.

He had played well over 200 games for his former club Liverpool, winning three European Cups and four league titles. I'm not sure he'd last too long in the Premier League now, and the same could also be said of our centre-half, Glenn Keeley, who was also in the ref's book before half-time. They certainly don't make them like those two any-more!

The game finished 2-2, after I set Chris Thompson up to win a penalty for our goal-machine Simon Garner to convert, and I must have made an impression in my first-ever professional game as I got the man of the match award for the Rovers. Looking through the scrapbook my mum put together, I was really chuffed with the match report from chief reporter Peter White in the *Lancashire Telegraph*. I'll forgive him for getting my age wrong!

"Rovers could also reflect on the bonus of a definite addition to the senior squad in 19-year-old Mark Patterson. Playing his first full league game, the Darwen youngster made one of the best debuts I have seen from a Rovers player. Full of skill and trickery, not to mention confidence, he played his full part."

I got nine out of 10 and man of the match in a few national news-papers, so all in all it was a fantastic debut. By the following midweek, Peter was eulogising over my performance. I promise I never paid him. He'd got some quotes from the gaffer. Under the headline 'Rebel who has made his mark', and featuring a photograph of me with a very dodgy tash, it read:

"Ewood hopes for the future were given a significant boost on Sat-urday when 19-year-old Mark Patterson (above-photograph with dodgy tash!) completed the transition from one-time rebel to a fully-fledged Rover…

"And manager Bob Saxton had no hesitation in putting a large part of Patterson's success down to the lad's attitude. He told me 'I knew he wouldn't let us down. When he first came to Ewood he was a bit of a rebel, which isn't always a bad thing. Now he's settled down and the bottle he showed as a kid came out on the field. As long as he continues to channel that confidence in the right manner, he'll be okay…"

Looking back at these extracts I think Bobby Saxton nailed it with what he said. I'd definitely been a cocky little so-and-so when I was an apprentice. Bobby was no doubt referring to the fight, amongst other stuff I got involved in as I came through the Rovers system, from a 12-year-old to now being a fully-fledged first teamer. I would go on to have a rocky second season. But I had made it, playing for my club, at Ewood Park, with my mum, dad and family watching. Nothing can compare to the feeling of pulling on the shirt of the team you support. And no-one could ever take that away from me.

I came down back to earth a little bit the following week, when we lost 4-2 at Sheffield Wednesday in front of over 16,000 at Hillsborough and Mel Sterland booted me all over the pitch. It was still a great experience! Mel was a hard bastard and he had me in his pocket. Strangely, I really enjoyed it, but less so when Noel Brotherston regained his fitness and I dropped out. I played once in the next seven games, a match at Shrewsbury that was unusual because it was played on a Sunday and unlike now, games were very rarely played on the Sabbath. The Shrewsbury midfielder Bernard McNally didn't play because his religious convictions meant he couldn't play on Sundays, but I think he'd also seen the weather forecast – it poured down all game, and there was also a howling wind!

Then, a few weeks later, Noel got injured again and I began a long spell of playing on the left wing – including a game against Leeds. It was notable not only because Simon Barker made his home league debut, but also because Leeds had Peter Barnes in their team. I had another half-decent game in a 1-1 draw, but it felt so surreal to be playing against someone I idolised as a kid. I got his autograph in the bar after the game!

After getting my debuts out of the way, the next target was that first goal and it arrived against Grimsby in December 1983, making me one of the 10 youngest scorers in the club's history. It was memorable probably only to me, though, as it was an absolute fluke! I made it to the byline and tried to cross the ball, and as the goalkeeper tried to read me I mishit it past him. Obviously, I told the lads that I meant to do it, saying I'd seen him make a movement outwards, but it was a load of bollocks and they knew it. We ended up winning 1-0, me scoring the winner in front of my mates for my hometown team and at the Darwen End. I actually went on to score some great goals at Rovers, but you never forget your first. Even if it was a fluke!

In all, I played 27 times that season, scoring seven times from the left wing and keeping Noel, a fans' favourite, out of the team. He got injured a few times but even when he was fit, I managed to keep my place. Noel, bless him, died tragically young just a week before Rovers won the Premiership, and I'll never forget listening to a radio interview he gave in which he said I was a top prospect. I had total respect for him and that meant, and still means, a lot to me.

I made it two goals in two games with a volley from the penalty spot at Cardiff's Ninian Park, and I was starting to get some plaudits from both experts and fans. But it was back down to earth with a bang in the return match with Brighton at the Goldstone Ground. Brighton's old pros had probably overdone it with their Christmas and New Year celebrations as I was quickly into my stride, jinking up and down the wing.

We got a penalty and as I'd been cracking them in in training, I got the gig. Unfortunately, with my eagerness, I managed to smash it over the bar. Brighton then got a penalty of their own and as I stood on the edge of the penalty area, Jimmy Case must have decided that he'd seen enough of me dancing up and down the wing and took matters into his own hands. As the ball hit the roof of the net, he stamped down on the back of my Achilles and I went down like a sack of shit, in shock and pain. I just about spotted that it was Jimmy Case running away laughing before I hit the deck. With no TV cameras, and with everyone watching the penalty, Jimmy had taken the opportunity to teach what he must have considered an upstart a lesson. I had to be taken off.

Being a bit of a fiery customer, I vowed to myself to get Jimmy back. It didn't matter that he had been around the block and was an ex-Liverpool legend. I wasn't going to let him get away with it and I would sort him out the next time we played against each other. My chance for revenge came the next season, when we played them again. From the age of 16 an old pro had taught me to just knock the ball a bit too far in front and then 'top' – or go over the top of – the full-back, or whoever it was you were up against, and hope that the ref thought you were going for the ball. My young, naïve mind thought that that trick had already worked for me in the past, so why not against Jimmy Case? Well, of course, Jimmy was far too smart and experienced for me. As I lunged at him, he jumped up and split his legs and I slid through them. Jimmy then expertly landed a knee straight on my chest. I couldn't breathe at this point and was winded to fuck. There was nothing wrong with my ears though and I could hear Jimmy, in his nasally, Scouse accent, laughing: "Don't fuck with me, son!"

The older lads in the Rovers team were laughing their heads off. It wasn't a great experience for me at the time, having 13 stone land on my chest, but looking back that is what it was all about: learning your trade against seasoned pros. Another game that stands out from my first season, apart from my debuts and scoring, is the return game against Man City at Ewood Park. It was a freezing-cold January afternoon and the snow on the ground felt like it was covering concrete underneath. After losing 6-0 at City in September, we beat them 2-1 in front of over 18,000. Around 10,000 of those were City and I had a bit of a blinder, winning the man-of-the-match award and plenty of accolades in the process.

We also drew with Newcastle, 1-1 at St James' Park. Keegan, Beardsley, Waddle and McDermott where in their lineup – I bet they didn't have to worry about fishing balls out of the River Tyne to save money! We finished the season sixth in the table, a bit of a disappointment for the fans considering we had missed promotion by goal difference under Howard Kendall the season before. However, when you look who went up that season, you can sort of see what we were up against. Chelsea had paid Reading £175,000 for 21-year-old Kerry Dixon before the start of the season; Wednesday were averaging over 22,000 for home games and Newcastle were inspired by Kevin Keegan.

By the end of my first season as a professional me and Simon Barker were being touted as the young bloods of the future for Rovers. I had won a North West young player of the month award, beating all the young First Division players as well as those in the same division, and was on the verge of being selected for England's U21 side. Simon did go and play for them and I was really proud of my contributions, wanting to make an even greater impact the following season.

So it was hugely disappointing for me how my second season

worked out. I ended 1984-85 with only nine appearances to my name and no goals. Noel Brotherston was fully fit and returned to form, I got injured and with frustration, the bad attitude I wrote about previously was very much still there. I was only 19, but I wasn't happy about not playing, which probably didn't go down well with the gaffer and his backroom staff. Looking back now, I realise I was out of order. But just like anyone would, I just wanted to play.

In many respects, on a very limited budget, the club had a great season both in the league, coming agonisingly close to promotion to the First Division and also getting to the fifth round of the FA Cup before getting knocked out 2-0 by Ron Atkinson's Manchester United in front of a bumper crowd at Ewood Park. I suppose us being in the top six all season made it difficult for Bobby Saxton to change the team and it was that close that we still had a very slim chance to win promotion, even on the last day of the season. We had to beat Wolves at home, but then unfortunately had to hope that Manchester City got beat at home to Charlton and Portsmouth lost away at Huddersfield.

Before the game began there was a bit of humour to break the tension in the dressing room, unless you are a Wolves fan. By the time they played us Wolves hadn't won for 21 games and were already relegated. They were managed at the time by Tommy Docherty, the former Manchester United boss, who sadly recently passed away. As we were going through our set-pieces, our dressing room door burst open. It was Tommy. "Well lads, all the best today," he said as he walked in. "I've just been sacked, so I don't give a fuck." With that, he turned around and left. We won 3-0. Unfortunately for us Manchester City romped to a 5-1 win. Portsmouth also won 2-0 so we actually finished fifth, only missing out on promotion by one point.

The mention of Portsmouth that season will probably be having a few older Rovers fans' blood boiling. Football fans in general might remember or have seen footage of 'The Battle of Ewood Park' which was also played out on *Match of the Day* with John Motson commentating. Jimmy Hill's summary at the end was something else. In reality the defeat against them probably stopped us going up, as Portsmouth won 1-0 and it was our third defeat on the trot.

The match was a bruiser to say the least. Portsmouth had a bit of a nasty reputation, with a number of players who were willing to mix it, including Mick Tait, Mick Kennedy, Kevin Dillon, and centre-forward Paul Wood. Some of our lads were no shrinking violets either and gave as good as they got. Keels, Brannigan, Fazackerley, and Rathbone had played hundreds of games together and if one got kicked or were hard done to, as in this game, they all got stuck in. Anyway, the must-win game was 0-0 at half-time so both teams had it all to play for in the second half. An incident between Mick Kennedy and Jim Brannigan lit the fuse and the game exploded. Jim then went through Kennedy and got booked. Paul Wood then went in high on Glen Keeley with a really naughty challenge which ended up with them both rolling around the floor. Not acting as you see some players now, but involved in a proper fight on the edge of the pitch.

They were quickly joined by the coaching staff of both teams. It was chaos. Keels didn't bide his time too long before seeking retribution and he absolutely nailed Wood with an eye-watering challenge. Keels was sent off and so was Wood. Portsmouth won but that wasn't the end of it. There was more than a friendly argument in the tunnel as both teams went for it. Anyway, if you want to see footage of something that epitomises 'Old School' football from the early 1980s, have a search for footage of this game.

Getting so close to promotion and not getting there was gutting for the players and the fans but this was put into perspective after the game when it became clear that something tragic had happened over in Bradford. We would find out in the coming days and weeks that 56 fans were killed and hundreds of fans were injured after a fire broke out in the main stand at Bradford City's home ground, the Valley Parade. Fans who should have been celebrating their team winning the Third Division trophy never made it home. By the end of May, the Heysel Stadium disaster claimed the lives of 39 more football fans. It showed that stadiums in England and across Europe weren't fit for purpose.

10

INJURY STRUGGLE TO SURVIVAL

By the time my third pre-season as a professional came around, I was 20 years old and a married man! I'd proposed earlier in the year and luckily Lindsey had said yes. I was very young and didn't really know what to expect being newly married and even though I knew what pre-season would bring, it didn't make it any less of a shock to the system.

After two months off, it was time for that first-day-back weight check. In fairness, most players didn't come back in that bad shape but pre-season always felt like you were going back to school after your summer holidays. It might be the best job in the world, but you still didn't want to be there. We'd start off with stretches and then a long run, ease us in… and then bam! The second day would be the proper start.

We'd booked our place on another Isle of Man Tournament so we got about 90 per cent fit in two weeks back in training and then went over to the island, getting pissed all the way on the ferry. It was a fantastic trip and Bobby Saxton was spot on with us. We played three games and he told us if we were playing the next day, we couldn't drink the night before. So if we weren't playing it was beers all the way. The trip definitely helped our team morale, but I can't say it had the same positive effect on our fitness.

We stayed in the Palace Casino hotel again which was a top hotel with cabaret on. The previous year, the singer Alan Price, of the

Animals and *House of the Rising Sun* fame, had been on stage, letting us sing along with him, and that night it was Tony Christie, singing the song made even more famous by Peter Kay. *"Show me the way to Amarillo..."* Us Rovers lads took it upon ourselves to be his back-up singers, blasting out the words from the bar area. But unlike Alan Price, Christie was having none of it. He eventually stopped halfway through the song, telling us in no uncertain terms that we were ruining it for the rest of the punters!

We'd then move on to Whispers nightclub to carry on the drinking and banter. In another lull in the music at around 2am, there was an announcement. "Can Mark Patterson go to reception please? Mark Patterson to reception, please." Half-cut, I made my way to the phone and picked it up. I was that pissed I wasn't even thinking who it could be.

"Is that Mark?" said my dad on the other end of the phone.

"Yes, dad," I said. Before I could ask him why he was calling me at this time and how the fuck he knew I'd be there, he started to give me a blasting.

"You do know you are fucking married, don't you?" he asked. "Your wife's here in bits. You haven't spoken to her for three fucking nights."

I have to be honest; I was enjoying myself that much that I had forgotten I was married. We'd only got hitched a month earlier, so the missus was a bit tearful and wondering what I was up to and when we got back home, I got the full interrogation. Lindsey wasn't convinced that I had just been playing football, but I honestly had! After that, I made sure that I called her regularly on every trip. In between getting drunk and having a great time, of course.

***

At the start of the third season, after the Isle of Man trip, I was back in favour. When we had a few injuries before the first game of the new season up at Sunderland, Bobby told me and Simon Barker that we would be playing in central midfield together. I ended up scoring a great goal in a 2-0 win and we grabbed all the headlines and accolades. We ran the show on the day in the middle of the park and

11 games into the season, I was still playing there. I'd scored five or six goals by then and my confidence was sky-high. I was also being watched by First Division side West Ham, although I didn't know it at the time, and QPR wanted Simon. He eventually signed for them and ended up playing over 300 times.

I felt on top of the world. Then, very suddenly, it all went wrong. We were away at Millwall, never the friendliest of grounds, when our goalkeeper, Vince O'Keefe, came out to claim the ball. He did so, but also smashed into me in the process. I got an absolute clattering, much to the enjoyment of the Millwall fans behind the goal as well. But I knew it was serious straight away. It turned out to be a torn medial ligament, and I'd also damaged my cruciate ligament for good measure.

I was out for five months in the end and it was during that time I found out how close I had come to signing for a top-flight club. I was sat in the stands one day, with my knee still heavily bandaged up, when someone tapped me on the shoulder. It turned out to be a West Ham scout. "I've been watching you a few times this season and we were thinking of making a bid before you did your knee," he said. I think he could tell how gutted I was. "Don't worry," he added. "Get yourself back to fitness and I'll keep my eyes on you."

When I eventually did make it back into the team in early March we had gone from near the top of the table and promotion contenders again, to really struggling near the bottom of the division. I was obviously glad to be back, but in the remaining games of the season I knew that something had gone. I knew it would take me a few games to get back into it, but I'd lost the spark. It didn't help that I'd been pushed back onto the left wing – we called it the graveyard shift, feeling that we'd never really get into games if they were tight.

And it was getting really tight at the end and it actually looked like we were going to go down. After a run of 10 games without a win, including only four draws, we looked down and out before, out of the blue, we pulled off a 6-1 home win against one of my future teams, Sheffield United. I'm hoping one or two of you reading this were in the 4,736 crowd that day to witness my only hat-trick of my career!

Unfortunately we then got beat 3-0 away by Charlton, which confirmed their promotion and left us needing to beat Grimsby on the last day of the season and hope others lost, otherwise we were down. Luckily, we won 3-1 at home to Grimsby and Carlisle lost their last two games and were relegated.

The fans would probably say we didn't deserve to, but we celebrated staying up with an end of season piss-up to Magaluf. For many of us it was our first end-of-season abroad trip, so we kicked the arse out of it. We were half-pissed before we got to the airport and by the time we were in the air, the beers were flowing and our songs were drowning out the pilot's voice. As we were getting off the plane, a few of our fellow passengers let us know what they thought about footballers. "Overpaid piss-pots" was their verdict. What must they think of them now?

We didn't mean anything by it – we were just being like any group of lads are when they are away. A bit too boisterous and not really considering the families that were on the plane. Within 10 minutes of checking into our hotel, we were on the beach – one of the lads had brought a boombox with them, with the Beastie Boys' *Fight for your Right* the song of the week. We were dancing on the sun loungers, some of us puffing away on our big cigars and thinking this was the life, when a couple of the Guardia appeared. They ordered us to get down from our loungers and respect the people round us.

Glen Keeley argued back, and their response was the Spanish equivalent of: "Get the fuck down, or you're coming with us." Keels wanted to take it further, but we managed to calm him down. The partying carried on for the next three days. It was my first trip abroad but wouldn't be my last to Magaluf, which seemed to be the go-to place for a large number of professional football clubs through the 1980s and 90s. We returned home to a long summer break, before pre-season training – and the dreaded weigh-in – came round once again.

11

THE BEGINNING OF THE END

1986/87

After a great start to my career at Rovers, it started to go pear-shaped for me and being a local lad, it really did seem easier for the fans to turn on me. The Riverside section of the crowd were particularly hard on me, but it didn't always stop there. At times I would be out in Blackburn and would be confronted by supporters, who took great pleasure in telling me what they thought of me.

On one occasion me and Lindsey were out with our friends, who were mostly Rovers fans, and I was approached by a bloke in the Ribblesdale pub, in the town centre. He asked me if I was Mark Patterson and had bet his mate a fiver I was. I knew what was coming. As his mate handed over the fiver, the loser turned to me and started having a right go. Before he could finish his rant, my mates stepped in and told him where to go in no uncertain terms.

After near-relegation, the 86/87 season was make or break for Bobby Saxton. Even though his hands were tied with the lack of finances, fans had seen unfancied teams such as Oxford and Wimbledon make it out of the division. And like they had against me, they had started to turn against him.

Even though he took one of my potential spots in the team, Bobby made a shrewd signing in bringing Scott Sellars in from Leeds United and our bright start to the season – which included Simon Garner scoring four goals in a 6-1 thrashing of Sunderland – wasn't used as a springboard. We lost the next four out of five games and only drew the other.

When we faced a tricky away fixture at Reading, the gaffer came up with a novel way of trying to raise morale and get us back to winning ways. We set off down south just after lunch on a Friday as usual and as we passed Birmingham on the M6, Bobby Saxton got the driver to pull the bus over.

He jumped off and got the driver to open the baggage compartment and pull out a few crates of beer. In those days every team who played away always had crates of beer onboard for the journey home. We thought Bobby was taking the piss at the start, but he wasn't. Before long, a party atmosphere had developed. It was clear what he was trying to do; get a bit of camaraderie going and build up the team spirit. Before long, the beers were flowing and the fags were out, the card school got bigger and bigger, and the craic was great. Don't get me wrong, it wasn't a full-blown session – just a few beers to lighten things up.

Back then, we didn't wear tracksuits to away games and had to get suited and booted for our evening meal. So we checked into the hotel and unpacked our suits, before making our way down to the dining room. More often than not there would be a carvery waiting for us, followed by a selection of sweets. Some would take full advantage and go over the top with the portions – often, if a lad was having a bad game, he would get reminded about being a greedy bastard the night before. Still a bit giddy from the beers, I think most of us probably went over the top.

On the morning of the game, we met at reception as usual and went for a walk to blow off the cobwebs. Then we had a team meeting in the conference room, where the gaffer named the team and the two subs. He then went through the set pieces – who's picking up for corners, who's on the post, who's on the edge of the box, who's in the wall. No stone was left unturned. I'd like to say his novel approach of relaxing us before the game had worked, but we were 3-0 down by half-time.

To be fair, Reading were flying at the time and I think it was more to do with the quality of their team than anything we had done.

Not that Saxo had seen it that way when we made our way into the changing room at half-time. As far as he was concerned, we had let him down. "Well, what the fuck was that?" he asked. "I can't believe what I'm seeing. For Christ's sake, you would think you'd been on a fucking bender the way you're playing. Well, we won't be taking that approach again, will we? Now just get out there and show me and the supporters that we are better than that."

We at least managed to have a better second half and kept the score down. We only lost 4-0. His idea may not have worked, and Bobby Saxton isn't remembered that well for his time at Rovers compared to other managers, but he did a great job under the circumstances and you'll struggle to find a player who played for him at Rovers who will say a bad word about Bobby. He was a real man's man and a great man-manager. Being a bit naïve at the time, I didn't realise how good he actually was but the lads who had been around for a while, the older pros, loved him, which said a lot. He was just a genuinely nice man, but in football that often doesn't count for much. Unfortunately we only won one game in the next ten and Bobby was sacked just after Christmas.

Tony Parkes took charge as caretaker boss for the first of what would be many successful times and took us through January undefeated, including a 4-3 win in a Full Members' Cup game against First Division Oxford. The Full Members' Cup was set up after all the English clubs had been banned from playing in European football after the Heysel disaster and featured all the First and Second Division sides except for the top six, who played in their own little competition, the English Super Cup. Don Mackay then came in as manager in early February 1987.

I was just returning from injury when Mackay became manager and was pencilled in for a reserve game away at Leeds, to get some game time under my belt. Tony and Don went up to Leeds in the car, and Don told me I'd be going with them. I was really chuffed and thought that he must have fancied me as a player. Anyway, not for the first or last time in my life I was to be proved wrong.

I was in my early 20s by this stage and Leeds had a blonde lad in midfield, probably about 19. He was putting himself around and did me twice; bad fouls that you didn't need when you were coming back from injury. So, when he tried it a third time, I just gave it to him. I let the ball go out of my feet and just cut him in half, dropping him to the floor. I think he got the message, anyway. The lad would go on to play for England… a young David Batty.

I wasn't looking for a medal when I came off at half-time, but I was just showing that I could give it and take it. Don Mackay was having none of it, though, and came straight over to me. "If you ever tackle like that again," he said, "you'll never play for me again. I don't like my teams doing that."

I couldn't believe what I was hearing. "He's just fuckin' cut me in half twice," I retaliated, "and you want me to let him carrying on do-ing it? I don't give a fuck, I'm looking after myself, fuck what you say…."

Needless to say I didn't get a lift back home in his car and we didn't get on for the rest of our time together at the Rovers. I think my number was up before he'd even got started properly. Although I didn't get on with Mackay, I have to give him some credit as he over-saw Rovers' first competitive trip to Wembley in nearly 37 years when we beat First Division sides Chelsea and Ipswich 3-0 in the quarter-finals and semis of the Full Members' Cup.

I even managed to get on the scoresheet against Chelsea and then appeared on the hallowed turf of Wembley, for my beloved Rovers, in the final against another First Division club in Charlton. Unfor-tunately it was only for the last 20 minutes. Being a local lad, not starting was a big blow for me as a large number of family and friends were in the near 30,000 Rovers contingent. It was also the start of Wembley not being a good place for me, but more about that later.

We won the final 1-0 with a goal from Colin Hendry and as we paraded the trophy around the ground to our fans, one of the lads pointed out a huge flag hanging from under the scoreboard. It was from a battleship that one of the lads had served on and written on it was: "ANCHOR BLUES DARWEN." I got hold of the cup and held it aloft, pointing to them and raising my fist in celebration. After a night in a hotel in Luton and a civic reception at Blackburn Town Hall the next day, I went straight to the Anchor and the boys carried me into the pub and straight to the bar. It was bouncing. All the regulars had been at Wembley and it meant so much, to them and me. These were the lads that had backed me, been there for me in the tough times. And I'll never forget that.

In the end it turned out to be half-decent season for us as we finished a respectable 12th, after being bottom at Christmas, and added a trophy into the cabinet. I knew though, that I wasn't Mackay's cup of tea and he definitely wasn't mine, even though he did start me in the first six games of the 1987/88 season. I actually started off well with a goal in the first game, a 2-2 draw at Hull City, before an even more satisfying equaliser at Maine Road in a 2-1 win over Manchester City. Then, a back injury kept me out for nine games. I was gutted as I was playing well and we then drew Liverpool in the second round of the League Cup, so I knew I'd miss out at playing at Anfield in the second leg after a 1-1 draw at Ewood.

New signing Howard Gayle, a born and bred Scouser, played his part in this game and it meant so much to him. A Toxteth lad, Howard was the first black player to sign and play for Liverpool and even had a European Cup winners' medal from his short time at the Reds after coming on as sub in the second leg of their semi-final against Bayern Munich in Munich and helping them to a 1-1 draw. Liverpool went through on away goals and went on to win the final.

Unfortunately, like me, Howard was injured for the second leg. I was gutted about missing the chance to play at Anfield but ended up having a brilliant night with Howard, who took me to the game in his car – but with a few detours! He first took me to Chinatown and treated me to a lovely meal before we went to Toxteth. What I hadn't realised is that Howard had managed to get his hands on a couple of dozen tickets for the game. We ended up stopping on every street corner and various locations as he dished out the tickets to family and friends. If the police had seen us I'm sure we would have got asked a few questions, but it was all legit! Once all the tickets had gone we made our way to Anfield. The lads played well, only losing 1-0 in front of a great crowd which was swelled by Howard's friends and family.

That was to be the highlight of my last season as I only played

13 games in total, scoring one more goal. The final inclination that Mackay didn't want me was when we played Birmingham at home. He named his team and to my surprise, I was starting. Then he put the team up on the tactics board. I was out on the right wing – I was a little surprised, but at least I was playing. As we set up for the kick-off, I glanced across at the full-back I was playing against. It was a young Julian Dicks.

Dicks later made his name at West Ham but even then, he was as naughty as they came. It didn't take too long before I was flying over the touchline on the Riverside. The next 90 minutes were possibly the worst I played for Rovers. Not only was I getting smashed on the pitch, but the fans in the Riverside stand were booing me. That night there was no pub crawl; just a table in the corner and waiter service!

***

In February, 1988, me and Lindsey had our first child, our beautiful daughter Jade, and Lindsey had to finish work. I was still only on around £170 a week and with football agents lower down the league still a long way off, I sat down with Mackay and told him about the missus being pregnant in the hope that I could get a new contract and a pay rise. That meeting really showed me that my Rovers career was well and truly over.

It was a really strange meeting anyway. I was sitting opposite Mackay, but for some reason he'd got Tony Parkes to sit at the back of the room, behind me. It felt like he was trying to intimidate me. After hearing me out he offered me a measly £10 a week pay rise. In other words, he wanted shut of me. I was fuming and told him that a tenner wasn't going to make much of difference to my predicament. His reply was: "Well, I didn't get your missus pregnant, did I?"

"So, what we are saying then is I'm gone?" I asked.

"Yes," was the reply.

The meeting sealed my fate. My only proper dealings with Don Mackay was an ill-fated lift to Leeds and me trying to negotiate a new contract and he threw that in my face, so I went to Preston North End at the end of that season. I had been at the Rovers for over 10 years, from being a young boy, and thought I deserved better, but in truth I was glad to get away because of the stick I had started to get from the terraces. My game time had gone down and down after Bobby Saxton left, and the whole thing had started to turn sour.

I used to go into the Anchor pub after the home games and mates, who were big Rovers fans, would come into the pub telling me that they were sick of sticking up for me at the games. They'd actually had fights on the terraces when other Rovers fans had started having a go at me. In the end, I was relieved when Preston came in for me. I was totally out of favour with Mackay and I knew it was time for me to leave. Don't get me wrong, I'd had some great times at the Rovers and had loved it, but when your time's up, your time's up.

It may have finished on a sour note, but nobody can ever take what I achieved at Rovers away from me. I played in 101 league games, scoring 20 goals, plus 20-odd cup games and helped win a cup final at Wembley. I played with a great bunch of lads and made memories for life. And even lined up with a World Cup winner...

When people ask me who the best player I ever played alongside was, they are often surprised with my response. Outside Blackburn, most people won't remember the two amazing loan signings Rovers made in the 1987-88 season. Steve Archibald came first on a season's loan from Barcelona, where he had helped them win their first La Liga in 11 years and also played in a European Cup final. His legs had gone a bit, but he was a superb signing. His first touch was still instant and he could hold the ball up superbly, getting other players involved. He also chipped in with a few goals as well, in the 20 games he played for us that season.

But then on transfer deadline day, which in those days ran until April Rovers – challenging for a play-off place – pulled off an even bigger coup. Archibald had managed to convince his ex-Spurs team-mate, the great Argentinian genius and World Cup winner Ossie Ardiles, to come and join him at unfashionable Blackburn Rovers!

I'm still not 100 per cent sure whether it is true or not, but the rumour was that it was Jack Walker's cash that was funding the loan deal, before he officially started putting his money into the club. Either way, Ossie was potentially available for the last eight games of that season. The hope was that he would inspire us to promotion to the old First Division, now the Premier League and always the promised land for any club. I was out of favour by this point under Mackay but to train and play with such a great player was a real honour.

Around that time plans to redevelop Ewood Park were revealed, although I knew in my heart that I wouldn't be around to play in the new revamped stadium. The Warburton steeplejack family got the contract to dismantle the Riverside stand and shortly after the announcement, they began the work. The stand was built in 1913, bringing the capacity of Ewood Park up to an unbelievable 70,000! In the 1980s football fans, not just Rovers', had stopped going to football in their droves. Dilapidated stadiums, football hooliganism and unemployment were up and attendances were down.

The flooring in the original stand was lengths of Canadian pine and many were still in excellent condition. My older brother, Tony, was building aviaries for his birds at the time so when I mentioned the stand was being demolished, his ears pricked up. He was, and still is, a wheeler-dealer. The following day I nipped over to the workers' brew cabin on the Riverside terrace, opened the door and introduced myself. They invited me in and within five minutes we were chatting about football whilst smoking Park Drive cigarettes and drinking mugs of coffee done on the stove. I asked Tony Warburton and his brother John if my brother could have a few lengths of the pine. They agreed and as the conversation went on, I realised John and my brother Tony had a lot in common, mainly hunting, shooting and dogs. After an hour or so I left the cabin and nipped round to out Tony's to tell him the good news.

The following day after training we took the trailer down to the ground. Tony decided to take his 52-calibre black powder elephant gun, thinking it might help him strike a deal for the pine with the Warburtons. He and John wandered off with the gun whilst me and one of the lads loaded the trailer. All of a sudden, there was an almighty bang. Fuck me, I thought as I hit the deck so quickly along with the workers. What the fuck was that? I turned around to see Tony and John pissing themselves. John had tested the gun, firing it against the Riverside wall.

For weeks after there were rumours flying around Ewood that

the gypsies, who had a site over the road, had been taking care of business. There was even a rumour a player had been shot at! Tony got his wood but John wasn't convinced with the gun. After all, there weren't many elephants knocking about Ewood.

I spent quite a bit of time with the Warburtons and the gang in that brew cabin, where there was always a Park Drive and mug of coffee waiting for me. At that time I would rather be on the terrace than in the company of Don Mackay. I went on to become good friends with Tony Warburton, who later became a scout – first for Blackburn and then for Aston Villa. Funny old world.

Speaking to him recently, he reminded me of when he was recovering from a knee injury whilst working on the Riverside. We had gone down dog shit city, or Pleasington as it's better known, for training in the morning. The club physio at the time was Jack Cunningham, who was mates with Tony's brother John. Jack came onto the pitch and beckoned Tony over, offering to have a look at his knee whilst the players were out training. Tony, a lifelong Rovers supporter, was surprised at the offer but couldn't get in to the physio's room quick enough.

As he entered the room there was a player lying back on one of the treatment beds with a newspaper covering his face. He lowered the paper and acknowledged Tony. Tony nearly fell over when he saw it was Steve Archibald, who had recently signed from Barcelona. It reminded me of when I played against Peter Barnes then stood next to him in the players' lounge at Preston.

Steve and Ossie were superb professionals. Ossie was 35, but still had all the tricks and could do things with a ball that us mere mortals could only dream about. On top of that, he was a real gentleman and also a real funny bloke. And, as I was to find out to my cost, also a bit of a card shark! Come the last game of the season, we were in a position where we had to beat Millwall, on their own ground, to get into the play-offs. They had already won the title. On the coach down to London, the cards soon came out. We started playing three and seven card brag and shoot pontoon before Ossie, who spoke good English after his long spell as a Tottenham player, then got us on to playing seven card stud poker.

Before long I was in the money; well, pound coins to be exact. The new pound coins had come out a few years earlier so the stakes were upped to £1 minimum bet. I couldn't believe my luck, not only was I was playing cards with a man I had watched lift the World Cup on TV when I was 13, I was quids in against him as well. The epic card game was only interrupted hours later as we neared Millwall's ground. We were joined by a police escort, front and back of the coach, whose role it was to hopefully provide us with safe passage to Cold Blow Lane and the Old Den.

You'd think that the natives would have been happy enough, with their team already promoted as champions of the Second Division. Oh no! They still seemed restless, with their not-too-friendly hand gestures, and different objects were soon bouncing off the windows of the coach as we neared the ground. Everyone knew Millwall's reputation and we were glad to make it into the safety of the stadium. The lads were off the coach sharpish but I was a bit slower, weighed down by my tracksuit pockets full of around 200 pound coins! By half-time in the card game, with the second half to take place on the way home, I was more than a week's wages up!

I wasn't in the starting line-up – surprise, surprise – but still had to go out and warm up, and that was intimidating enough. As you jogged out of the tunnel of the Old Den you were protected by a cage structure keeping you safe from the Millwall fans, otherwise known as horrible bastards, and to be fair it was needed. Coins, spit and verbal abuse were thrown at you with equal venom as you made your way onto the pitch. It had been the same for years.

Mackay may not have been the first name on my Christmas card list, but he tried to get us in the home fans' good books before the kick off by walking to the centre circle and picking up a stuffed lion, Millwall's not so cuddly mascot. He then held it up like a cup and saluted all corners of the ground in recognition of Millwall's achievement of being champions.

Our manager was convinced we could take advantage of Millwall already being promoted and ambush their celebrations. The hope was that their players had already been out on the lash, celebrating their success, and wouldn't be as up for the game as us. He was right, as we dominated right from the start. The problem was that it led to even more unrest and I wished I was still in favour with Mackay. The safest place to be was on the pitch, compared to the dugout and its proximity to the home fans.

When me and Keith Hill, the other substitute, dared to do a bit of stretching and warming up as the game was being played, we were met with grown men – hairy-arsed dockers, not kids – hanging off the fences, giving us slit throat gestures and pointing directly at us if we dared to look up. "Yeah, you, you fackin cants," they said. "We'll fackin do you two after." Suffice to say, me and Keith moved quickly back to the dugout, which at least gave a bit of protection.

Near the end of the game, when the home fans started chanting: "Champions" and: "On the pitch, on the pitch, on the pitch" the ground was bouncing in celebration mode. But it was also obvious that they weren't too impressed with us daring to be 4-1 up, and me and Keith could sense that trouble was brewing. We decided that the best place to be as the final whistle blew was at the entrance to the cage and, knowing what was coming, we quickly scarpered down the tunnel, followed by the rest of our players and coaching staff.

It was absolute mayhem as we tried to regroup in the changing room. Millwall's fans had invaded the pitch as the ref blew his whistle and, after a count-up, we realised Nicky Reid and Simon Garner were missing. The pillocks had decided to go over to our fans to celebrate reaching the play offs! Bad mistake. After a few minutes, Nicky made it through the door, in just his jockstrap. The home fans had ripped his full kit off. Then within a minute or so, our top scorer staggered through the door. Garns was as white as a sheet and holding his jaw. He'd taken a crack off one of the Millwall nutters.

At this point, with everyone accounted for, we barricaded ourselves in the changing room as it sounded like all 15,000 Millwall fans were coming up the tunnel. I can honestly say that we were all shitting ourselves, but it wasn't long before the police got everything under control. Maybe the Millwall supporters remembered that they actually had something to celebrate.

If the Guinness Book of World Records team had been about, we would have easily recorded the fastest ever getaway from a football ground. While the Millwall players were still celebrating with the Second Division trophy on the pitch, we were back on the coach and heading back up to Blackburn. It wasn't long before the tinnies came out and I held my own again at seven card stud. Back at Ewood Park the chairman, Bill Fox, let us celebrate reaching the play-offs in the impressive boardroom. It had a fantastic oak table which we all sat round, the beer and banter was flowing and before long, the little Argentinian Ossie wanted to play cards again.

You can't say no to a World Cup winner, can you? Unfortunately by now my alcohol intake was impairing my judgement and I lost my £200 winnings from London, plus another £170 on top. It was over two weeks' wages, but at the time it didn't really matter. You win some, you lose some – not many can say they have played with a World Cup winner and even fewer can say they've been skinned at cards by one. Thanks for the memories, Ossie!

I didn't get a sniff in the play-offs against Chelsea, who had finished fourth bottom in the First Division – it was all done a bit differently then. We unfortunately got beat 2-0 in the home leg and 4-1 at Stamford Bridge. It would be a number of years before Rovers and myself would make it to the First Division. In fact, it was that long they'd given it another name by then!

In July 2021, one of my former Rovers teammates sadly passed away. Full-back Ally Dawson was a Rangers legend, playing over 300 games for the Scottish giants before joining the Rovers in 1987. I only played with him for a short time but what a lad he was.

In the 1987/88 season the Rovers team were treated to a couple of nights north of the border, in Alex's old stomping ground of Glasgow. It was my first trip to Scotland as a player and I wasn't disappointed. We were awarded the obligatory night out so after a few beers in the hotel bar, the taxis were called and off we went.

Alex still obviously knew a lot of people in Glasgow and had left the hotel earlier to meet a few. He returned to us in in the first bar, after driving there in his good friend's Ally McCoist's VW Golf. Through a twist of fate, England rugby union legend, and Rovers fan, Bill Beaumont was in Glasgow and also met us for a few pints until we moved on.

There were that many bars along one street that we just moved along from one to the next. Ally seemed to know everyone and it was a fantastic session. Before I knew it, it was midnight. Not late, I know, but I was a gallon and a half deep and a bit knackered. I asked Ally if he knew any taxi numbers and he obliged, but he jokingly threw me the keys to Ally McCoist's car.

I jokingly started walking out of the bar, which was still packed, before turning back, but by now Ally was back in conversation with one of the lads. Well, in my pissed-up state and tiredness, I thought: "Fuck it, I'll take the car." I was sure that Ally wouldn't mind. After all, he did offer me the keys. How wrong was I?

My roommate Chris Price was knackered too and was going to get a taxi as well, so he joined me. I know now it was wrong, and how we got back to our hotel with the car and us in one piece I will never know. We crashed out in our room until the early hours of the morning until we were woken to the door being kicked in. What the fuck was going on?! We soon heard our answer … "Hey, you little cunt, get out here now."

"Ally, calm down, don't do anything stupid." said Don MacKay, for once trying to look after my wellbeing.

"I'm not doing anything stupid," Ally replied. "I'm going to fuckin' kill him."

Fucking hell, I thought. If I'm honest, I was expecting by now that I was going to get a good pasting. But between Mackay one side of the door and Chris Price on our side, pleading with Ally to leave it to the morning to sort out, he left. In fairness when we went for breakfast, Ally just gave me a look, then a smile and a nod which told me I wasn't going to get a good hiding after all. RIP Ally; a top bloke.

12

PASTURES NEW

June 1988

You would think I would have been distraught at being told I was not wanted by Rovers, my boyhood club, but sadly it was completely the opposite. Through a combination of injury, bad form and falling out of favour, my promising career had started to go downhill and so when I got a phone call at the end of the 1987/88 season, saying Preston North End wanted me, I jumped at the chance.

Preston manager John McGrath had come in for me with a £20,000 offer and even the prospect of dropping down a division didn't bother me. I just needed to get back playing every week. My old mate Mickey 'Basil' Rathbone had already left Rovers for North End the season before and had told me how great the atmosphere around the club had been when he had arrived. The season before Basil signed, McGrath had taken Preston up from the old Fourth Division in his first season in charge.

It was miraculous – before McGrath took over, Preston had finished second bottom of the bottom division. Proud Preston, one of the founder members of the Football League, had finished 91st out of 92 teams, and had to apply for re-election. McGrath had then managed to assemble a squad of old pros, free transfers and young lads and somehow get them promoted. They had then held their own in the Third Division in their first season back up.

With no agents knocking on my door, I took my dad across to

Preston with me for company and left him having a fag in the car as I went to meet McGrath in one of the Deepdale lounges. He was some unit, and I could see why Mickey Rathbone had described him as a bit scary. He was six-foot plus, with a craggy face and a proper deep Mancunian accent. I was a bit nervous as he introduced himself. "Hello, how are you, son? I'm John McGrath, have you come on your own?"

"No, I've come with my dad," I replied.

"Where is he then?"

I've left him in the car."

"What the fuck have you left him in the car for? Get out there and get your dad in here now!"

I was 23 but felt about 12 as I jumped up and headed for the door.

McGrath was a real gentleman with my dad, offering him a cigarette as he shook his hand. He then asked me if I smoked and if I wanted one. I was still on 10 a day around that time but I thought he was testing me, so I said I didn't smoke. I didn't fancy another potential bollocking! We negotiated a deal – can you imagine a 23-year-old lad negotiating his own deal now? – and I somehow got a better wage than I had been on at Blackburn, in a division above. It was around £325 a week, for two years, and I also got a £15,000 signing-on fee – £7,500 per season, with the first instalment included in my first wage.

It was obvious that because I'd come through the youth ranks at Rovers, they'd kept me on shit money, so the increase was a bit of a bonus straight away. I don't think my dad could believe the figures as he sparked up another fag in celebration and offered my new boss one. By the end of the meeting McGrath had both me and the old fella laughing and joking, but he finished off, in a serious tone, by telling me that he wanted North End to continue to play an attacking brand of football and I would be going straight into the team. We shook hands. McGrath nearly broke mine. Just from that one meeting, I knew that I was going to enjoy myself at Preston.

I officially signed for Preston on June 15, 1988 – the same day England lost 3-1 to the Netherlands at the European Championships, on their way to coming home pointless after the group stage. We had the most hooligan-related arrests out of all the teams competing, despite doing a Scotland and coming home early. Wimbledon were the reigning FA Cup winners after shocking Liverpool. The No.1 single in the British charts was *The Tardis* by *The Timelords,* which looking back now seems very apt. And I was about to enjoy a great season with John McGrath, playing some football ahead of its time. It was an era when most teams, like Wimbledon, were playing route-one but we played out from the back and, in assistant manager Les Chapman, had one of the funniest and most bonkers blokes I ever came across in football.

Antiques and outer space were two of his hobbies and, according to some North End programme notes, the astrologer Patrick Moore was the man he would most like to meet. Unfortunately for me, in the first week of pre-season training I thought Preston's very own Doctor Who, manager McGrath, was going to turn into a Dalek and exterminate me before I could show him my silky skills.

I couldn't wait to get my hands on my first pay packet at the end of the first week of pre-season, thinking of that extra £7,500 signing-on fee. I remember being handed it just before training, ripping it open and looking at my Pools winning. But when I looked at the figures at the bottom of the printout, it was considerably less than I was expecting. Don't get me wrong, it was still a very decent amount for that day and age, but not the £7,500-plus I was expecting. I was gutted and marched down to the wages fella to get it sorted.

He looked down at my wage slip as I explained with a few expletives that I'd been short changed. "Oh, I understand where you are coming from and can see why you thought it would be more," he said. "But it's all changed now. From the start of this season, you have to pay tax on your signing-on fee." For fuck's sake, I thought. It could only happen to me. My first ever transfer signing-on fee and I end up paying tax!

I stormed off to training, feeling sorry for myself. But not half as sorry as I was a couple of hours later, when the gaffer heard that I had been giving the wages clerk a bit of earache. Just before the end of the session I was asked to report to the manager's office. At the time I hadn't put two and two together and wasn't sure what it was about.

As I walked in, though, I could tell by the faces of Les Chapman, coach Walter Joyce and chief scout Fred O'Donoghue that it wasn't to congratulate me on my efforts in training.

I'd just about shut the door when McGrath started to rip me to bits. "Who the fuck do you think you'se are?" he asked. His loud aggressive tone shocked me. No, to be fair, a bit more than that. It shit me up big time.

"What have I done, gaffer?" I asked. "What have I done?" My nervous voice sounded like I'd sucked some helium out of a balloon.

"I'll tell you what you've done," he replied. "You've been into the wages department and been asking for more fuckin' money. I told you it was £7,500 each season before tax. It's not the fuckin' wages clerk's fault that you didn't understand that. You don't go and see other people if you think something is not right. You come and see me!"

I stood there like a naughty schoolboy as the gaffer absolutely tore into me. I nervously glanced at the coaching staff and they looked a little embarrassed, but I could also tell they weren't going to be acting as my defence team. McGrath continued to hold court before finishing with some words of advice. "Now fuck off out of my office. You've started on the wrong foot here, so you better fuckin' sort yourself out."

When I look back now, I realise that McGrath was breaking me down and showing me who the boss was. In those days football was a small world where a lot of people knew other players and managers, especially in the North West. Fred O'Donoghue was a great man. He had originally scouted me as a young lad and got me to sign for Rovers before moving to Preston in 1985, so he knew me inside out. At a relatively young age I had become part of the furniture, but this was a new start. The gaffer was showing me he was the boss. He was a big imposing man who had the fear factor, and there was nothing wrong with that. I was maturing by now and realised afterwards where he was coming from. Probably not at that moment, though, when I had to go and change my underpants!

13

PARACHUTES TO PLAY-OFFS

1988/89

Preston had finished 16th in Division Three in the 1987/88 season, after their famous promotion a year earlier, and had managed to hold their own in the higher division, with a great number of the promotion-winning squad including David Brown, Ian 'Dusty' Miller, Bob Atkins, Alex Jones, Gary Swann, Gary Brazil, Mickey Bennett, Oshor Williams and Sam Allardyce.

They had then added players such as the ever-reliable Mickey Rathbone, exciting midfielder/winger Brian Mooney and striker Tony Ellis to the squad, while myself and Neil Williams, signed from Hull City, were added in the summer months ready for the 1988/89 season.

John McGrath may have been as mad as a box of frogs but he was also ahead of his time in the way he did a lot of things. He may have been old school in his playing career – he was a hard, no-nonsense, tough centre-half who had played at the top level in the 1960s and 70s for Newcastle and Southampton – but as a manager he was totally different and forward thinking, looking for unusual ways to get the best out of us.

Before the start of the 1988/89 season this began with some unconventional pre-season training – a few days training down in Aldershot with the elite of the British Army, the Parachute Regiment! It raised more than a few eyebrows at the time and possibly a few "what the fuck are we doing that for" comments – out of earshot of the gaffer, of course – but by the end of the trip it no doubt got the results that he was looking for.

McGrath had played for 20 years, with nearly 500 professional games on his CV, and so had been through the same necessary but monotonous pre-season training schedules season-in, season-out. Thinking outside the box, he wanted us to do something a bit different, with the same result of getting us fitter and team bonding. The paras training, including going over their assault courses, certainly was different. We were only used to running on flat surfaces and the odd hill run, so for a start going up and over assault courses, using our upper bodies, was a killer and also a test of our bottle and nerve.

As well as individual fitness training, para style, the physical training instructors (PTIs) had us doing team assault courses showing us the importance of teamwork. That, and the team bonding in the bar at night, proved to be massive successes. I'm not sure if I was saying that when I woke up in the mornings with aches and pains in muscles that I didn't know I had, but the PTIs really put us through our paces. It was extremely tough, but really enjoyable. We then had more than a few beers in the mess each night with the instructors and their fellow soldiers and the banter in the bar with my teammates and our new friends was brilliant.

However, something seemed to happen on every pre-season or mid-season trip I went on, and the Aldershot one was no different. Luckily, this one didn't involve me! After finishing a grueling fitness session, Mickey Rathbone called his missus and got the sad news that his dog Max, who had been present at many a Rovers' training session, had passed away.

Now Mickey was the most placid bloke I'd ever met, and still is. But any dog owner will tell you that when you've had a dog for a long time, they become like a son or daughter to you. That was definitely the case with Mickey. So, what he didn't need was our goalkeeper, David Brown, hearing the news and thinking it would be good banter to start taking the piss.

Browny was already sat at the bar when Mickey came in and ordered a beer, and he started winding my mate up straight away. Then every so often he would start whistling and clicking his fingers to summon his imaginary dog to him. I told him to shut the fuck up myself, but he was having none of it.

There was one whistle and command too many and Mickey just got up, walked over and stuck one on him! Mickey Rathbone, the most mild-mannered pro you'd ever meet, had had enough. He caught Browny with a cracker. Browny went down against the bar, slid down it and ended up like a pile of shit on the floor. Mickey didn't say a word, but just turned and walked out of the bar. I went after him to see if he was okay and then returned to a sheepish David Brown, who was dusting himself off. I told him in no uncertain terms that he had deserved what he had got.

The aftermath just showed the type of man Mickey was, and still is. He came back and apologised to Browny. Mickey confided in me that he couldn't believe he'd resorted to violence, but I thought it was brilliant. Browny had gone too far and got his comeuppance. He never took the piss again, anyway! And the little spat didn't dampen morale.

On the last morning of training after another late night in the bar we even managed to turn the tables on the PTIs who had been whipping us into shape as we got them doing our type of training. We were put into two groups, one group running around the outside of the football pitch whilst the other group did long sprints. After about four long sprints, when we were just getting into it, there was a massive cheer as one of the PTIs puked up the previous night's beer and pizza on the side of the pitch.

Looking back, it makes me realise that squaddies and professional footballers, and the lives they lead, are very similar in some ways. Both are among a group of blokes day-in, day-out and the testosterone flies about as a result. But there were a few differences, too. They were more disciplined than us and were ready to go one step further. Crazy guys!

One of our pre-season fixtures was a Manx Cup game at Blackburn. It was my first game back at Ewood Park, we won and afterwards, me Lindsey and some friends ventured up to what was then the Beechwood pub in Blackburn. We had a few beers then left, and were followed out by a few young Rovers supporters – who were having a go at me and sounding like they meant it. Fortunately, I had my golf clubs in the boot. I took out a club, which fortunately deterred the lads from coming any further – but the whole episode confirmed that, sadly, I had made the right decision to leave the club I loved.

The first thing I had to get used to at Preston, apart from my new teammates, was the plastic pitch which had only been laid in 1986. Being classed as a midfielder/winger at this stage in my career, the plastic pitch was great for my pace, skill and trickery, but it couldn't half catch you out with the uneven bounce and the speed of the ball. It had undergone repair work over the summer and so my league debut for Preston, against Port Vale, was the first game I had played on it. And it showed. I was subbed in the second half as we lost 3-1 but, to be fair, no-one on our side covered themselves in glory.

After another defeat, this time on the road at Huddersfield, we knew we needed a win and the good old fixture gods decided we had a home game against our local rivals, Blackpool. Coming from Darwen and being a Rovers fan, whose main rivals are of course Burnley, I hadn't realised how fierce the rivalry was between PNE and Blackpool. All week, in the build up to the game, everywhere I went in Preston the fans and staff at the club just kept saying "Come on, we've got to beat the Donkey Lashers!"

I really didn't know what they were on about at first but by match day I knew how important it was to the fans. I only went and scored the winner against our main rivals, in front of just under 9,000 fans. Early in the second half, Tony Ellis had jinked his way to the edge of the box and shot. I just took a chance and followed in and as Barry Siddall, the Blackpool 'keeper parried the ball, I ran and slotted it in. We managed to hold on and the PNE fans went mad at the final whistle. From that goal onwards, things just went from strength to strength for me.

The two themed headlines in the national Press after my winner against Blackpool made me laugh. 'Speedy Patterson turns tide', said the *Sunday Express,* and the *Sunday Mail*'s was: 'Mark stirs up Lancashire hotpot'. All good fun! The Blackpool game started a decent run for us, including me banging in two goals in a six-goal thriller against Chester City. Gary Brazil also scored his 50th goal for the club in a 3-2 home win against Southend.

We came from 2-0 down with 15 minutes to go and Brazil scored the winner in injury time. The home fans went nuts. Hope you like that one! By the way, the referee for that game, Trevor Edward West from Hull, was a detective sergeant for Humberside police. How far the game has progressed! I'm glad we all kept on the right side of the law during that game.

We had our tails up as a team, and I wasn't expecting the mass bollocking we got at half-time in the next game, a night match away to Bristol Rovers. It was one of those nights and in the first half we just couldn't get out of the blocks. We kept making mistakes, were second to the ball all over the park and went in 1-0 down at half-time.

As soon as we got in the changing room, the gaffer's arms started going and you could tell we were going to get it with both barrels. McGrath went through the full team back to front, explaining their shortcomings, starting with Browny, then the full-backs and then on to the centre halves.

Sam Allardyce, by this point in his mid-30s and something of a veteran, was sat back, arms and legs crossed, chewing gum, with a 'Seen it, got the t-shirt' look on his face. To be fair, he had been one of the stalwarts in the Preston defence that had seen them promoted under McGrath. McGrath turned to Big Sam and told him, in no uncertain terms, to get rid of the gum.

Sam gulped it straight down and sat up straight. I'm not sure if he did it out of respect or was just shocked and did it without thinking. Either way, with the mood McGrath was in, it was probably the right thing to do at the time. The gaffer carried on through the midfield lads until he got to me. "Paddy, sometimes you are a world beater, son, but tonight you are all over the place and you can't trap a bag of cement," he said. "What's going on with you, you little cunt?"

I didn't reply, but I made sure I upped my game and played better in the second half. The rest of the lads pulled their fingers out, too, but we still lost. At least we knew where we all stood with the boss. We had got a bit ahead of ourselves and he put us in our place.

McGrath had a great way of motivating the team and whether it was one of his legendary funny analogies or a bollocking, it usually hit the spot. It had definitely worked this time as we then went on an eight-match unbeaten run from early October to late November, which included five wins and three draws.

Opposing defences couldn't cope with our forward play, and our plastic pitch, and we scored 18 goals in the eight games. The goal tally was split mainly between Gary Brazil, who scored a hat trick in a 5-0 home win against Gillingham; Tony Ellis, who scored five in eight games, from all over the place; and me, with two in two. That was backed up with some superb performances from Mooney, and even Mickey Rathbone got a nosebleed and a goal against Mansfield.

Tony Ellis was a great player, and a bit of a lad. He was from Salford, into the Manchester scene and allegedly had a few 'connections'. He drove a shiny black Astra GTE, which was his pride and joy. Tony polished it every day after training and took pride in taking anyone who was the slightest bit interested for a spin in it. He came in to training one day shaking his head, saying he may have got himself into some trouble with the boys in blue as the police had paid him a visit and he was facing a charge of animal cruelty! When he started telling us the story there was a few lads struggling to contain themselves.

"Every fuckin' night for weeks now, when I get home from training, and I've been in the house for about five minutes, I have a look out and next door's cat is asleep on the bonnet of my car, taking advantage of the warm engine," he said. "Well, I've warned the next-door neighbour that I'd do something about it if he doesn't stop it from climbing on my bonnet, it could bloody scratch it or summat. Anyway, last night I decided to take matters into my own hands when I saw it climb on my car again.

"I got my baseball bat out and walked up to it being all nicey, nicey. 'Here kitty, kitty, here kitty kitty…' I got close enough to take a proper swing at it, but the little shit scarpered. I chased it, but it was like Big Sam chasing me. I was never going to catch it. The next thing I knew I got a knock on the door from PC Plod. The neighbour had seen me and rang the friggin' police, and they are now going to get back to me about whether they are going to prosecute!"

Tony was one of a number of great characters within the squad and he also certainly knew where the net was. His goal record that season was fantastic and luckily, I don't think he got a police record after his little run-in with his neighbour.

The great little run on the pitch pushed us up to sixth in the table and into the early play-off places. We then went to Molineux to play Wolves, the league leaders, obviously in great spirit and good form. It would be a real test of our mettle as they were five points clear at the time. Well, Steve Bull, the Tipton Terrier and future England international, ran our ageing defence ragged, scoring four goals in a 6-0 mauling. Once again, we were lucky to get nil! I felt sorry for our defence, but even sorrier for our large contingent of magnificent fans who had travelled in their thousands and still clapped us off at the end.

We rallied with eight wins and three draws in our next 11 home games, including two great wins against clubs I would go on to play for. We beat Bolton at home on Boxing Day, an 11.30am kick-off on police orders, and then won 2-0 against Sheffield United, with yours truly opening the scoring. Both games had 11,000-plus gates and the feel-good factor was definitely back at Deepdale. Sadly our home form was not matched away and the Wolves game had started the rot. We lost another five away games on the trot, and even a goal by me away at Fulham couldn't cheer up me or my teammates.

However, the Fulham game stands out in my mind for two reasons. First, the goal I scored was a worldie free kick. Secondly, Gary Brazil christened me with my nickname that would stick for years to come: Gizmo from the film *Gremlins*. Fucking Gizmo. Even now when I bump into big Sam Allardyce now it's: "Gizzer, how are you mate?"

In the end, we didn't get a single away point from the end of November until the middle of February and Blackpool beat us 1-0 in the local derby return fixture. We had let down another huge away following and received another McGrath telling off during that week. He described it in his programme notes for the next home game, against Bristol City: "I pulled the players to one side this week to talk things over. Sometimes it does you good to clear the air and I hope to see some significant improvement this afternoon."

We took the bollocking on the chin and won 2-0! We then lost away to another team I would go on to play a few games for, Southend, before a morale-boosting first point away at promotion-chasing Lancashire rivals Bury. By this time Gary Brazil, who along with striker John Thomas had blasted the club to promotion, had moved to First Division Newcastle for £200,000 with us getting a great lad, Ian Bogie, as part of the deal. The gaffer had also brought in Tony Philliskirk from Oldham Athletic.

Around this time, we had a midweek, mid-season break to Frodsham in Cheshire. Now this was the clear-the-air type of activity I enjoyed. A few days in a posh hotel, with a bit of training and the added bonus that it was Les "Chappy" Chapman, the assistant manager, who was in charge, as I think John McGrath must have wanted a few days in the office on his own.

We had a couple of cracking days and nights and for once this time I'm happy to report that it wasn't the players getting up to mischief, but the assistant manager. I don't know whether he was still pissed from the drinking session in the nightclub beneath the hotel the previous evening, or he just felt free from the shackles of the gaffer. But when we met Chappy outside the hotel the next morning for a "hangover cure" cross-country run as agreed, it was soon apparent that the club's number two was like Apollo 13 once was... on another planet.

Just after we set off, leading from the front, Chappy sprinted off out of sight. We carried on in the same direction, laughing, joking and jogging, knowing that we'd catch him up eventually. We were running at a steady pace and a few hundred yards ahead there was a long row of trees that arched across the road, making a tunnel shape. As we began running through the tunnel, branches began raining down on us and there were some really strange squawking noises coming from the tree top.

Chappy came down from the trees, with us all laughing. But as soon as we started jogging again, he once again sprinted off out of sight. Five minutes or so, further along, we came over a hill, ran across a field, and came across a bloke with a golden Labrador running towards us. He had a look of terror on his face, shouting something. He looked like he was shitting himself, and we soon realised why. Chappy came out of some rocks at the side of the hill, bollock naked and waving a branch about. He looked like he'd escaped from a mental home.

He got dressed and we set off again, before he sprinted off for a third time. We eventually got back to the hotel, thinking at every turn that Chappy would jump out at us. The hotel manager met us as we made our way in. "Who's in charge of you lot?" he asked. "Come on, who's in charge?" We could see Chappy in the plush hotel's wishing well fountain, before getting out and spurting some water out of his mouth. A few of us pointed together at our assistant manager. "Him, mate," we said. "He's in charge." The look on the manager's face will live with me forever.

Taking that point at Bury and the midweek break was a turning point in our fortunes. It helped us get our promotion push back on track with three emphatic wins on the trot, which sparked off a long undefeated run. We scored 14 goals in those three games, including a 6-0 win over lowly Chesterfield and a 5-3 victory over Brentford. Tony Ellis had left his feline worries at home and was purring like a cat on the pitch, banging in a hat-trick against Chesterfield. He scored eight goals in eight games. Tony Philliskirk also started scoring for us as well, linking up brilliantly with Ellis.

I took over penalty duties from Gary Brazil and scored a penalty in all three games. I then netted one in a 3-2 win over Northampton, in front of more than 9,000. I took four penalties in eight games, and scored them all. I'm still quite pleased about that! The run had taken us to fifth place in the table, but I suppose all good things must come to an end. Our run did, with a 1-0 loss at our arch rivals Bolton.

We were then the April Fools, losing 4-1 at home to our promotion rivals Fulham on April 1. Amazingly, it was our first Deepdale defeat since the first home game of the season seven months earlier. I know it helped us and gave us a bit of advantage training and playing on the plastic pitch, but what makes me happy now is how much the loyal Preston fans must have enjoyed that 17-match unbeaten run. In those 18 games we scored 45 times. I'm no mathematician, but my calculator tells me that it was 2.5 goals per home game. We kept them coming after that, too, and finished the season off in similar fashion.

Unfortunately, by the time we played Notts County at home with six games to go, we had picked up one point from a possible 12 and were in danger of missing out on a play-off spot. Cue a John McGrath team talk. Every motivational talk in the dressing room by John was something to behold, but I think we all knew that we were getting ready for one out of his top drawer. It always followed the same routine. McGrath would get Chappy to take us out for a warm-up and then get us in at quarter to three to give us a team talk, whilst we put our shin pads on and listened to whatever he had to say. His garden analogy one is still my favourite.

"Right lads, sit back down and listen," he said, after going through his tactics and reminders of set plays. He didn't start until every man was sat down.

"Back home, I have a garden that's got loads of beautiful flowers," he continued. "There's roses, daisies, some yellow ones, some red ones and loads of pink ones. But sometimes I get weeds. I fuckin' hate weeds, they spoil my garden. So when they appear, I rip them up and throw them in the bin."

At this point he was walking around the changing room, ripping out imaginary weeds.

"Now, I look at you lot like my garden, lovely roses and daisies, reds, yellows and even some pinks. Beautiful flowers. So, get out there and play like you're my beautiful colourful flowers and not those fucking weeds, because you know what happens to weeds. They get ripped out and fucked off."

What the fuck have I just listened to? I was thinking. It was like nothing I'd ever witnessed before. Not one player laughed. We all looked at each other, bemused, but no-one laughed. We went out and played like his beautiful flowers, winning 3-0.

I will always remember April 15, 1989 for two reasons. One, as a memory of that brilliant John McGrath team talk and that the PNE fans would have left the stadium happy. But it was also the semi-final of the FA Cup at Hillsborough that day and those shocking scenes unfolded, mostly whilst everyone at every other ground in England would have been enjoying a game of football. Nobody should go to a football game and not come home.

More than 56 fans died at Bradford and almost 100 at Hillsborough, with so many more left with physical and mental scars for the rest of their lives. Like Bradford, the Hillsborough tragedy would help to change football for the better. It's just so sad that so many had to lose their lives for it to happen.

Victory at Chester City – with, I'm sure, more of our away fans there than home – strengthened our play-off chances and two of my most important goals of the season sealed a 2-1 home win against Reading. With two away draws, we were assured of sixth place and a play-off semi-final game against third-placed Port Vale.

We capped the season with a six-goal thriller against Wolves – luckily, this time they didn't score all six – and I scored with virtually the last kick of the game to make it 3-3. We had a traditional walk around the pitch to thank the fans for their brilliant support in a superb season, but the play-off semis proved two games too many. Port Vale had finished 12 points ahead of us, only missing out on automatic promotion on goal difference, so it was always going to be difficult but in the first leg at Deepdale, we went 1-0 up.

It could easily have been two or three early in the second half before the game had to be stopped as there was a small fire in the stands. With the game taking place only a month after the tragic scenes at Hillsborough, no chances were rightly taken and the 3,000 Port Vale fans in the Town End were evacuated, with most of them being brought onto the pitch. As it turned out it was something and nothing, but the game was suspended for nine minutes and when we returned to continue, we had lost tempo and conceded to draw 1-1.

We took a massive following to Vale Park. After going one down, I managed to get on the scoresheet with a cracker of a goal, if I do say so myself. I've watched it a couple of times on YouTube. Well, maybe more than a couple. Brian Mooney was involved in a short corner routine, crossed it, and someone had a swing at it but missed the ball completely. I was between the penalty spot and the 18-yard box when the ball came to me. I quickly took a touch to get the ball out of my feet and then curled a left footer into the top corner, to send the massive contingent of North Enders into ecstasy.

Sadly, it was short lived as a couple of defensive mistakes in the second half allowed Darren Beckford in to complete his hat-trick. Port Vale went on to clinch promotion with a two-legged aggregate victory over Bristol Rovers, while we came up just short after a great season. I think the fans would have taken it before the start of the season but I know it would still have hurt. Still, we knew we had entertained them especially at Deepdale, where we had lost only two games all season and scored 56 goals, at an average of more than two a game.

Attendances were up, and a number of Prestonians followed us the length and breadth of the country. Personally, that season would be my best ever in terms of scoring, with 15 league goals – finishing second only to main striker Tony Ellis. I'd only missed four league games all season. And, more importantly, had really got my appetite back for football.

14

THANKS FOR THE MEMORIES

1989/90

I t was really disappointing to lose in the play-off semi-finals after having a great first season, but I was absolutely raring to go again. Well, as keen as I could be for pre-season, anyway! The Preston fans and the local media seemed to have really taken to me, and I shared the *Lancashire Evening Post's* 'Starman' award for the season with Brian Mooney, after we both won eight man-of-the-match gongs in the league from the then-LEP sportswriter, Paul Agnew.

Me and Mooney also shared a couple of player-of-the-year awards given out at the end of the season by various supporters' clubs and associations. I was chuffed with them and also to share them with Mooney – we had forged a great partnership on the pitch and off it as well, rooming together on away trips. We signed a few new players that summer – including striker Graham Shaw from Stoke, winger Steven Harper from Port Vale and a young Irish centre-half on loan from Arsenal, Pat Scully – but frustratingly lost Tony Philliskirk, who had built up a great understanding with Tony Ellis but signed for Bolton Wanderers.

Our pre-season destination before the start of the 1989-90 season was Keele in Staffordshire, and our digs would be at Keele University. Les Chapman was again in charge of us whilst we were away and in his first game programme notes, John McGrath wrote: "The short break down at Keele was excellent…" If only he knew.

Chappy must have told him that everything had gone well. In reality, it had gone a bit pear-shaped. We actually did have a great few days to start with, and it finished with Chappy allowing us out into town on the last night. We'd been training really hard and wanted to let off a bit of steam. But, as usual, a few in the pubs wasn't enough for us and we ended up in a nightclub. We were a little worse for wear but were generally just having a good blow-out.

A big group of us hit the dancefloor, throwing some shapes and just having a great laugh. A couple of the lads then started having a bit of fun with some girls, which didn't go down well with a group of local lads. I could see what was going to happen and before long, Tony Ellis started getting bumped into. Tony wasn't taking any shit and squared up to one of their lads, before a couple of handbags were thrown.

All the players on the dancefloor tried to break it up and after a while order returned. We went back to having a laugh and prancing about but before we knew it, the local lads were squaring up to Tony Ellis once again. It looked like nothing was really going to happen as we stood our ground, but one of the locals threw a cheap shot at our full-back, Neil Williams. We didn't know it at the time, but the punch had broken his jaw.

We made our way back to the digs and I gave Chappy the bad news about Neil getting injured. He started fretting straight away. "What's the gaffer going to say?" he asked. "Oh, for fuck's sake…"

When I got back to our university accommodation block, I nipped into Warren Joyce's room and Brian Mooney was in there. I just ambled in, expecting to join in the conversation, but for some reason they both started to have a go at me, which really pissed me off. They hadn't even been on the dancefloor helping out. They'd been sat at a table along with a couple of other players.

I told them what happened, but they were having none of it and said I should have done more. Mooney got personal and started firing accusations at me, which was out of order. He wasn't there when it kicked off. It was getting a bit heated so I decided to go back to my own room, before I got too pissed off.

Mooney and me had become good mates, which I think is what

angered me even more. I laid on my bed, stewing it over, before the red mist came over me. "Fuck it," I thought. "I'm not having it." So I went back to Joycey's room and banged on the door until he let me in. Mooney was sat on a chair against the wall, so I sat down on the edge of the bed, three or four yards from him, hoping for an apology. "Listen Brian, take it back," I said. "I'm telling you now, fucking take it back. You're having a go at me but you weren't even there. So take it back."

Mooney shook his head. I told him again, with my voice raised. Mooney looked at Joyce, then back at me. He shook his head again. "No."

I jumped off the bed. Brian got up off the chair at the same time so, thinking he was going to hit me, I got the first one in. The punch knocked him back down onto the chair and against the wall; when he tried to get up, I went for him again. Joyce then grabbed me around the waist with both arms and dragged me out of his room. Back in mine, I started to think about the repercussions of smacking Mooney, so I went to see Chappy to tell him what had gone off.

Poor Chappy couldn't believe what had happened. He knew he was in for a bollocking off the gaffer for letting us get out of control. But I got up the next morning and went for breakfast in a defiant mood, knowing I was in the right. But Mooney was John McGrath's golden boy and to be fair, he'd had a superb season, especially on our plastic pitch. He was a fans' favourite and definitely one of the manager's.

Mooney hadn't surfaced for breakfast just yet, and I had a word with my two closest mates at the club, Micky Rathbone and Dusty Miller. I asked them to jump in if it kicked off and if anyone else joined in. Both being great lads, they said they would. I wasn't bothered if Mooney wanted to carry anything on as I was still angry, but I knew that if Joycey or Micky Bennett, who were good friends of his, got involved I would be struggling.

Anyway, Chappy told me that we needed to sort it out before we went back to Preston. When Mooney turned up at breakfast, he had a black eye, but there was still no apology. I was still keen to sort it out man to man, but Mooney wasn't having any of it. He wouldn't speak to me at all, other than saying: "Nah. I'll do you, don't worry, but not now. But you *are* getting done."

On the day I brushed it off but when we got back to the club, we never really got on after that. Things weren't right between us and I started to take his initial threats more seriously. Mooney was an Irish lad who lived in Liverpool and travelled in every day by taxi. Micky and Dusty, who I shared a car with, used to have to listen to me worry about it every single day. I think I probably went through every Liverpool and Irish gangster 'what could happen to me' scenario.

It all eventually came to a head at training at Deepdale one day and there was a black cab parked up outside the ground, next to where we usually park. Mooney got out as we pulled up, and then the driver walked to the boot of the car. As we walked past, the driver just stared at me, nodding, giving me the daggers all the way. My paranoia may have got the better of me; I was thinking he may have had a baseball bat in the boot. Anyway, nothing happened, but even Mick and Dusty were a bit unnerved.

I'd had enough of the scare tactics and confronted Mooney in the changing room. "You're bang out of order with these scare tactics," I said. "You'd better sort it out. I'm not having it."

Luckily, that was the end of it and we started speaking a bit more after that. But sadly it was never the same after Keele. Just like my body was never the same after playing on that plastic pitch for a full season! It was like playing on concrete for 90 minutes. Nothing like the superb, 4G astroturf pitches that are played on now. They were more like carpets and although it was great to play free-flowing football on once you get used to it, anyone stupid enough to slide into a tackle or fall over when fouled ended up with burns all over their legs and arms. Waking up on the morning afterwards and having to peel the bed sheets off your wounds wasn't the best or most painless start to a Sunday!

I was feeling far from 100 per cent and after the first league game of the season, a 3-1 defeat away at Rotherham, my back, hip and leg pain got too much. I had started walking like a 90-year-old and was struggling to get upstairs. I was actually pleased when I was diagnosed with sciatica, rather than needing a major operation. The pain went from the centre of my back, into my pelvis and arse cheek and down the back of my leg. Frustratingly, rest – and keeping off that plastic pitch – were the orders from the doctors and physios. It meant I missed the next 15 games and unfortunately during that time, the team didn't continue its good form from the previous season.

I eventually made my comeback against fifth-placed Shrewsbury, marking it with a penalty in a 2-1 win. Looking back at the team-sheets from that day really makes you think how quickly time goes and how much your paths cross as players and managers in football. For instance, out of the 11 who started that day for Shrewsbury, three of the players went on to be my teammates at Bolton Wanderers: Tony Kelly, Mickey Brown and the Wanderers fans' favourite, Super John McGinlay.

Shrewsbury had plucked John out non-league football and he was soon repaying their faith with goals. Tony Kelly had already been christened 'Zico' by some Stoke fans, and would be a fantastic team-mate at Bolton, where I would do all the hard work and then give him the ball and he'd do a bit of magic.

Mickey Brown was also a great lad, who played a season with me for the Whites and although I didn't line up alongside two of the other Shrewsbury players, you'll recognise their names straightaway if you're of a certain vintage or know your football... David Moyes and Asa Hartford.

By coincidence, Mickey Rathbone came on as sub for Brian Mooney that day and I wonder if he tackled his future boss, Moyes? Moyes would go on to manage PNE and nearly get them to the promised land, the Premiership – just falling short in the 2001 play-off final against one of my future clubs, Bolton Wanderers. Who was Preston's physiotherapist that day? None other than my good mate Mickey Rathbone, who retrained after he retired as a professional footballer. Moyes would then take Mickey to Everton as head of sports medicine.

Hartford was Shrewsbury's player-manager at the time, and was a bit of a legend. He would have been 39 and had 50 caps for Scotland, earning him a place in the Scottish FA's Hall of Fame, and also played in the final stages of two World Cups. He was still playing as well as managing at that ripe old age – 18 years after failing a medical at Don Revie's Leeds, after it was discovered that he had a hole-in-the-heart condition. Wikipedia tells me that Asa made 744 professional league appearances and Google tells me that overall, it was 973 if you throw in cup games. Respect!

A few weeks later, we went to Hillsides Park for a second-round FA Cup tie against Whitley Bay, from the Northern Premier League, and lost 2-0. Paul Agnew, in his column in the next PNE matchday programme, called it "one of the blackest moments in the history of this famous football club". I think that was fair enough. We had no excuses. They just wanted it more on the day and deserved to go through to the third round.

Apart from that woeful defeat, we were holding our own and starting to go back up the league. The gaffer was still coming out with some great team talks, but also had the habit of getting names wrong. He once bollocked Graham Shaw at half-time in a game for getting knocked off the ball too easy. "Shawy, you need to beef up lad," he said. "Starting on Monday, you're going to go the gym and get on the weights. By the time we've done, you'll look like Arnold Shoemaker."

He'd somehow got Willie Shoemaker, the American racehorse jockey, mixed up with Arnold Schwarzenegger and at first, didn't take too kindly to us all bursting out laughing. Then someone explained to him there was probably about 10 stone difference between them and Shawy probably had Shoemaker's build already. Shawy was certainly different to the rest of the lads, in that he actually had a few brain cells. We used to see him sat in his car after driving up from Stoke for training, reading the *Daily Telegraph*. We thought he was taking the piss at first!

Whether he knew it or not, John McGrath was a very funny guy and you never knew whether he was being serious. I'll never forget the day he told me Preston had turned down an offer for me from the Spanish team Osasuna. The late Michael Robinson, once a great player for Preston before he got a massive move to Manchester City, eventually finished his career with Osasuna in La Liga and then became a scout for them. Apparently, he was at one of the games when I played a blinder, setting one up and scoring another.

On the Monday after the game, McGrath pulled me into his office and told me that Osasuna wanted me, but he wasn't prepared to let me go. To this day I still don't know if he was serious or if he was pulling my pisser. But it soon became apparent that Preston were looking to cash in on me, to help their ailing financial position. Tony Ellis had already been sold in December for £250,000, and I heard that Bury had already put in a bid for me, which McGrath turned down.

I was still playing well, picking up a number of man-of-the-match awards and scoring a few goals after coming back from injury, but the plastic pitch was getting me down and between games, I was struggling with the sciatica. So, when McGrath said that he had accepted a £100,000 bid from Bury, plus former PNE favourite Nigel Greenwood, I must admit that I wasn't overly disappointed to be leaving. I'd had a brilliant first season at Preston and had been playing well again, but I felt it was a win/win – Preston were getting five times what they had paid for me, and I was getting away from that pitch.

I have nothing but great things to say about my time at Preston, though, and especially the stewardship of John McGrath and Les Chapman. They bounced off each other. Chappy was a great assistant manager who would go on to manage the club and although he was absolutely bonkers, he was fantastic with me. He went on to work as Manchester City's kit man for 22 years, into their glory years of winning the Premiership. But he was much more than the kit man. One of the City players called him "the heart and soul of the club" and you can see why.

I'm not eloquent enough to put into words how brilliant a manager John McGrath was to play for, and how much the forward-thinking, attacking style of football that he had us playing complemented my game at that time. But doing some research around my Preston days, I found this brilliant paragraph by the author of 'Back from the Brink', Edward Skingsley, about Preston's fight for survival and the promotion season of 1986/87. To me, his description of John McGrath's managerial style is absolutely spot on and a fitting tribute to a fantastic man, who sadly passed away on Christmas Day, 1998.

"A tough old style centre-half for Bury, Newcastle, United and

Southampton, he turned out to be the most perfect managerial fit North End could have wished to find; old school, focused, no-nonsense, communicator, motivator, psychologist, thinker, tactician and, of course humorous."

Unfortunately, I didn't go to the gaffer's funeral, but I know it was a great turn out and even on such a sad occasion, Chappy managed to raise a smile or two. Halfway through the service, his phone started ringing as he'd forgotten to switch it off. The ringtone blared out around the church. "We wish you a Merry Christmas, we wish you a Merry Christmas…"

Thanks for the memories, gaffer and Chappy.

15

BURY DAYS TO SLEEPLESS NIGHTS

A round the time I travelled to Bury to speak to their manager, Sam Ellis, decisions were being made that would change football forever. It was the week that Lord Justice Taylor published his report into the Hillsborough Disaster, recommending that all top-flight stadiums should be all-seater by 1994 and that the rest of the Football League followed suit by 1999. There were massive implications that would start to change the face of football.

This time, I didn't take my dad over, driving the 11 or so miles to Bury on my own and resisting the urge to have any tobacco in case my new gaffer didn't approve. I was down to only having one or two fags with a beer by now, so I was getting better. I sat down with Sam, his number two Mike Walsh and local businessman Hugh Eaves, who was the major shareholder and essentially bankrolling the club at the time.

Bury had finished 13th in Division Three the previous season and due to their proximity to the two big Manchester clubs, and the other local teams in the area, they only averaged just over 3,000 loyal fans per season. But on the day we were sorting my contract out, they were sitting seventh in the table and pushing for a play-off spot. Since Sam Ellis had arrived in the previous summer they had made a number of signings, including tough tackling defender/midfielder Andy Feeley from Brentford, centre-half Alan Knill from Swansea, big target man Tony Cunningham from Ellis's former club, Blackpool, and Preston lad, goalkeeper Gary Kelly, from First Division Newcastle for £70,000.

My new gaffer-to-be made me feel very welcome. There was no offer of a fag, but big Sam Ellis's all-round friendly demeanour made me feel really at ease. Sam made it clear that the aim for the season was at least the play-offs. It was already a done deal with the transfer and, with no agents knocking around still, I somehow managed to get myself a decent pay rise to £400 a week and another decent signing-on fee of £25,000 broken down into three payments – and taxed, of course!

I shook hands with them all as Sam told me I would be going straight in the team to play Shrewsbury at home on the Saturday. The team had hit a bit of a slump and had lost the last four league games. I knew about one of them, as I'd played in the Preston team that had beaten the Shakers at Gigg Lane a couple of weeks earlier. Sam was no doubt hoping I could help to stop the rot.

On the way out he introduced me to the chairman of Bury, Terry Robinson; aka Selwyn Froggitt. To be fair though, Terry looked more like Selwyn Froggitt than Selwyn Froggitt himself and when he said he was pleased to meet me, I was dying to say: "Magic our Morris". For any non-Bury fans and younger lads and girls who are reading this, Google or visualise Greengrass out of *Heartbeat* and there you have it; Terry Robinson!

The Bury team was absolutely teeming with characters on both the playing and coaching staff. In my first training session I met the legendary Wilf McGuinness, the former Manchester United Busby Babe – and briefly, their manager, who had become Bury's physiotherapist, coach and kitman. What a character Wilf was, and he would quite rightly get a fantastic testimonial year while I was at Bury.

From the first training session it was clear that the lads were a great bunch. The captain Andy Hill was held in high regard, being part of the team that had won promotion under the previously very well-liked manager, Martin Dobson, who had unfortunately been sacked the previous April after a bad run of results. Apparently, it also hadn't gone down well that he'd allegedly been touting himself to other clubs.

Andy had been made captain when he was 19, contrasting wildly to the 'seen it, done it, got the T-shirt' veteran full-back Kenny Clements. Kenny had the best mop of hair and 'tache at the club, possibly in the league. I was a little bit in awe when I first met him as he was a Man City legend to me when I was a young lad. He had played in the same team as my City heroes Peter Barnes and Colin Bell through the 1970s and although he was coming to the end of his career at Bury, he was still doing a great job for them as a utility defender.

Charlie Bishop was also a top lad; in fact all the players in the first team -including midfielders Jamie Hoyland and Phil Parkinson, striker Liam Robinson and fans' favourite, tricky winger David Lee, to name a few – seemed fantastic lads. I could see that there was a great camaraderie in the team, even with the recent poor run. The gaffer and Mike Walsh really enjoyed the banter and I think it helped that, like most of the lads, they seemed to enjoy a beer or two as well. Sam was a real ale drinker and apparently didn't mind the lads having a few beers after the game and on the away trips, just like at my former clubs. It was just the way it was then. They were both ex-players, with over 700 league games between them, and they just got it. Their man management skills were fantastic.

I made a half decent debut in a 0-0 draw, with defender, Peter Valentine coming back after a long injury to shore up the defence, but we went on to lose three of our next four and couldn't buy a win. Liam Robinson missed a penalty in a dreary 0-0 draw at Wigan and we showed a little bit too much fighting spirit against Tranmere, when Liam was sent off along with Tranmere's Neil McNab. Then our skipper Andy saw red as well… after the final whistle! I think he'd had enough of some strange decisions being made by the ref and, in no uncertain terms, had told him so.

After an away defeat at Crewe the natives were definitely getting restless and, in fairness, had every right to be. We had gone nine games without a win at this stage, dropping out of the play-offs and down to eighth after being second in early December. The gaffer then pulled a masterstroke.

After training on Heaton Park one day during the week, he announced that after the following home game against Notts County, we would be going away for a mid-season break, straight after the game. He wouldn't elaborate on the destination, but just said we should bring our passports with us. Striker Kevin Hulme, a local lad, unfortunately didn't have a passport, but Sam told him not to worry and that he'd sort it out. Even if he had to smuggle him on the plane.

We called Kevin "Reggie the Roofer" – yep, you guessed it, he used to be a roofer – and he was made up. We all were. Hugh Eaves was definitely throwing money at the club so a few of us started to think, or hope, that it could be Magaluf. The rest of the week in training flew by as the excitement grew and by the day of the game, everyone was absolutely buzzing. I loved a mid-season break, as a great way to relax and recharge the batteries. And as you may have gathered from the antics at my other clubs, the craic was usually great too!

Any outsider looking into our changing room that day would have wondered what was going on. The floor was strewn with suitcases full of holiday clothes, flip-flops, speedos and sun cream. The promise of a mid-season break abroad did the trick as we beat County 3-2. I scored my first goal for the club as an added bonus, and we were like kids in the dressing room afterwards. We boarded the coach, opened a few crates of beer and headed south towards Manchester airport. Imagine the looks on our faces, then, when we drove straight past the airport turn off and carried on… towards Wales.

The gaffer and Walshy had done us big style. After a bit of a moan about the piss-take, we did what all footballers did in those days and continued to get increasingly hammered on the coach until we got to the hotel somewhere in north Wales. We had a couple of great days, and nights. It was team bonding, early 1990s style, at its best.

On the last night, most of the lads got pleasantly pissed before making their way to bed and by the end, it was last men and a woman standing. By the early hours there were just a few left, including the gaffer, Walshy, David Lee, Gary Kelly, Peter Valentine, the club physio, Mandy, and myself. I'm not sure whose bright idea it was, but we started to get stuck into a massive jar of pickled eggs that were on the end of the bar.

Peter Valentine decided that he was Cool Hand Luke and had one too many eggs before he regurgitated most of them back into his near-empty Guinness pint glass. Like a true pro, though, he then got himself a fresh pint of Guinness and washed the taste down, before carrying on and knocking a few more back.

Eventually the gaffer and Mike called it a night, and not long afterwards, me, David Lee and Kell decided we'd had enough as well. Now, what you don't do when you are on the piss with a group of footballers, even if you are the assistant manager, is leave your bedroom door open. As we noticed Walshy had done in his pissed-up state. It was too good an opportunity to miss and as Mike was dead to the world, we sneaked into his room, giggling like schoolboys.

We got his toothpaste from the bathroom and went to town on our victim, who didn't come round one bit as we covered his hair, eyebrows and 'tache with toothpaste. We squirted some in his ears for good measure before heading off to bed, pissing ourselves.

The next morning, we went down to breakfast, expecting to see Mike quizzing everyone to find out who the culprits were. But to be fair to him, he played it as cool as you like and didn't even mention it. It wasn't until years later, at a dinner for ex-players, that I revealed to Mike that we were the guilty three. Remembering it well, Mike just laughed his head off about it. As I knew he would.

At a more recent get-together, as we were reminiscing about our time at Bury, Mike told me a great story about when he and Sam signed Andy Feeley at the beginning of the season that I joined. The escapade summed up how alcohol, rightly or wrongly, played a large part in football in the 1980s and 90s. Feeley had a tough reputation and Sam and Mike had wanted to sign him to put a bit of bite into the team. They decided to meet him at a pub where the two of regularly drank, that also did bed and breakfast.

The 'talks' went really well, and late into the night, and the alcohol flowed. Around 10 pints of real ale and lager later, the three of them staggered off to their rooms. Mike and Andy then started getting a bit giddy and boisterous in the corridor on the way to their rooms before

Andy landed an 'accidental' punch on Mike. The next morning, when they met for breakfast, the assistant boss had a shiner. Andy couldn't remember a thing about it and the deal was done!

It may not have been the trip abroad we were hoping for, but our midweek jolly certainly worked as we went on a great run to get our promotion push well and truly back on track. The break had definitely done Reggie the Roofer good as he scored his first-ever league goal for Bury in a 1-0 win over Northampton. I was especially grateful he did, because I had managed to miss a penalty! A couple more wins put us back in the play-off picture and an unlucky 2-1 away defeat to eventual champions Bristol Rovers didn't dampen our spirits.

Training during the week was tough, but really enjoyable. Thursdays would not only be going through tactics and shape, as at other clubs, but would be based around a full no-holds-barred 11 v 11 game, which we christened 'Shinpad Thursday'. The ex-Bolton manager Ian Greaves was now on board as a coach and it seemed it was him who encouraged the Thursday mash up. Everyone got stuck in, knowing that the gaffer and Mike were watching and that Sam ultimately picked his team from who performed on that day. The tackles would be flying in from everywhere, so the wearing of shin pads was a must.

It was probably a little unconventional, even in those days, but it worked. We won four of our six games after the Bristol Rovers defeat, drawing the other two and scoring 15 goals. David Lee was on fire, scoring four on the trot – including a great goal at home to Blackpool. Not to be upstaged, I also scored an absolute cracker after a long run and finish in a 2-0 win, which will have no doubt made my friends at PNE happy. We hammered Huddersfield 6-0, the same scoreline they had beaten us by the season before, with six different scorers, and our biggest league crowd of the season so far packed Gigg Lane for a 2-0 win over local promotion rivals Bolton.

That secured our play-off place, with two games to go, and we were now just two wins away from Wembley and a chance of promotion. We finished the season with a defeat away at Reading, which I think the small section of travelling fans would have forgiven us for – as most of us were still a bit hungover from a good old-fashioned knees-up in the social club after the Bolton game. A 2-0 win against Cardiff sent us into the play-offs in good spirits and for the record, we kept seven home clean sheets on the run since that Notts County game and also won 10 away games, which I think was some kind of record. It was amazing what a mid-season piss-up could achieve!

I had thoroughly enjoyed the season, playing in every league game since I signed. My goal scoring tally had gone down, but the enjoyment and injury-free level had gone up. We finished fifth in the table, so played fourth-placed Tranmere in the semi-finals and whoever wrote the Bury 'Man for Man' section of the programme for the first leg had enjoyed my contributions too.

"Mark has been a revelation since his signing at the beginning of February from Preston," read my section in a rundown of every player. "Slotted in very well on the left-hand side of midfield/attack. Has shown what a highly skilled player he is with what must rank as one of the best goals scored in years v Blackpool. Has brought in greater balance to the team. Good rapport with the fans."

We went into the semis against Tranmere cautiously confident. We had beaten them in the league at Prenton Park, but they had returned the favour by winning at Gigg Lane. As it happened, there was nothing to separate us in the first leg and we couldn't get an advantage to take away for the second leg. There was even a chance of a Wembley derby game in the play-off final, with Bolton facing Notts County in the other semi-final.

But unfortunately, it wasn't to be. The highest scorers in the league that season were too good for us on the night of the second leg in front of over 10,000 fans, which included a great following from Bury. At 1-0 down at half-time, we still had a chance but it proved not to be our night when Phil Parkinson handled a cross from Tranmere's centre-forward, Jim Steel. Ian Muir sent Gary Kelly the wrong way from the spot and I'm afraid that was that. Ours was a very quiet changing room after the game and I was as gutted as anyone at my second play-off defeat in two seasons. Another chance of a Wembley appearance gone.

I took my mind off the disappointment by spending a month, like every other England fan, watching Italia 90. New Order continued to keep the football world in motion and it was a World Cup that many say changed the face of English football for the better, with England getting to the semis and the tears on Gazza's face. I have to agree. How the beers flowed!

It was a great summer of love for English football and Lindsey helped to make it even more special by making our family complete when our son, Scott, was born on June 24. Having a newborn son was worth the sleepless nights that quickly ensued. Like a lot of the Bury lads, I still managed to get a quick family holiday in before returning for pre-season. We all came back humming the tune to Pavarotti's classic, *Nessun Dorma*, and a few of the lads weren't that far off his weight either. But no names shall be mentioned!

16

PAYING THE WAGES

August 1990 to January 1991

A new season always brings new hope for fans of any football club and it's the same for any professional footballer. Bury fans had reason to be optimistic, too, with Hugh Eaves splashing the cash throughout the summer and bringing in four new players to show the club's intent for the season. Together, the four – Ronnie Mauge, Roger Stanislaus, Colin Greenall and John McGinlay – cost £430,000. That was a massive amount for a small club in those days and no doubt the signings signalled Bury's promotion intent to all our Third Division rivals.

It's a pity our poor pre-season results didn't reflect that, but you have to remember that we were running off the World Cup excesses. Our preparation this time took us to the sunny climate of Frodsham in Cheshire again – same place, different team. On one of the days we were given the afternoon off to do what we wanted. At the time, Gary Kelly, David Lee and me were car sharing and the best of mates, so we decided to go into Frodsham together for a look around. We saw Andy Feeley and Andy Hill mooching around in the town and had a bit of banter with them.

They were great lads but kept themselves to themselves and were handy, let's say. You didn't fuck with them anyway, but that didn't stop us playing a practical joke on them. I can't remember whose idea it actually was, but we decided to get a bag of maggots from a fishing shop we passed. Knowing that the two Andys were still in Frodsham when we got back to the hotel, we managed to persuade the reception staff to lend us the skeleton key for their room.

We put the maggots in their toothpaste, in their hair and shower gel, under their bed sheets and in their pillowcases. We were pissing our sides as we thought of the best places to hide them, before handing back the key and heading back to our rooms. We got down for our evening meal early and waited for them to come down. We made sure not to tell any of the other players – knowing that our lives wouldn't be worth living if anyone grassed us up. When both Andys came down together, they just sat down and didn't say a word. We kept our gobs shut until Andy Feeley turned to us.

"Did you see a fishing shop in town, lads?" he asked. We just started laughing our heads off, knowing that we had been sussed.

"You fucking cunts," he said. "We'll get you back for that…"

To be fair, they were both laughing. Both took it in good spirits, and it went down well with the other lads when they found out what had happened.

We got off to a great start to the season with a 2-1 win at home to Chester City and yours truly scored the first goal of the new season. Throughout my career I have been lucky to score a few screamers, but this wasn't one of them as I was in the right place at the right time to slot in from inside the six-yard box. John McGinlay started off his Bury career with a goal on his debut, a penalty, and we were up and running with three points.

We continued in good form, with big Tony Cunningham scoring a few goals and me finding the net again in a win over Rotherham which took us up to third. Shin Pad Thursday was becoming even more intense – we certainly weren't going to be physically bullied by any other teams in the division – and the ground had the extra bonus of stinking like cat piss, courtesy of a ginger cat that had been sort of adopted by the club in pre-season. The kit woman looked after it, but the moggie didn't seem to bother where it did its business and so, before long, the whole place stank of cat piss.

One day, it got too much for Mike Walsh, who put the cat in a box and said he was going to let it out at training on Heaton Park. I'm not sure if it ever made it but hopefully it went on to live happily ever after. Unfortunately for Mike, the heartbroken kit woman had witnessed the catnap. So, when she reported it to the RSPCA as missing, she let them know that the last time she saw the cat was when the assistant manager gathered the poor little mite into a box and was taking it away.

I don't think it was the same RSPCA officer who had spoken to Tony Ellis, but Mike did have a bit of explaining to do. Luckily, he was a great talker and managed to explain his way out of the situation, but the kit woman didn't speak to him for a while after that.

On the field, we were gelling well as a squad and the new lads were settling in nicely, but our results were very mixed. Of the 12 games after the Rotherham win in early September, we won four, lost four and drew four. We just couldn't get a winning – or at least unbeaten – run going, even if we had our moments, like a cracking 2-2 home draw against our rivals, Bolton.

They had gone in 1-0 up and early in the second half, we got a free kick. It was about 25 yards out, honest, and I fancied it straight away. I caught it sweetly, watching it go over the wall and into the top corner, to the delight of our fans. Alan Knill then made it 2-1, but unfortunately, we couldn't hold on for a famous win as Tony Cunningham gave away a penalty.

One win in seven games saw us drop down to ninth place and for a club that had invested so much money in the summer, it wasn't good enough. And the fans were rightly letting us know. A cracking 3-0 revenge win over Tranmere, who had lost the play-off final to Notts County at Wembley, should have seen us kick-start our season. But it all started to unravel after an unexpected FA Cup first-round defeat against local non-league side Chorley.

Having been beaten by a non-league club at Preston the previous season, I knew it wasn't going to be easy against Chorley but we actually didn't play that badly. We just couldn't put the ball in the back of the net, which didn't help. Then the pressure started to build as Chorley scored from a close range shot and then a header from a corner. We managed a consolation goal but it was a major scalp – for, coincidentally, a team I would go on to manage when my playing days were over.

In the following weeks there were a lot of repercussions from the game. Apparently, Hugh Eaves, the major shareholder, was verbally abused on Chorley train station and Sam Ellis' position was called into question. Within weeks, Sam had left the club to join Peter Reid as his assistant at First Division Manchester City and Eaves was not happy with the criticism, pulling the plug on the finances. I think it might have also had something to do with his business situation at the time but he essentially stopped bankrolling the club and paying the players' wages.

The extent of his financial dealings didn't become apparent until the late 1990s, which would coincide with my second spell at the club, through to early 2000, when the club unfortunately ended up going into administration. From a non-technical point of view, let's just say that him pulling the plug on the finances left the club in the shit! It was shockingly sad to see Bury's recent further demise and expulsion from the Football League in 2019. To see 124 years of football history go down the drain is disgusting really, with all the money that is swishing around football. I hope for their great loyal fanbase that they can rebuild and fight their way back into the Football League as soon as possible.

Some good and bad news arrived when, in mid-December, Mike Walsh got the manager's job, which all the players were really pleased with. The bad news was that the club didn't have enough money to pay the players' wages – which wasn't the best position to be in, especially over Christmas and New Year. I then got called into the new boss's office and told that I would be paying the wages. Not me personally, but my transfer fee to Bolton would. Mike was apologetic as we got on fantastically well, but Bolton had come in with a £65,000 offer for me and the club's dire position meant that they had no alternative but to accept.

So, my leaving late-Christmas present to the Bury faithful turned out to be a spectacular equaliser against my former club Preston. It came more or less on the stroke of half-time after my old mate Brian Mooney had put them ahead, and came from a punt upfield from our goalkeeper Gary Kelly. The ball was flicked on by Tony Cunningham and I managed to do a little dribble before smashing in right footed

– yes, right footed – into the top corner from outside the box, giving Gary's brother Alan Kelly no chance.

I did say nearly on the stroke of half-time because we then got a penalty for handball. I stepped up confidently and smashed the ball towards the corner of the net, only for Kelly to pull off a brilliant save and tip the ball over the bar. I took eight penalties and scored all of them for Preston, but that was just a great save by Alan. Luckily for me, my miss didn't cost us the game as in the second half Tony Cunningham and Liam Robinson both scored and we ran out 3-1 winners.

My final game for the Shakers was a 3-1 defeat at Bradford City on New Year's Day, 1991. I knew I was going to miss some of the great friends I had made at Bury – particularly the car-share lads, Gary Kelly and David 'Didsy' Lee, even if Didsy wouldn't let me and Kell into his new car until we had finished our fags. We just used to have the craic all the time although I had once nearly fallen out with Kell after a misdemeanour by him in a card school on the way home from an away game.

After a few blind hands I had looked at my cards and thought I was in the money, with a jack flush. Happy days indeed, but Kell gave me a nudge under the table and gave a quick shake of his head, as if to say he'd seen my hand and he'd got an even better one. Now please don't think this happened every time because it didn't, but I took the hint that he had a better hand, stacked my cards and watched the game unfold.

When the cards were revealed Kell won a big money pot … with ace high! I was fuming inside but I couldn't show my emotions because I would have been accused of cheating. When we got to the relative privacy of the car back at the club, I went berserk. Kell and Didsy just started pissing themselves laughing. In the end, just like the trip to Wales, I saw the funny side, but just made sure I didn't sit next to Kell in card schools again!

I was extremely disappointed to have to leave Bury. We had a great set of lads and I'd made some fantastic friends in the relatively short time I had been there. We had been unlucky to miss out on promotion in my first season and with all the new signings, the club had been showing their ambition to get promotion in the second season. That was until the finances went to pot, obviously.

So, the next stop on my Tour de Lancashire, after Blackburn Rovers, Preston North End and Bury, was Bolton – another of the original 12 founder members of the Football League. They were also less than 10 miles from my home in Darwen. I had no idea it would be my most successful club.

17

NEXT STOP BOLTON

In early January 1991, I sat down with the Bolton manager and his assistant to sort out my next contract. I was 25, in my eighth season as a professional, and had played just shy of 200 league games at the equivalent of today's Championship and League One level. I'd also scored 49 league goals, which wasn't a bad return at all. I had played and won a trophy at Wembley for my hometown team and had been involved in two play-off campaigns. All in all, I felt, not bad for a lad from Darwen at that stage of my career.

The manager I sat across from was Phil Neal, whose own playing CV was ridiculous. He is still the most decorated English footballer in the history of the beautiful game, having won... eight top-flight league titles, a British-record four European Cups, one UEFA Cup, one UEFA Super Cup, four League Cups and five Charity Shields, for Liverpool. He also scored in two European Cup finals and holds the Liverpool record for consecutive appearances – a crazy 417 games in a row, between October 1976 and September 1983. He didn't miss a single game for the equivalent number of years I had been playing professionally. Throw in his 50 England caps for good measure and it really does make me realise how lucky I was to mix with some real football greats during my career.

His assistant, Mick Brown, wasn't from bad footballing stock either. Mick managed Oxford in the late 1970s before joining Ron Atkinson as his assistant at West Brom and when Ron got the Manchester United job in 1981, he took Mick with him. Phil's trophy cabinet may have been bulging but Mick had two medals that eluded Phil – two FA Cup wins, from his time at Man United. Mick lost his job when Big Ron got the sack in 1986 and Alex Ferguson took over. But over the next season-and-a-half at Bolton, he showed he was a brilliant coach.

In fact, he was the main man with the players on the training pitch. Phil may not have been the best manager I ever played for, but he was, and still is, a lovely bloke. He had been in charge at Burnden Park for four seasons when I signed, and he hadn't found management as easy as he found playing. Another record he holds, but would rather he didn't, was being the first Bolton manager in the club's history to take one of the founder members of the Football League into the fourth tier. They did bounce back up the very next season, though, and Neal did take them to Wembley twice in the Sherpa Van Trophy – a 4-1 victory over Torquay in the 1989 final making up for losing 3-1 to Bristol City three years earlier.

After losing in the play-offs the previous season, I was joining a club on a 13-game unbeaten run since October, lifting them from second bottom to a play-off position. They were also about to play the cup holders Manchester United in the fourth round of the FA Cup at Old Trafford. It turned out that the amount of cash that Bolton would get from the bumper tie with their fierce, local rivals paid for my transfer. Unfortunately for me, the Chorley cup defeat in November meant I was cup-tied!

Still without an agent, I again negotiated my own contract and signed for the same money as I had been on at Bury, albeit with the added bonus of a signing-on fee that worked out at £10,000 per season. With Bolton being Bury's local rivals, and with me playing and scoring against Bolton in the last few seasons, I knew the Bolton lads quite well already. Three had been teammates elsewhere. Steve Thompson was the same age as me but had already played nearly 300 games for the Whites when I signed, and football is a small world; me and Steve played together for Lancashire schoolboys at the age of 15. Paul Comstive had stopped diving into rivers and eating pies and had gone on to play for Wigan and Wrexham before landing at Bolton, while Tony Philliskirk was a former teammate from my Preston days.

Tony was banging them in for fun already that season and scored for the fourth game in a row against Bradford City, when I made my debut off the bench. It was by no means a classic game, but it was certainly a poignant and emotional day for our goalkeeper David Felgate. He had been Lincoln City's 'keeper on the fateful day of the Bradford fire disaster at Valley Parade six years earlier.

My home debut was the following Saturday, January 19, and I was lucky enough to get a mention in Phil Neal's programme notes. "First and foremost, this afternoon I would like you all to extend a very warm Burnden Park welcome to Mark Patterson, the latest addition to our fold," he wrote. "Those fans who followed us to Bradford last week will have seen a glimmer of the qualities that I am sure will justify our investment." Cheers Phil, no pressure then! The Bolton fans did indeed give me a warm welcome and I was glad I went straight into the team in my second game. Forgive my French but fucking hell, Burnden Park was a cold ground. I was glad I wasn't on the bench!

Even within a few days of being at my new club I could tell that there was a great team spirit, probably because a number of players had been there a number of seasons together. There was a great mix of lads, including a number who were coming through the youth set up – most notably Alan Stubbs, Neil Fisher, Nicky Spooner and Mickey Jeffrey – and older homegrown players, including Steve Thompson and Julian Darby. These were all mixed in with seasoned pros such as club captain and right back Phil Brown, Felgate, Comstive, and Philliskirk, defenders David Burke, Barry Cowdrill, Mark Winstanley and Mark Seagraves, midfielder/striker Scott Green, winger Stuart Storer and Philliskirk's strike partner, David Reeves.

My old teammate Thompson scored the winner to beat Shrewsbury and keep our unbeaten run going, before the game that everyone wanted to play in – and I couldn't. The lads more than held their own in front of over 43,000 fans at Old Trafford and I took the opportunity to sit with 10,000 Bolton fans in the away end, who never stopped singing all game. In a great gesture before the start of the game, United let Bolton's 1958 FA Cup winning team parade on the pitch in front of the fantastic visiting support and although the lads weren't able to repeat those heroics, they put on a great display. This really opened my eyes to see the potential of this once massive club.

In Division Three terms, our next league game had a great crowd of just under 10,000 as we took a sizeable following to our Lancashire rivals and another one of my old clubs, Preston North End. I got a great reception but by the end of the game the PNE fans must have been sick of us ex-players as Tony Philliskirk scored both goals in a hard-fought 2-1 win. His goalscoring partnership with David Reeves was once again flourishing and by early February the Bros Brothers had already scored 21 goals. Tony scored the bulk of them, with 14, but David was doing all his running, setting him up and chipping in with a few goals himself.

Games were coming thick and fast and frustratingly I had started to feel a pain in my lower abdominals, but when you are playing well and getting good results, you take the painkillers and get on with it. We were soon up to third and hadn't been beaten for 18 games. Could we keep the run going? Aided by a stroke of luck, we could. We were supposed to be playing Exeter away next, but the game got switched to Burnden Park and we took advantage of not having to travel all the way down to Devon in midweek, beating them 1-0. Tony took a rest from scoring, but his striking brother didn't and a David Reeves goal settled the match.

Goalkeeper David Felgate and right back Phil Brown had been ever-present from the start of the season and, in fact, Mr. Consistency and pub landlord Phil had not missed a game since his £17,000 transfer from Halifax in June 1989. He wasn't quite in the Phil Neal category yet, but what a bargain buy! Barry Cowdrill had made the left back spot his own and Mark Winstanley and Mark Seagraves had a great centre-half understanding. Barry Cowdrill then only went and scored a blinder away to Reading to become the first defender to score all season and earn us a 1-0 win and when we took 3,000 travelling fans to Tranmere on a Friday night, I thought I had better open my account if Barry had started scoring. A late equaliser was my first ever goal in Bolton colours.

In a gap in midweek fixtures the manager organised a team-bonding session in Blackpool with the young lads included for their first trip. Some went to play golf and some of us went round the pubs. I like my golf but decided to have a day out around Blackpool's finest ale houses, joined by the young guns Stubbsy, Mick Jeffrey, Nicky Spooner and Neil Fisher. We had a cracking day but by the time it came to Spoon's round, some of the golfers had called it a day and joined us. Suddenly it looked like costing him quite a few bob, so I helped him out and put a bit of dosh in his pocket.

If the younger ones needed a hand, we were there for them but they weren't mollycoddled like the young lads are today and had to do an initiation ceremony when they made it to the first team. It meant them standing on a table, bollock naked in the middle of the dressing room, singing a song whilst having boiling hot tea bags thrown at them, leaving red burn marks where they hit. And just to finish off, boot polish was smeared around their bollocks!

I recently spoke to Nicky Spooner about it and he said it was a great craic – maybe not at the actual time, but the banter was great. He reminded me of how on their first overnight trip away to Peterborough when the young lads were together in their rooms, a handful of 'senior' pros burst into their room with pillows and a fire extinguisher and they got a good blasting. Back then it was just the norm. Imagine that happening now…

Back on the football front, we extended our unbeaten run to 23 games with a 3-0 win over Fulham. I scored another to go above Barry in the scoring charts, and Phil Neal celebrated his 40th birthday with the Third Division manager of the month award for February. What a great record to be part of – half a season undefeated. Team spirit and morale was sky high ahead of a midweek trip to lowly Mansfield, who promptly beat us 4-0.

The wheels came off the promotion bus spectacularly. We had no injuries, except me hiding mine, and no excuses – we were just well and truly beaten. It would be comforting to say that this was the start of Mansfield's rise from fourth-from-bottom to a top half finish, but it wasn't. They went on to finish bottom of the league and we ended up finishing 3 points below champions Southend. It wasn't that defeat that cost us as we then went on to lose two out of the next three away games, but this was one that got away!

After a great home win against Wigan our home unbeaten run then came to an end against, of all clubs, our local rivals Bury. I took some stick from the travelling support as John McGinlay scored a hat trick on a rain-sodden midweek night and a dampen-your-spirits 3-1 defeat ensued. We were still within touching distance of automatic promotion but really frustratingly for me I was now getting severe pain in my lower abdominals and a scan showed that I needed a double hernia operation. I was being nursed along by now and couldn't train fully or travel long distances as I needed daily treatment.

Our consistency had also gone and frustratingly I couldn't play in three away defeats to Exeter, Bournemouth and Cambridge United, who had come on the outside rails and would eventually finish as champions. Cambridge had only come up the season before and their direct style introduced by manager John Beck might not have won any popularity contests, but it would win them the Third Division title.

Unfortunately I couldn't make it through to the end of the season and had to watch the last four league games from the sidelines after going under the knife. Without me, the lads managed to win at home to Orient, draw at Rotherham and then a magnificent 2-1 win at Swansea to take the chance of automatic promotion to the very last day of the season. We had to beat Chester at home and hope for other games to go our way. The lads did their bit with a nervy 1-0 home win, with Tony Cunningham scoring again, and almost 13,000 fans in our highest crowd of the season hoped it would be enough. But Grimsby, whose result we had to better, hung on for a 2-1 win. Their fans were sent home ecstatic; ours, when news filtered through, were gutted. We had come up short on goal difference.

Even a point at Mansfield, or anywhere else, would have given us automatic promotion and although it would be hard for the lads not to feel sorry for themselves, they had to put the disappointment out of their minds as they prepared for another crack at the play-offs. Standing in their way for a place in the final, and a trip to Wembley to face Tranmere or Brentford, were their local rivals and my old team. Bury.

You really had to tip your hat to Mike Walsh, who had done a magnificent job to get Bury to the play-offs. By this time, the Bury finances were in freefall and as well as me departing, they had sold John McGinlay to Millwall, Tony Cunningham to us and captain Andy Hill had got a well-deserved dream loan move to Manchester City. Mike had shown what a top man-manager he was and although my loyalties were now with my new club, I was really pleased for them.

Tony Philliskirk's prolific form continued as he scored a goal in each leg to seal a 2-1 aggregate victory and a Wembley date with Tranmere. I was absolutely gutted to be missing out on another chance to play at Wembley and was just hoping that the lads could get us promoted. It was always going to be tough against Tranmere, but we had finished five points above them and took four points out of six against them in the league. So the lads went into the game feeling confident.

How sad it was for everyone concerned that for the second year running, we came up just short. A tight, very even match saw few chances for both sides and, for once, none fell to Tony Philliskirk. Julian Darby nearly scored with a thunderbolt that was brilliantly saved by Eric Nixon and Paul Comstive unfortunately screwed what was possibly our best chance wide in a tense second half. The game was 0-0 in extra-time until Chris Malkin followed up a great save by David Felgate to score from near the penalty spot. It was absolute heartache for over 20,000 Wanderers fans, and the players and staff of Bolton.

For me watching from the stands it really was a matter of what might have been. I'd had a decent first season and felt if I hadn't been forced into what in those days was a big operation, I could have either helped to get us automatic promotion or made a difference in the final. After the game I spoke to a number of Tranmere players who told me they were happy not to see my name on the teamsheet before the game. Football is a game of ifs, buts and maybes, and this was just another one of those moments.

18

NEAL DOWN AND OUT

1991/92

The start of the 1991/92 season brought some good and bad news. The good was that my double hernia operation and continued recovery meant I was nursed through the pre-season and missed the usual monotony that came with it. The downside was that I also missed the first couple of league games, two 1-1 draws against Huddersfield and Swansea. I made my comeback as a sub in a Rumbelows Cup replay against York City at Bootham Crescent, albeit not in the best of circumstances. Young first team debutant Neil Fisher saw claret after a nasty clash of heads which needed more than a few stitches. Football can be cruel as he'd been celebrating scoring a goal on his debut only minutes earlier.

The game was level at 1-1 with half an hour to go, and I got straight into it – going on a bit of a run through their defence and scoring what turned out to be the winning goal. It felt great, especially when the draw came out and we were paired against Brian Clough's Nottingham Forest. I wondered if Cloughy would remember my apprentice duties in the away changing room at Ewood?

Before then it was back to the bread and butter of the Third Division and when we played Orient in our next game, winning 1-0, I got a rather nice mention in Phil Neal's programme notes. "Getting back to the York game, I've got to make a special mention of Mark Patterson who came on for the last half hour and scored the match winner," Phil wrote. "I'm delighted for 'Paddy' because he has worked very hard indeed to fight his way back from his recent operation. I don't think many people realised the problems he was having last season, when we never saw him on the training ground because he was always either resting between games or having treatment. He's gone through the pain barrier in the name of Bolton Wanderers and, although we saw plenty of him last season, I think we are going to see a new player from now on in Mark Patterson."

As I mentioned, Phil was not the best manager I played under, but he was an absolute gentleman and he also made a signing that would help to kickstart Bolton's glory years of the early 1990s, even if it wouldn't help him keep his job. Bringing in Tony 'Zico' Kelly for £100,000, along with his teammate Mickey Brown from Shrewsbury, turned out to be an inspired move. Even in the opening games of the season you could see what a talent Tony was and in the following seasons he would become both a players' and a terrace favourite. But that was only when the next manager helped to sort out his nutrition and his fluid intake.

It was no secret that, like many of us in that era, Tony liked a beer or three and wasn't too concerned with his diet. It didn't stop him being one of the best players I ever played with but, when he arrived at Burnden Park, Tony wasn't in the best shape. He didn't even try and hide his love of a beer and a burger. Tony was a proper Scouser, Huyton born, who'd started his footballing life as a trainee with the mighty Liverpool in the early 1980s. By the time he arrived at Bolton he was just about to turn 27 and his footballing journey had taken him firstly to non-league Prescot Cables, before he played nearly 300 league games for Wigan, Stoke, West Brom and Shrewsbury. He was a great character, as his answers showed to the 'profile' questions in one of the matchday programmes not long after he joined.

Weight: Varies – 2lbs lighter than Barry Cowdrill
Nickname: Chico Zico Fatman
Favourite food: Salads – I've had enough of them!
Favourite drink: Lager
Hobbies: Drinking and eating
Which three things would you take on a desert island: My wife, food and drink.

When you consider that Mark Seagraves answered the profile question about the biggest risk he had taken in his life with: "Going out for a drink with Tony Kelly", you sort of get the picture of the type of man Tony was. A lovable rogue, but one of the most gifted and well-respected lower league midfield players around.

Results showed that we didn't start the season off that badly and after our first loss away to Darlington, when the double act scored one each again, we welcomed West Brom to Burnden Park in a game that many thought would be two of the teams battling for automatic promotion. West Brom were in the Third Division for the first time in their history and we were looking to avoid being involved in the play-offs. A brilliant 3-0 win ensued, with Tony Philliskirk scoring two and Mickey Brown netting his first goal. This was followed by a great 2-1 away win at Bournemouth, with Phil Brown scoring and taking us right up the table.

Looking back, with the Forest game looming, the competition to start in the game at the City Ground probably meant that everyone had raised their game. Until the game away at Bradford, anyway, when our defence forgot how to defend and conceded four goals.

Luckily, Julian Darby had brought his shooting boots and scored two, David Reeves notched again and I scored my first league goal of the season, the 50th of my career, from the penalty spot in a 4-4 draw. My goalscoring ratio may have been on the slide, and would continue to, but at the time I was averaging nearly a goal every four games. Looking back, that wasn't bad for a little winger from Darwen.

When it was my turn to appear on the programme's profile page, my family details amongst other answers showed that I was settling down to some extent. But like Tony Kelly, I still loved the banter. In those days – well up until the next season – that was to me what football was all about; playing, the banter, drinking and family.

Nickname: Paddy/Gizmo. [As I mentioned before, that came from Gary Brazil, from my playing days at PNE. "Yes, Gizmo, pass it..." The cheeky fucker.]
Family details: Wife Lindsey, kids Jade 3, Scott 1.

Favourite drink: Tea. [I think I may have thought the interviewer meant non-alcoholic drink.]

Biggest influence on your career: Don Mackay (he kicked me out of Blackburn). [Carrying on the theme that unfortunately I didn't get on with Mackay – ironically around this time he would be relieved of his Rovers job after a poor start to the season. By that time the Jack Walker era at Rovers had officially started and Mackay's replacement would astound the football world … Kenny Dalglish!]

Player for the future: Alan Stubbs (when he can pass a 10-yard ball). [I don't think I needed a crystal ball for this prediction. Stubbsy had come through the youth ranks and had already played in the first team but what a great career he went on to have at mainly Bolton, Celtic and Everton, his boyhood club. What a strong character and role model as well, overcoming testicular cancer whilst he was at Celtic. At the time of this programme interview, though, he was still only 19, so I'll give myself a bit of credit with this prediction!]

Biggest risk ever taken in your life: Drinking with Andy Feeley and Sam Ellis. [Enough said about this, as I don't want the Bury fans on my back!]

Ambitions: To win promotion and to make my landscaping business successful. [My crystal ball did work with this one, both on the pitch and with the business.]

When the Forest game eventually rolled around, we were up against one of the best sides in England and would face three players who would later become Premiership greats: Stuart Pearce, Roy Keane and Teddy Sheringham, Forest's record £2.1m signing from Millwall. But despite their star names, we travelled to the City Ground full of confidence and it was an absolute pleasure to play there, on a Tuesday night in September against the full-strength former European champions in front of a cracking crowd of over 18,000.

We were hammered 4-0 with a young Roy Keane running the show, scoring the first goal and setting up the third. I have a photograph somewhere with me running away from him with the ball, which is a great memento – what a player he became. The second leg a few weeks later was another lesson in attacking football with Forest banging five past us. At least we scored two, even with Forest now boasting Des Walker in their line-up.

October 1991 came and went with two wins and two defeats, one of the latter an emphatic 3-0 home defeat to Fulham which ended our undefeated start to the season at Fortress Burnden and didn't go down well with the supporters. Maybe it was the overcompensation from my double hernia operation in the summer, but I started to get lower back and hip problems and was diagnosed with a sacroiliac joint problem. It meant I had to have a steroid injection and rest up through November and December. I really don't know how Phil Neal managed to get through seven years without an injury. Frustratingly for me and the club, I couldn't seem to get through seven months.

Without me in the team the lads went through November undefeated and drew another non-league side away from home in the first round of the FA Cup. It could easily have been Chorley again, but Emley beat them in a replay and although I wasn't playing, I still felt nervous about the prospect of another giant-killing. I needn't have worried, the lads doing a professional job and winning 3-0 in front of a great crowd of over 9,000.

We beat Bradford City 3-1 at home in the second round to reach the heights of the third round, where any Third Division side would be hoping for either a home tie or one of the big boys away. We drew fellow Third Division side Reading at home, giving us great belief that we could progress, and Tony Philliskirk kept up his habit of scoring in every round to help us to a 2-0 win. Another home tie followed in the next round, albeit a slightly disappointing one against Second Division side Brighton. Our league form had started to dip around our cup run and we dropped out of the play-off places.

Speaking to a few Bolton fans recently, they tended to dismiss Phil Neal's reign as Bolton manager and in some respects, it wasn't the most successful. But in January 1992, the gaffer made two signings that would prove to be invaluable for the club. A young talented lad called Jason McAteer was signed on a free from non-league Marine and Andy Walker arrived on loan from Celtic. The loan move would ultimately become permanent, and what a signing it was. Andy netted with his first touch of the ball in a 2-2 draw at Exeter, and hardly stopped scoring for the rest of the season.

Even better, coming from a Scottish club meant that Andy wasn't cup-tied for the Brighton game and again, we came out on top in a close game. Andy opened the scoring from close range before Brighton equalised. I should have probably scored when I scuffed one past the post after running through, but I made up for it by setting up the winner. Well, when I say setting up the winner, I mean I flicked a ball over the top and a Brighton defender gave a penalty away with a handball. Tony Philliskirk dispatched it into the bottom corner to put us through to the fifth round for the first time since 1980.

This time we finally managed to get paired against a First Division club, Southampton, with the added bonus of a home tie. Over 20,000 fans turned up on a cold but sunny February day to see their famous old club potentially get through to the quarter finals of the oldest, most famous cup competition in the world. But by half-time their dreams – and ours as players – looked in tatters as we trailed 2-0 to two carbon copy goals.

Matt Le Tissier floated a corner to the back post, the Southampton centre-backs Richard Hall and Razor Ruddock charged in, and Hall scored with a downward header. Minutes later, same side for the corner, same cross and same type of header. We went in at half-time 2-0 down and gutted. However, with the experience now in our team, with Tony Kelly pulling the strings in central midfield, we started to cause Southampton more and more problems until, with 12 minutes to go, Scott Green, who had only just come on, chased a ball down and pulled it back to Tony Philliskirk, who whipped in a ball to the front post. Who else but Andy Walker stole in and slotted one in, with the Southampton defence asking for an offside, which wasn't given. Game on.

It set up a great last 10 minutes and we poured forward looking more like the First Division side. Tony Kelly then threaded a ball through the eye of a needle to Tony Philliskirk who crossed again to find Scott Green steaming in at the back post to score with a diving header. The home fans went absolutely berserk and we went close to winning it in the six minutes that remained.

It wasn't to be, but at least it set up another money-spinning tie for the club. The replay can only be described as a heartbreaking epic. Unbelievably, on a Wednesday night in late February, over 3,000 Bolton fans made the four-hour-plus trip to Southampton. It would have been absolutely brilliant if we could have won for them, and we nearly did. Deep into injury time, we were winning 2-1.

A young Alan Shearer, who was already earning many plaudits, had opened the scoring after David Felgate came for a ball he probably shouldn't have, but then Andy Walker scored a delicious chipped goal with Southampton 'keeper Tim Flowers stranded outside his box. It led to an unbelievable finale and it looked like we had scored the winner in the 89th minute, after a world class save by David Felgate had kept us at 1-1. Julian Darby then smashed a right foot volley into the roof of the net, right in front of our fans. We had done it and just had to hold on for a famous victory.

Then, deep into injury time, Southampton midfielder Barry Horne picked up the ball 40 yards out and ran forward as we backed off. He then let fly with a speculative shot from around 35 yards. To be fair it moved a bit in the air but I think if David Felgate is honest with himself, he should have just tipped it over the bar. Instead, he dived backwards and pushed it into the back of the net. It was 2-2 in the 94th minute. Gutted.

It took the wind out of our sails and in extra-time, Horne again had a shot from outside the box. This time a deflection gave Felgate no chance. Our luck was out, and it was heartbreak for our superb travelling fans. Unfortunately for Phil Neal the rest of the season just petered out and it was a slow death before his six-year reign as Bolton manager came to an end.

A big win in the last game against Stoke, where I actually managed to score a great right foot volley, couldn't hide the fact that we'd had a poor second half to the season. I'd missed an absolute sitter just before I scored and that about summed up my campaign. At least I would still have a job. We finished 13th, which wasn't good enough for the Bolton board and Neal was sacked. While on our summer jollies we found out that the new manager would be Bruce Rioch, who had recently left Millwall. I didn't know much about him at the time, but I certainly would over the next three years.

19

RIOCH'S ARMY MARCH TO GLORY

1992/93

New season, new manager, new division – sort of. It was all change in the football world at the start of the 1992/93 season and as if by magic, Bolton moved from the Third Division to the second. It was the first season of the new Premier League and my boyhood club Blackburn Rovers now had Jack Walker fully on board and had made it to the promised land. With Kenny Dalglish as manager, they were very much in the money and had outbid Manchester United to sign Alan Shearer for a then-British record of £3.6m.

There was also a new ruling; to try and sex up football the backpass rule had come in, meaning goalkeepers couldn't pick the ball up if it was passed back to them by a teammate. It was carnage at first as 'keepers and defences up and down the country struggled to come to terms with it.

I was now in my ninth season as a professional footballer and had played under five different managers. I was fortunate to have had a great relationship with all of them, except for Don Mackay, and, in some way or other, each manager had helped my game. I would play for a few more before the end of my career, but none would have the influence that Bruce Rioch did. In hiring Bruce, the Bolton board and chairman, Gordon Hargreaves, made a decision that would catapult the famous old club back into the big time. On a personal level, Bruce would educate me on what it really meant to be a professional.

Phil Neal had proved that being an unbelievably successful player didn't automatically mean that you would be a successful manager. Bruce was no mug as a player, winning a First Division league title at Derby and playing 24 times for Scotland, but he had also won promotion twice as manager of Middlesbrough, taking them from the third tier to the first. After being harshly sacked when they were relegated, he took Millwall to the 1991 play-offs but resigned after a poor second season.

I knew the clubs he had previously managed but I didn't know that much else about Bruce. But it didn't take long for him to show who was boss and although I had always been a bit rebellious throughout my career, I soon learned that you didn't argue with Bruce Rioch. He was the son of a Scots Guards regimental sergeant major, and it really came through in how he managed! He didn't take any shit; and you either bought into his philosophy or you wouldn't get anywhere near his team selection.

His training methods were totally different to all the other managers. For a start, he was the first manager I had played under who made the team train in the afternoon. I know it sounds daft now, but in those days most professional teams did just a morning session and that was it. Not with Bruce though. He would have us in every afternoon, Monday to Thursday, and it was always 11-versus-11 on Burnden Park. After a few weeks we could play the system with our eyes shut.

Although it wasn't a really physical session, because it was all about shape, it was still totally alien to what we knew and took a bit of getting used to. Bruce also started to educate us individually. Diet sheets were handed out and we were made to look at our nutrition and how much water we were drinking. "What the fuck are carbohydrates?" asked one of the lads. I had to admit I didn't know much about them myself.

Rioch also made it clear that he wasn't going to be a manager who would have a pint with his players, and boozing and smoking was an absolute no-no. I suppose my maturity had caught up with me as I absolutely loved his work ethic and the realisation that playing football was a job. A brilliant job, but a job that you had to put a lot in to get a lot out.

We had a great start to the season with a 2-0 home win against Huddersfield, started with a quickfire goal from who else but goal machine Andy Walker and a late one by Julian Darby. I had a great game myself, with a hand in both goals, and nearly scored from 50 yards out due to the backpass rule. Huddersfield's 'keeper had to come out to clear a dodgy backpass and when the ball came to me near the halfway line, I hit it straight over his head. I'd still be telling stories about it now if a defender hadn't got back and cleared it.

Bruce brought in his assistant manager, Colin Todd, from Bradford City and looking back at the programme from that day, it's clear what Bruce's intentions were and how he felt he could make Bolton successful. "For our part, we have a single-minded attitude, a determination to produce a successful football team and, along with others, to make Bolton Wanderers into a successful football club," he wrote. "There are 92 managers this afternoon starting out... and it's a fact of football life that there can only be a few successful teams come the end of the season. I want to lie on the beach at the end of the year and be one of them."

Even though we were unlucky to lose away at Brighton in the next game, we won the next two home games, 2-1 against Reading and then a cracking 3-0 victory against Blackpool. Sadly I missed the Blackpool game with a niggling injury and only played once, off the bench, in the next four games, but Andy Walker was flying and our new 'keeper, Keith Branagan, showed his class with some unbelievable saves in a goalless draw away at league title favourites Stoke City. Bruce had signed him on a free from his old club Millwall, and that day we realised what a brilliant addition he would be.

After five games we had made a really decent start. The formation was being drilled into the squad. We were all eating better and drinking plenty of water. I think a lot of us really started to believe that this could be our season. And then it all went a bit pear-shaped. It wasn't for a lack of effort – in fact, perhaps it was because of the new training regime that we picked up several injuries, including my own. We missed Andy's goals while he was out injured and it probably helped make up Rioch's mind to bring in a striker.

He went back to his old club Millwall and bought none other than

Clockwise from above: Me, my brother Sean and my mum outside our house; The mill wall and rows and rows of alleys back in my home town of Darwen, where I learned a lot; A postcard telling me I had been selected for a Blackburn Rovers coaching session; My Rovers identity card; The teamsheet from a reserve game I played against Liverpool, against legends such as Alan Kennedy and Ian Rush - with my name spelled as 'Paterson' on the teamsheet!

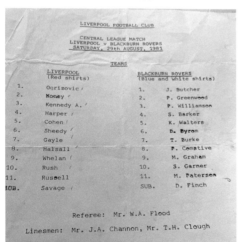

LIVERPOOL FOOTBALL CLUB

CENTRAL LEAGUE MATCH
LIVERPOOL v BLACKBURN ROVERS
SATURDAY, 29th AUGUST, 1981

TEAMS

	LIVERPOOL (Red shirts)		BLACKBURN ROVERS (Blue and white shirts)
1.	Ogrizovic	1.	J. Butcher
2.	Money	2.	P. Greenwood
3.	Kennedy A.	3.	P. Williamson
4.	Harper	4.	S. Barker
5.	Cohen	5.	K. Walters
6.	Sheedy	6.	D. Byrom
7.	Gayle	7.	T. Burke
8.	Halsall	8.	P. Comstive
9.	Whelan	9.	M. Graham
10.	Rush	10.	S. Garner
11.	Russell	11.	M. Paterson
SUB.	Savage	SUB.	D. Finch

Referee: Mr. W.A. Flood

Linesmen: Mr. J.A. Channon, Mr. T.H. Clough

BLACKBURN ROVERS FOOTBALL CLUB

IDENTITY CARD 1979-80.

Po... with club SIGNED SCHOOLBOY.
Admit via STAND "A" DOO
NAME MARK PATTERSON.
ADDRESS 25 LLOYD ST.
DARWEN.
SIGNATURE

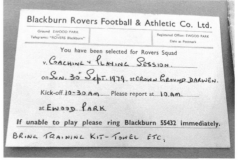

Blackburn Rovers Football & Athletic Co. Ltd.

Ground EWOOD PARK
Telegrams: "ROVERS Blackburn"
Registered Office: EWOOD PARK
Date as Postmark

You have been selected for Rovers Squad

v. COACHING + PLAYING SESSION.

on SUN. 30° Sept. 1979. at CROWN GROUND DARWEN.

Kick-off 10-30 AM. Please report at 10 AM.

at EWOOD PARK.

If unable to play please ring Blackburn 55432 immediately.

BRING TRAINING KIT - TOWEL ETC.

Overleaf: Celebration time after winning the Full Members Cup at Wembley with my boyhood club, Blackburn Rovers. I'm on the back row, being hugged by Vince O'Keefe.
Above: Soaking in the moment with David Lee, Alan Stubbs and Jason McAteer after Bolton's FA Cup win over Aston Villa in 1994. We made it all the way to the quarter-finals that season

Me and Super John McGinlay after winning the 1995 play-off final with Bolton at Wembley

Rebel who has made his mark!

PATTERS
STUNN
SETTLE

PATTERS
STUNN
SETTLE

by **RONALD KENNEDY**: Blackburn Rove

AGAINST opponents whose ambitions fo
screeching halt at the centre line, Blac
though that is not to say they won we
astonishing record of being unbeaten i
Oc

Mark's on his

MARK Patterson never had the opportunity to make up for the penalty miss that cost Wanderers a place in the quarter-finals of the Coca-Cola Cup.

His saved spot-kick against Norwich in Wednesday's Burnden replay turned out to be his last kick after almost five years as a Bolton player.

But Burnden boss Roy McFarland confirmed today: "We did not want him to go."

INSISTED

Patterson, a bargain £65,000 signing from Bury in January 1991, was the key to the Nathan Blake transfer – the reason why the deal took more than a week to come to fruition.

In the end the clubs agreed on a £1.2 million fee plus Patterson for Welsh striker and

And he's
to make a

Randell doubtful to face up finalists Brighton

PATTERSON, 19
SET FOR DEBUT

MIDFIELD man Colin Randell is the latest doubt for injury-hit Blackburn Rovers as they prepare to face last season's FA Cup finalists Brighton and Hove Albion at Ewood tomorrow and that could mean a full League debut for 19-year-old local boy Mark Patterson.

Randell is suffering ankle problems and, in fact, has had precautionary X-rays on a damaged joint. He looks a very doubtful starter as Rovers bid to restore

By PETER WHITE

their reputations, badly dented in last Saturday's Maine Road massacre.

With Noel Brotherston (ankle injury) and Terry Gennoe (thigh) also unlikely to be available, the manager's problems show little sign of easing and that makes a Patterson debut even more likely.

The youngster had his first taste of League action when Mr Saxton took the opportunity to use him as substitute for a spell late in the Manchester City game. If he plays tomorrow, he is likely to fill a similar role to that normally adopted by Brotherston—on the left flank of midfield.

There would be a vacancy on the substitute's bench for another of Rovers

young professionals as the injury jinx continues to haunt the Ewood club.

Mr Saxton said: "I'll sort the team out after today's training session but I don't think either Noel Brotherston or Terry Gennoe will be able to come into the reckoning. Collin Randell has seen the doctor about his ankle and we are just hoping that it doesn't prove too serious."

I expect Rovers to line up: O'Keefe, Branagan, Rathbone, Randell or Patterson, Keeley, Fazackerley, Miller, Lowey, Thompson, Garner, Hamilton.

Brighton are certainly attractive visitors but it's a tough game for Rovers to try to bounce back after their humiliating experience last Saturday.

They will have a star-studded side, including former England goalkeeper Joe Corrigan, who made his debut last Saturday, and ex-Liverpool ace Jimmy Case. There is a doubt about another international Steve Foster, who

A selection of newspaper cuttings from throughout my career - including me posing with John McGrath after signing for Preston from Blackburn Rovers, right. I particularly enjoy the 'Rebel Who Made His Mark' headline, above left!

Wa
war

DIVISION Three better
End next season! So sa
terson who is convinced
motion contenders.

Patterson arrived at Deepdale today to take the routine medical and make official his £20,000 move from Blackburn Rovers.

The chirpy 23-year-old midfielder, who played around 100 Second Division games for Rovers and collected more than 20 goals, said: "Preston is the only town club around here I would have considered leaving Rovers for.

"They are going places – you have only to look at team squad to see John

MARK PATTERSO

Mark Patterson (Rovers)

Full name: Mark Andrew Patterson.

Birthplace: Darwen.
Birthdate: 24.5.65.
Height: 5ft 7½in.
Weight: 10st 11lbs.
Married: No.

Car: No.

Previous clubs: None.

Nickname: Paddy.
International honours: No.
Favourite player: Bryan Robson.
Player for the future: Franz Carr.
Favourite other team: Spurs.

Child soccer hero: Peter Barnes, Coli Bell.

Favourite other sp Cricket, snooker.

Favourite other sport person: David Gower, Alex Higgins.

Most memorable match: My debut against Brighton.

Biggest disappointment: Being injured. Burnle winning!

Best stadium played in: Old Trafford, Villa Park.

ite singers: aye and son.

IT'S A DREAM COME TRUE FOR MARK OF THE ROVERS

TO BE a professional footballer is the pipe dream of ... Patterson of ...ven, it is a ... but for ... apprentice, provid... his football is up to standard the next step ...en will ... actually being signed on as a professional.

...Mark's interest in football ... to a very ...y age. Patter...on, says he was kicking ... as "great A pupil of Darwen ... High School, Mark...

CHAMPAGNE Charlies!

ON R IT

...lesbrough 0

...t part came to ...
...d well to win —
...to maintain their
...gue at home since
...e penalty area,

...ay ...me ...nds

...ark from their
...rs and knows
...In the end,
...ellars, Richard
...a Curcic, Andy
...e Burnett and
...Thompson to
...from injury, we
...was an area in
...were reasonably

...k's had five tre-
... years here and
...igning him means
...g to get regular
...football."

...son, who figure-
...ently in two prom-
...with Wanderers
... league ap-

h out Mark

...gnew

... look-out for Preston Nort
...e's latest recruit Mark Pat-
... End can be among the pro-

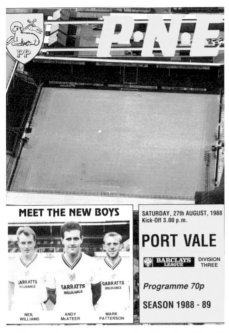

Above: A cover star on the Preston North End programme, shortly after signing at Deepdale and continuing my tour of football clubs in the Lancashire area!
Right: A typical old-school challenge in my Sheffield United days, away at Walsall

Back at Bramall Lane in Bury colours, not long after leaving United. It looks like Bobby Ford has gone right through me here - maybe he was taking some revenge for an earlier tackle?

Left: With two of my oldest mates from Darwen, Steve 'Eggy' Eggleston and Sam Stone - the three of us got up to some mischief in our time!

Right: Having a few words with referee Geoff Eltringham as Scarborough manager, after he sent me off during a game against Worcester City

Left: Watching the rest of the Worcester win with then-Scarborough chairman, Malcolm Reynolds (front) - who had sacked me a few years earlier!

Back at my old stomping ground of Bury, before they sadly went out of business

With my crazy kids, Scott and Jade. I am so proud to be their old man

Left: I met my lovely wife Andrea in 2011 and we got married three years later. My stepdaughter Lois is Manchester City-mad, and easily has more interest in modern-day football than I do

Right: I first set up a landscape gardening business while I was playing at Bolton, taking Bruce Rioch's advice for players to have a plan B after retirement, and I returned to it full-time after leaving football. My lad Scott works with me

John McGinlay. It was great to have an old teammate back with me and the Bolton fans soon forgave him for scoring a hat-trick against the Whites when he started banging a few goals in.

Around this time the club skipper Phil Brown also got injured. Rioch first made Julian Darby the captain, and then gave it to Tony Kelly – it seemed to jinx them both and neither had good games wearing the armband. I was secretly hoping that the gaffer would give me a chance to captain the side, and it duly arrived away at Chester City after we'd suffered three defeats on the trot. It's hard to describe the pride I had when I was first announced as captain. I had been unbelievably proud to play for my hometown club and to play for Preston and Bury, but to be told you were going to lead your club out as captain was very special.

I'd gone from being a cocky kid at Rovers, to finding my feet and playing many games as a professional footballer. But before the Rioch revolution, I was still smoking occasionally and drinking too much alcohol. Suddenly, through the education of Bruce and Colin Todd, I became a mature 27-year-old footballer. The captaincy could have been a short-lived gig when we went 2-0 down at Chester, but John McGinlay opened his account for us before super-sub David Reeves banged in the equaliser to stop the rot.

I was determined to give it my best shot as the captain. Well, my best header actually! In our next home game I scored the second goal in a 2-0 win with a rare one off my bonce! I'm not saying it was anything to do with me being captain, but we went on a brilliant league and FA Cup run. I also played my part off the field, too, and not a lot of Bolton fans will know that I was instrumental in bringing David Lee to the club. David had not enjoyed his time at Southampton and as a mate he told me he was desperate to move back to the North West.

I let Bruce Rioch know, and the rest is history. Bolton firstly managed to get him on a month's loan, which started with him having a great game in the 3-1 away win at Exeter, where he linked up brilliantly with Andy Walker who bagged a brace. We then went on a six-game winning streak, starting with an FA Cup first round victory against non-league Sutton Coldfield. It was great that the club welcomed back former player Barry Cowdrill – but even better that we managed to get past a non-league club with me playing!

From then on, we just got better and better. Bruce had moved me into central midfield, and I was reveling in a position I'd always wanted to play. We absolutely smashed Fulham at Craven Cottage and I can't tell you how proud I was to be captain against my old Rovers manager and nemesis, Don Mackay. We even gave Fulham a goal start before David Lee scored his first league goal for the club. Then the floodgates opened, with a fit-again Andy Walker scoring two and young Alan Stubbs getting in on the act.

You would think that things couldn't get any better than that, but they could. As a Rovers fan, imagine how I felt captaining a team against Rovers' bitter east Lancashire rivals, Burnley. We were on a roll and in front of well over 11,000 fans at Burnden Park we ripped Burnley apart. Club captain Phil Brown, Mr. Dependable, was back not only playing great at the back but he also managed to score. David Lee carried on his electric form with a goal and Andy Walker scored another two. A young Jason McAteer made his debut coming on late in the game. What a signing Jason would be.

I'm the proud owner of a newspaper clipping of my contribution on the day and a report from Gordon Sharrock, of the *Bolton Evening News*. "Mark Patterson has never given a better performance in a Bolton shirt," he wrote. "The Darwen terrier rolled up his sleeves and simply revelled in the thick of the Lancashire derby. But why shouldn't he? He has everything he has always wanted – a job in the centre of midfield and the captain's armband. Who could ask for more?"

Gordon had absolutely nailed it. Nowadays it is always brought up in any interviews I do and supporters always remember me as a hard-working pro. They appreciated my effort and, to me, that was never a problem. I just loved playing football and I always remembered what my dad had done for us, working for 12 to 14 hours a day for not a massive amount of money. That grounding, with Bruce Rioch's guidance, meant it just clicked for me.

I think Bruce saw that in me, a hard worker with a bit of tenacity. I was a real pain the arse, chasing lost causes, and I was always on to the other teammates, getting them to up their game. I think if you have one of those types of players in your team it keeps everyone on their toes. I'd bought into Bruce's philosophy and I enjoyed helping players, showing them how Bruce wanted them to play. I would then take that into games. I basically became his voice on the pitch. Yes, I could be a bit of a headless chicken at times, but it helped me get the armband. It was all about enthusiasm, effort and voice. Bruce might have been the sergeant major off the pitch, drilling his team, and I was one of his men leading by example on it.

A 4-0 rout of Rochdale in the second round of the FA Cup sent us into dreamland when we were paired with the current holders, Liverpool, in the third. The buzz around the club at this news, both with the players and the fans, was unbelievable, but Rioch and Todd weren't daft. They kept us all on our toes, by saying everyone had a chance to play against the cup holders.

Liverpool might have been going through a sticky patch at the time but still had the likes of Ian Rush, John Barnes, Steve Nicol and Rob Jones playing, to name just a few of their internationals. The Scousers in our club, Tony Kelly, Mark Seagraves, Alan Stubbs and Jason McAteer, were absolutely loving the draw and it inspired us to continue our winning ways.

Over the Christmas period we gave our fans some Christmas presents in the shape of maximum points from three games, starting off with a 5-0 home win against Bradford City. By the time we played Liverpool on Sunday, January 3, we hadn't lost for 12 games and had won the last six. There may have been a two-division difference between us, but anyone will tell you winning breeds confidence and we had Bruce Rioch and Colin Todd in charge. To the outside football world we may have looked like the underdogs, but they had us totally fired up believing we could win.

It was a frosty day with a noon kick-off and the pitch was still pretty hard as it got ever closer. Legend has it that the undersoil heating wasn't turned up high enough to thaw the pitch, to try and unsettle the mighty Reds. If that's the case, it certainly worked as some of their backroom staff were trying their best to get the game called off. Bruce was having none of it and had us out warming up, showing the referee that the pitch was more than playable. It paid off, and by the time the game started in front of a sell-out crowd of over 21,000 fans we weren't just warmed up – we were on absolute fire.

I was probably revved up more than anyone, with the honour of wearing the captain's armband as well, and any neutral watching the first half would have thought we were the FA Cup holders rather than the famous visitors in red. It took us six minutes to score the opener, John McGinlay rounding Mike Hooper before slotting into the empty net from a great low cross from Scott Green, and it was one-way traffic towards the Normid Superstore for the rest of the half.

McGinlay hit the foot of the post when he could have scored before more pressure brought a corner. I floated it over to the front post and it was flicked on for Mark Seagraves, a Scouser and ex-Liverpool player, to bundle a header over the line. The Bolton fans were going absolutely bonkers and I think the Liverpool players were glad to go in at half-time only 2-0 down instead of four or five. And that is not an exaggeration. Our dressing room was buzzing. Their defence had been all over the place and we went out in the second half firmly believing we could finish the job.

Unfortunately for us, an ineffective Michael Thomas came off early in the second half to be replaced by the lively Ronny Rosenthal. Not long afterwards he raced clear, only to hit the foot of the post – but the unlucky Mark Winstanley, chasing back, got his feet mixed up and the ball ended up in the back of the net for an own goal. We still had chances to seal victory but with eight minutes left, Liverpool had another huge slice of luck as Seagraves sliced the ball backwards when trying to clear upfield. A young Steve McManaman raced clear, Keith Branagan made a great save but the ball fell to the one player you wouldn't want it to fall to and Ian Rush was on hand to slot home the equaliser.

That was it, everyone thought. We had missed our chance. We'd wasted a 2-0 goal lead and let the FA Cup holders escape with a draw. I think the whole footballing world – including Wolves, who got a home draw against the winners when the next round was drawn – thought that Liverpool would make it through to the fourth round.

They'd had a scare and would put it right at Anfield. We were having none of it. Bruce Rioch had got us drilled, organised and the team spirit for the trip for Anfield on the 13th January was sky high, even after suffering our first league defeat for three months when West Brom beat us 3-1 at the Hawthorns.

Liverpool v Bolton Wanderers – FA Cup Third Round replay. January 13, 1993.

Anfield. A place you dreamed about playing at when you were growing up. I wasn't only going to be playing there, but I was also going to be captaining Bolton Wanderers in one of their biggest FA Cup games since they had won the most famous cup in the world in 1958. I had managed to get loads of family and friends tickets for the game, including my old man, and when we came out to warm up, we were greeted by 8,500 Bolton fans who had completely sold out and filled the away end and part of another one of the stands. It was absolutely incredible.

Two years before, I'd arrived at Bolton and missed out on playing at Old Trafford because I was cup-tied. Now I was playing against the most successful English team in the modern era and all I knew was that I was going to give it my all and make my dad proud. We were unchanged for the game and our dressing room perked up even more with the news that Ian Rush wasn't playing due to injury.

Again, unbelievably when the game started, we took control. With less than three minutes on the clock, Tony Kelly got the ball to David Lee who was out on the left-hand side near the halfway line. In an instant he took it on his left foot and as Mike Marsh, the Liverpool right back, came out to meet him, Didsy pushed it past him and raced clear down the left wing. He then put an inch-perfect floated left foot cross over to the far post where John McGinlay, after hanging in the air, met it and buried it past Mike Hooper, right in front of our fans. Cue unbelievable scenes.

Three minutes had gone and we were 1-0 up against the cup holders at Anfield. Instead of defending for our lives, we attacked for our lives and played the better football for the rest of the first half. David Lee had an unbelievable 45 minutes, terrorising Mike Marsh with his pace and his old-fashioned wing play, and with better finishing and a bit of luck could have had a couple of goals. Just like at Burnden Park, Liverpool would have been glad to hear the half-time whistle.

Surely it would be a backs-to-the-wall second half? It certainly wasn't. We didn't just hold on, we had chances to get the second goal. Liverpool threatened us a few times but this time our defence was magnificent. Then with 12 minutes to go, John McGinlay skipped away from a tackle and headed down the right wing. He looked up and sent in another inch-perfect floated cross and his strike partner, Andy Walker, scored a brilliant header at the back post. That was it. Game over.

Well not quite, but if anyone was going to score another it was going to be us. We got a corner and as I went over to take it, John McGinlay went down on the ground and the physio came on. I then had a bit surreal moment as I waited to take the corner. As I was soaking up the atmosphere and the noise exploding from the 8,500 Bolton fans, I could hear someone shouting my name directly behind me. Unbelievably, it was one of my mates from Darwen, Mark Walkden. Mark was a Liverpool season ticket holder and was with another lad from Darwen. He had come down from his seat to try and grab my attention. Well, he did, but he also caught the attention of the Liverpool fans and said he got slaughtered as he made his way back to his seat!

When the final whistle went, the scenes for the next few minutes were absolutely amazing as we made our way over to salute our fantastic and delirious fans, who Tony Kelly later described as the 12th man. Players picked out their family and friends in the crowd and applauded everyone who'd made the journey. As we started to make our way off the pitch, we realised that the whole of the Kop – not just a few hundred, but the whole of the Kop – had stayed behind to salute us and clap us off the pitch. Some fans and some football club, because when we got back to the changing room the Liverpool back-room staff, players and manager couldn't have been more gracious in defeat. Us? We were just overwhelmed.

We had the belief, but then we'd actually done it. I'll never forget Nat Lofthouse, that legend of a man and scorer in the 1958 FA Cup final, coming into the changing room and shaking all our hands and celebrating with us. I must admit that I'm not the shyest person in the world, but even I was taken aback with the local, regional, and national exposure we received from the media after the game and for days to come. Yes, some of it focused on the demise of Liverpool, but Bruce Rioch and the team got a lot of accolades, and rightly so.

Over two games, we hadn't just been lucky or even held our own; we'd actually well and truly outplayed the mighty Liverpool. I still have the *Bolton Evening News* pull-out and the amazing on-pitch photographs of the first 'White Hot' game and the iconic photograph of John McGinlay, David Lee and Andy Walker celebrating. They were magnificent, but I think they would be the first to tell anyone that it was the team, from one to 11, who were all magnificent.

Bruce was quick to acknowledge the magnificent support we had enjoyed at Anfield before our next game, a Second Division home clash with Plymouth and a dose of reality. Knackered from the Liverpool game and the celebrations afterwards, we struggled against Plymouth but showed our mettle and did the business on the pitch with a 3-1 win. More important than the win, though, was the news that Bolton had signed David Lee permanently. The £250,000 fee showed the club's intent. Mind you, we must have made a few quid from those two games!

Sometimes it can be a case of 'after the Lord Mayor's show' but if First Division Wolves were upset that they didn't get the more prestigious tie with Liverpool in the FA Cup fourth round, they were even more upset by the end of the game as goals by Scott Green and John McGinlay, and our magnificent defence, sent us through to the fifth round. We proved that the Liverpool game was no fluke and we could hold our own against higher league teams. It was a special time for our loyal travelling fans, and it was great to hear them at the end singing: "We are the one and only Wanderers!"

Our reward was another tie against a First Division club, Derby County, in the fifth round. We stuttered a little before that game, losing at Brighton after not scoring for the first time in 18 games, before drawing at Huddersfield and losing at local rivals Stockport County. But we still went into the Derby game confident that we could hold our own.

Unfortunately for us and our brilliant travelling fans it wasn't to be and we were beaten 3-1. The difference with the team after this setback, compared to the Southampton defeat the previous season, was that with Bruce Rioch and Colin Todd in charge, you weren't allowed to feel sorry for yourself and let the season slip away. Not a chance.

Rioch and Todd were relentless in their methods. Tactics, fitness, nutrition and hydration and the best dressing room spirit, which was probably never surpassed for the rest of my career, meant that at the end of that season there would be no heartache of the play-offs for me yet again. We won six of the next eight games, with the duo of McGinlay and Walker in irresistible form. The stand-out for me, the game that showed our automatic promotion credentials, was a 1-0 away victory at Burnley. McGinlay scored late on and the Bolton fans still sing: "Who put the ball in the Burnley net? Super John McGinlay..."

We also beat Fulham 1-0 at home, and no, I didn't shake Don Mackay's hand at the end. A double over Burnley and the double over Mackay? Things couldn't get any better. Sadly for me they actually couldn't, as injury meant that I missed the next six league games and the captaincy was handed back to club captain Phil Brown. But reflecting now, I have a real sense of pride to have represented the famous Bolton Wanderers as captain for 28 league and FA Cup games, helping us rise from 18th place in the league to the play-off places and still within reach of automatic promotion. It was an absolute honour to be captain over that period, and especially to run out at Anfield as the skipper.

The team was in such form and with everyone knowing their role it meant that, even with injuries, we just kept on picking up points. A young Jason McAteer had come in for the injured Tony Kelly and Alan Stubbs replaced the ever-reliable Mark Winstanley. They were 21-year-old lads coming in who could easily have been overawed. But because they knew the system, they just slotted in and excelled.

Jason reiterated this on a Bolton Wanderers podcast *Here we go again,* when he was recounting his time at the club. He also described me as being the hardest player in the world who would smash anything. Including the time I "cut him in half" in an 11-v-11 practice match!

Jason was the new kid on the block and although he had come from non-league, it hadn't taken him long to adjust to life with us. He just got better and better and grew in confidence as he picked up more and more game time.

During this particular session, though, he was showing off too many of his skills and was taking the piss a bit too much, so I just smashed him in what he described as a "naughty tackle." He did go on to say that I was in some ways just trying to toughen him up.

In truth I was, but I was also trying to teach him a lesson around not taking the piss. However, Bruce saw it as me overstepping the mark and I soon found out that, although I might have been one of his leaders on the pitch, Bruce was still the boss. He had a proper father-son relationship with Jason and I'd hurt his love child.

So Bruce brought himself on in this practice game and within a few minutes, absolutely smashed me. Of course it fuckin' hurt, but in those days you did your best not to show it! When I heard Jason call me the hardest man in the world on the podcast, it did make me laugh.

I know what he meant in some ways, because I could give it and take it and didn't take a backward step. But compared to old-school players like Millwall enforcer Trevor Hurlock, my old Blackburn Rovers teammate Glenn 'Killer' Keeley and the actual hardest player in the world, the notorious former centre-forward Billy Whitehurst, I was bottom of the league.

As I said, I didn't take backward steps in my career, but was rather pleased that Billy didn't play directly against me, but instead just used to terrorise my team's centre-halves and anyone else who went near him! Anyway, I don't think it did Jason too much harm as he went on to have a brilliant season, and career.

Even the loss of the prolific Andy Walker for the last seven games to a terrible knee injury couldn't stop us. We did have a blip in a 2-1 away defeat at Bradford City but after that, we won the next four games playing great football but also showing the grit and determination that Rioch had instilled in us. By the time we played Hull City away on a Friday night with three games to go we were really in the mix for automatic promotion. When Alan Stubbs got sent off in the first half and we then went a goal down, most teams would probably have folded. But not us. We hung in there, profited from a Dean Windass own goal and then who else but John McGinlay scored the winner in the dying minutes. We had an amazing following that night and at the end the noise they created was unbelievable.

In the penultimate game we played the champions Stoke City on a Tuesday night. They were already champions, but they were never going to lie down and let us win with their superb following swelling Burnden Park to a near 20,000 gate. It was fitting that local lad Julian Darby, the only Bolton-born player in the team, scored the winner in a 1-0 win. I just wished he'd left it later than the 12th minute to score as we didn't half suffer after hanging on for an eternity for the win!

So, after 45 league games our season came down to one last match to see if we could get to the First Division automatically. I really don't think I could handle another play-off final! We returned to training the following day but there was no sign of John McGinlay. In fact, we didn't see him again until Friday before the last game of the season. Allegedly he had gone on one of his benders, but Bruce knew how to handle him. The decision would be made following the game on Saturday what punishment he would receive.

The fixture gods had decided that we would play my former club Preston on the last day, with North End having to win and then hope other results went their way to stay up. I obviously didn't want my former team to go down, but this day was all about Bolton Wanderers. An absolute full house witnessed a really nervy performance, but it was all about just getting over the line. When we got a penalty with less than 20 minutes to go there was only one man going to take it. Super John McGinlay – even I was calling him that by then – scored it, and we held on for a famous victory.

The celebratory pitch invasion after the game was a sight to behold as every single Bolton fan stayed behind to salute the team. We got the chance, from the safety of the stand, to join in the celebrations and in turn salute them in what had been an unbelievable season. In the following days I think I drank more beer than I had done all year and I just about remember the open top bus ride to the town hall. What a season!

Bruce Rioch got just what he wanted. Keith Branagan played in 60 games that season, John McGinlay scored 22 goals and got away with his midweek misdemeanour, David Lee was magnificent. And what Rioch built, along with the discipline he instilled and the young lads he and Toddy had given a chance, meant that he was able to lie on a beach somewhere and celebrate promotion to the First Division.

20

ANOTHER WHITE-HOT SEASON

1993/94

Bolton were now one division from the promised land of the Premiership and if anyone could get us there, it was Bruce Rioch. His first season in charge had been brilliant, and it all started with the team bonding in pre-season. He was meticulous in everything he did and although I'd love to say that the second season started with the usual pre-season drinking session, it didn't. That was a definite no-no with Bruce and Colin Todd.

Bruce was a strong disciplinarian, but he also had a softer side and was a real family man. Under him, gone were the boozy pre-seasons and in came team bonding in an old stately home in Cheshire. We'd train hard for three days and then when it got to Sunday it was a family day, when the lads' families, including children, could come and visit us. It was completely alien to us but turned out to be a really nice touch.

Don't get me wrong, we still had a great laugh and Bruce and Colin Todd loved the banter, but there was a real change in the professionalism of the training and the nutrition and diet sheets continued. It started on the first day of pre-season and would be relentless for the whole season. At night, instead of the big drinking sessions, we were allowed a few beers and that was it. The craic on the first night was still great, and some of the lads started going on about the hotel being haunted. I still don't know if I was a set up, but on that first night something really strange happened. I had a single room – number 13.

I'm not really superstitious but everyone knows that number 13 is supposed to be unlucky.

"Do you believe in ghosts?" asked the receptionist as she handed me the key as everyone made their way to bed. I just laughed as I just thought she was taking the piss. It was a big old room and probably because I'd only had a couple of drinks, I struggled to get to sleep. It was a massive bed and I never slept with two pillows, so I threw one on the floor. About 4am, after I'd been tossing and turning, I woke up with something on my legs and shit myself when I realised it was the pillow I'd thrown on the floor a few hours earlier. I thought one of the lads must have sneaked in to try and spook me.

The next morning, I went downstairs and asked another receptionist if the room was haunted. She was adamant it was. "Every time I go past that room," she told me, "I cross myself." All the lads thought I was taking the piss, but it really freaked me out. I didn't sleep very well for the next few nights!

We trained hard on Thursday, Friday and Saturday before relaxing with our families on the Sunday before having a game of cricket in the grounds. Bruce showed how competitive he was by having a go at me, even though I was on his side. I was keeping wicket, he was bowling and, to be fair, he wasn't bad. One ball he bowled came through to me, so I rolled it on the floor back to him and he started bollocking me straight away. "Don't fuckin' bowl the ball along the floor," he said.

"Why?" I asked, laughing.

"We don't want to waste the shine on the ball do we? I'm wasting my time shining it up with you doing that."

The lads were loving it and I gave him some banter back. I told him in no uncertain terms that he couldn't bowl anyway, and added a few verbals in as well – loud enough so he would hear, but the women and children in attendance couldn't!

The 1993/94 season would mainly turn out to be another great season for both the club and for me, mainly for the club because we held our own and consolidated our position in the second tier and had an amazing FA Cup run, and mainly for me because I had a really decent season, scored the winner in one of the best games of our league season live on television and played against one of the best players in the world. But – and it's a big but – I also made a mistake in the biggest game of our campaign and Bolton fans still remember it almost 30 years later!

In the summer Bruce Rioch and Colin Todd once again showed how shrewd they were in the transfer market, bringing in striker Owen Coyle from Scottish club Airdrie for £250,000 and a young Geordie lad from Newcastle United, 19-year-old Alan Thompson. Both would turn out to be great signings. Owen was brought in to replace the prolific but injured Andy Walker, who wouldn't make an appearance until well after Christmas of the 1993/94 season, and Tommo was a breath of fresh air. He'd made 16 appearances for his hometown club, but Bruce had managed to talk Kevin Keegan into letting him go, and also convinced Tommo that a move to Burnden Park would be better than playing in the reserves at St. James' Park.

Tommo was young and naive when he arrived at Bolton, but a fantastic lad. He was having the craic with me one day after one of the afternoon pre-season training sessions and I was telling him that everyone knew how much he was on, so he could tell me. He wasn't the brightest of lads so he told me, in his Geordie accent. "Aww man, I couldn'ae believe it," he said. "£500 pound a week, man. I couldn'ae believe it…"

For fuck's sake, I thought. Five hundred quid a week at 19! From the slack-jawed expressions on my face and a few of the other lads, he twigged that we didn't actually know. But he turned out to be well worth the money. He had a great left peg and slotted into the left side of midfield.

I was troubling the scorers less and less with my move into centre midfield but I still managed to score a goal that most Bolton fans of a certain age will probably remember, and it was also live on ITV against Nottingham Forest. Although they had lost Roy Keane to Manchester United and Nigel Clough to Liverpool, they still had a great side – and not a bad left back in England captain, Stuart Pearce, either.

So, when Stan Collymore turned our makeshift centre-half Julian Darby just inside our half before showing a clean pair of heels and scoring, we knew we were in for a game. Poor Julian Darby. He was never a centre-half, but I think he played every position on the pitch for Bolton when injuries arose. He was a great servant for the club. I think the Bolton boo boys forgot that when they used to get on his back – just like some Rovers fans used to get on mine. Local lads always seemed to get harsher treatment from the terraces.

We then went 2-0 down to Forest when they scored a thunderbolt from 35 yards, straight into the top corner. Any other team might have laid down and died, but not us. Just before half-time, I hit a tame right-footed shot which the 'keeper should have held. Instead, he just pushed it out in front of my mate David Lee who smashed it in and early in the second half, we were all square. Tommo started repaying his wages with a lovely run and shot with the outside of his left foot for his first league goal in a Bolton shirt.

Then Stan the Man slid in at the back door to make it 3-2 to them. One thing that Bruce Rioch had made us though, was resilient and David Lee got his second to set up a grandstand finish. Seeing as we were on the box, I thought I had better get in on the act and with a few minutes to go, I was in the right place at the right time as Jimmy Phillips swung over a cross. I darted in and swept the ball in for 4-3, much to the delight of the home fans!

Scoring the winner meant a live interview after the match. Of course, I was chuffed to bits, but also gave it the "it's a team game" clichés. Blah, blah, blah. That night I ended up in a curry house in Darwen and some lads were taking the piss because they said I was talking posh in the interview. Me talking posh? Behave. I had recorded the game so when I put it on the next morning, I couldn't believe it. My accent had changed completely – I *was* talking posh!

We carried on picking some decent points up, winning a few and losing a few, before we were involved in another 4-3 game. This one however, was more memorable for the manner of our loss. With 20 minutes to go, playing away at Watford, we had romped into a 3-0 lead with goals from Jason McAteer, Didsy and Tommo. When we came off at full-time with a 4-3 defeat to our name, I don't think anyone fancied going into that dressing room. You win some, you lose some, I suppose!

***

Does anyone remember the Anglo-Italian Cup? I can imagine some of the older readers thinking: "Ah yes, that shit cup" while the young 'uns think: "The Anglo what?" The competition had a few guises but when we played it had replaced the brilliant Full Members Cup – medal winner, remember! – and was played between English and Italian teams from the second tier of their respective leagues.

We made it to the main group stage in November 1993 and played Brescia at home. It was a cold November night, and the stats show that there were 3,021 fans present. I wish there had been a lot more there as I came up against possibly the best player I ever played against – and managed to get booked for clattering him!

Georgi Hagi was a Romanian international and had already played for Real Madrid for two seasons before signing for Brescia. He was that disappointed that Brescia had got relegated in his first season that he had the balls to resist signing for another top foreign club, because he wanted to stay and get them back up. That was great news for all 3,021 people who were at Bolton that night. We played out a very entertaining, sometimes very niggly 3-3 draw. I was marking Hagi and was all over him like a rash.

Well, to let the truth be known, I couldn't really get near him until I thought I could nick the ball off him just as he wrapped his foot round it. Unfortunately, I clattered him instead and got a booking. He was giving me some verbals in Italian and I returned him some back with my down-to-earth Darwen accent. A few minutes later I witnessed a bit of magic as David Lee chased him down near his own corner flag. I'm still not sure how he did it but as Didsy went to put pressure on him, Hagi somehow backheeled the ball over Didsy's head before turning and running off. Everyone else just stood in awe.

So, you thought Bolton in Europe under Big Sam was the first time the Whites played away in Europe? Well, there might have been others, but I was in the changing rooms at Pisa after a 1-1 draw when we heard machine gun fire outside. We genuinely thought someone had killed the English referee and linesman, who had disallowed a Pisa goal in a game that finished 1-1.

When the game did end, the hostile crowd – all 1,000 of them, it seemed – starting booing and hissing the officials and then some of the fans followed them – and obviously us – down the tunnel. I'd not even played due to being diagnosed with a torn muscle in my stomach but didn't want to miss out on an away game in Europe. Barricaded in the changing room, I wished I hadn't bothered. It was like being at Millwall again. All of a sudden from the corridor we heard shouting before a machine gun went off and we all hit the deck. What the fuck was going on?

The 'machine guns' turned out to be firecrackers, but we still got a police escort to the airport. We also ended up drawing 1-1 away to Ascoli just before Christmas, with just 12 Bolton fans in the crowd, and exited the Anglo-Italian Cup undefeated. For the record, Brescia went on to win it at Wembley against Notts County on their way to winning Serie B.

My mate Hagi finished the season at the 1994 World Cup, getting Romania to within a whisker of the semi-finals, and was chosen in that year's all-star World Cup 11. He then signed for Barcelona and was rated as one of the best players in the world in the 1980s and 90s… and I clattered him. Sorry, played against him!

I had been feeling the injury long before the Brescia match, but I kept quiet and carried on playing. Bruce was building a great squad and I didn't want to miss a match in case I didn't get back in. My pre-match routine included a hot bath, which did little to ease the pain once the game had started. Every time I played a long pass the pain got worse, until I couldn't play anymore. I was sent for a scan, which meant I had to have dye injected into my abdomen. I've got to say, it was more painful than Jimmy Case jumping on my chest.

I was diagnosed with an abdominal tear and was sidelined for eight weeks, around the time that our 1993/94 FA Cup run began and given my previous luck against non-league clubs, it probably wasn't a bad thing for Bolton that I was injured for our first-round tie against Gretna. Yes, Scottish side Gretna! People don't just get married there, it turns out; they have a football team as well who, at that time, played in the second division of the Northern Premier League.

It was a first-round tie for us but Gretna had won five games already to get to this point, and the first thing they did after the draw was made was to change the fixture from their place to Burnden Park. Fair play to them. They made some extra dosh out of the switch and it would be a great day out for their 2,000 fans in a crowd of over 6,000.

It would also be a great day for their players – in those days the bigger clubs didn't put their reserve side, under-23 or youth sides out in the FA Cup, as they do today. We had our strongest side out, and the conquerors of the FA Cup holders the year before were expected to dispatch Gretna easily. Of course, the romance of the FA Cup ensures that it doesn't work like that and a fairy tale for Gretna nearly ended up in a nightmare for us.

Watching from the stands I didn't think we were going to get the chance to play any of the big boys in a later round, as little Gretna played brilliantly against a full-strength team including Tony Kelly, Jason McAteer, Alan Stubbs, Owen Coyle and John McGinlay, to name a few. After 25 minutes Gretna were 2-1 up and held on to the lead until 11 minutes to go. They matched us all over the park and I don't know about the lads on the pitch, but up in the stands the Bolton fans and officials were getting a bit twitchy. FA Cup glory one season, disaster the next?

Luckily, Scotsman Owen Coyle scored the equaliser in the 79th minute and then got on the end of a cross from another Scot, John McGinlay, to head the winner with four minutes to go. Gretna had a great day out and we were lucky to be in the hat for the second round. Next up were Third Division side Lincoln City and although on paper a 3-1 away win looks straightforward enough, it definitely wasn't. It was a great cup tie. We were level 1-1 at half-time and it took a brilliant goal by our skipper Phil Brown, who smashed one into the top corner, to break Lincoln's resolve before Owen Coyle finished them off.

We'd done it again. For the third year running we'd made it to the third round, and to be drawn against Everton at home was perfect for us. We'd beaten their great Merseyside rivals the season before and by the traditional third round day in January we'd only been beaten once in 16 league and cup games. The only defeat had come five days earlier, against-high flying Wolves, while our opponents went into it having lost five of their last six matches and also their manager, Howard Kendall resigning.

We went into the Everton tie fully believing we could win. And with a full house roaring us on at Burnden Park – including the great Nat Lofthouse, who had just received an OBE in the New Year's honours list – we nearly did. Everton weren't having a great time of it, but still had a decent side out with players determined to impress the new manager. They had the great Neville Southall in goal, Andy Hinchcliffe, Dave Watson, Peter Beagrie and Paul Rideout were all playing. But just like Liverpool the season before, they were lucky – and happy – to get a draw and take us back to Goodison.

They did take the lead in the first half through Rideout, but were lucky to go in 1-0 up. We started the second half well and after a bit of pinball in the box I poked in the equaliser – much to the delight of the Bolton fans in the near-22,000 crowd. It was a brilliant feeling to score in such a big match. We then really went for it but unfortunately missed a load of chances to win the game.

We then beat Southend away but then lost at Millwall. I think everyone just wanted to stay fit and be involved in another potential upset and once again, we arrived on Merseyside as the underdogs. The Press thought we had missed our chance, but Bruce Rioch and Colin Todd again had us fully prepared and we were confident we could give them a great game. It actually turned into an even more dramatic night than at Anfield. Cue 'White Hot 2'.

Not that you would have put money on us to win when Stuart Barlow scored his second goal of the night to put Everton 2-0 up just after half-time. But not for the first time, the character, camaraderie, desire and never-say-die spirit that Bruce had drilled into us, and perhaps all those extra sessions, saw us stage a dramatic comeback – culminating in an extra-time winner! I spent the night having a right old ding-dong against Mark Ward, who was a fiery little bugger. Two little, short arses kicking the shit out of each other for the whole game. Mark was a great lad who unfortunately ended up on an extended holiday at Her Majesty's expense after we had ended up playing non-league football together at Leigh RMI.

Firstly, John McGinlay scored and then, with time running out and six minutes of normal time to go, a boyhood Everton fan scored against the team who rejected him as a 13-year-old. Stubbsy pounced on a rare Neville Southall mistake, and the 8,000 travelling fans went absolutely bonkers.

For some reason it seemed inevitable that we were going to win it and in the first half of extra-time, Owen Coyle raced through and slotted a great goal which proved to be the winner. That also seemed a bit inevitable – Owen had been dropped the previous weekend by Bruce Rioch for comments he'd made to the Scottish Press. All was forgiven and everyone was all smiles as we celebrated in front of our fans. What a night!

You can imagine the buzz that went round the club when we then drew the FA Cup and League Cup holders, the mighty Arsenal. This time I don't think anyone fancied us that much, as Arsenal were a different kettle of fish to Liverpool and Everton. When we played the Merseyside clubs, they were relatively poor sides compared to their previous standards but when Arsenal came to Burnden Park, for a *Monday Night Live* special on *Sky Sports*, they were third in the Premiership and were dripping with England internationals. David Seaman, Lee Dixon, Tony Adams, Paul Merson and Ian Wright all played on the night and again, we did ourselves unbelievably proud. It was a cracking game, which had the superb commentary team of Andy Gray and Martin Tyler purring.

We played some great football in the first half on a Burnden Park pitch that was cutting up everywhere. John McGinlay did a brilliant spin off one of the England defenders and slid in Jason McAteer, who confidently slotted past David Seaman. The celebrations were short lived when, who else, but Ian Wright slid in at the back post for 1-1 at the break. The second half carried on in the same way but I wasn't a happy chappy when one of their players ran into me and won the free-kick. I was totally pissed off when Tony Adams scored with a deft header for a 2-1 lead for the Arsenal.

Game over? Not on your life. Bruce threw Andy Walker on off the bench, with me making way. I was pleased for Andy as he was coming back from eight months out, and I was blowing out of my backside after chasing Paul Merson around. Andy didn't score but one of our other strikers, Owen Coyle, did with five minutes to go. Another replay. White Hot 3? You bet!

A 3-1 league revenge home win against Watford sent us down to Highbury in high spirits. But surely we couldn't beat another Premiership club in their own back garden. Could we? Anfield, Goodison and now Highbury. Three amazing old grounds steeped in tradition. A Wednesday night in early February 1994 will probably be one that the Arsenal historians will want to erase from their history books. The mighty Arsenal had only lost once in 28 cup matches, but that didn't mean anything to us with the self-belief we had. By the night of the game, we also knew that if we somehow managed to win we would play another Premiership team, Aston Villa, at home.

Off the pitch, we were in awe of these players, many of them internationals. But when the first whistle went, we forgot all that and went flying into the tackles. I was giving it, and taking it, and loved both sides of it. I remember thinking momentarily just how amazing it was to be involved. Once that whistle had gone, it was just them against us. Bruce had taught us to believe in ourselves and his words were embedded in our brains. "Win your individual battles, and play as a team." And that's exactly what we did.

On 20 minutes we had the audacity to go ahead. John McGinlay steered one past David Seaman after my corner had been cleared and hooked back into the Arsenal box. We had taken 4,000 fans to London on a Wednesday night, and they probably thought the worst 15 minutes later when Arsenal equalised. But they needn't have worried.

Again I tired near the end and with 18 minutes left, Bruce took me off for Andy. In extra-time, many would have backed the experienced Arsenal side to overcome us, but the lads were having none of it and with five minutes of extra-time to go, Jason McAteer raced onto a dodgy backpass and smashed it in for 2-1. Minutes later, David Lee broke through and instead of taking the easy option of passing to John McGinlay to run the ball into the corner, he put Andy Walker through. He finished brilliantly for 3-1, and it should have been four. Tony Kelly curled a brilliant free-kick over the wall and into the top corner of Seaman's goal, but the ref ordered it to be retaken as he hadn't blown his whistle!

It didn't matter in the end as it finished 3-1. We celebrated with our fans, and Ian Wright was a class act that night. He had played non-league until he was 21, and so knew what it was like in the lower leagues before he hit the big-time with Arsenal and England.

As we walked up the narrow stairs back to the changing room, Wrighty had waited for us and congratulated every single one of us by name, saying how we had deserved to win. He was right, and we celebrated accordingly. We were getting used to this. Bring on the Villa!

Our game against them, 11 days later, was live on the BBC and once more, we more than held our own against Ron Atkinson's high-flyers. We matched up against some household, brilliant players in Steve Staunton, Ray Houghton and Dean Saunders but it turned out to not be our best performance in the brilliant cup run. Our strikers, for once, were kept quiet by a great Villa defence, marshalled by the legend that was Paul McGrath, and it would take something special to beat Villa that day.

Up stepped a defender to provide it, as Alan Stubbs smashed a 30-yard free kick into the bottom corner. We held on for another famous win and we were one step from Wembley with the semi-finals now being played at the famous old stadium. White Hot 4? Unfortunately not.

We drew our local rivals Oldham at home in the quarter finals. What an opportunity. Unfortunately for me, it led to the single worst moment of my life as a footballer. To be fair, if the word 'Wembley' isn't mentioned, I ended up being very lucky as a footballer, suffering no professional team relegations, apart from at Southend at the end of my career, but I was only on loan for five games and they were already doomed anyway. I had 19 years in the game and this Oldham moment still stands out as my lowest feeling in football.

Oldham were a good Premiership team at the time but, as the conquerors of Everton, Arsenal and Villa on the way to the quarter finals, we really fancied our chances. We were the last team left in the competition who had been in it since the first round and another full house anticipated another great cup win. I was actually having a really decent game; Oldham had come to stop us playing and mix it up, and it had turned into a real battle. We'd had a few chances, but it was heading for extra-time before I fucked up. Massively.

Oldham had possession on the left wing but the cross eventually landed at my feet, 12 yards out, just out on the left-hand side and facing our goal. Out of the corner of my eye I saw Jimmy Phillips, so rather than just clearing the lines I tried to pass it to him. Instead I played it straight to Darren Beckford, who smashed it in. I didn't even get the chance to redeem myself as Rioch hooked me straight off for Andy Walker.

I remember watching it on TV the next day and the television cameras panned in on me on the bench, sitting there with my head in my hands and looking gutted. But that was Bruce. He was hard and he didn't mind telling you or showing you if you had fucked up. Martin Tyler had been doing the commentary and when he spotted me after the game, he said he was surprised I'd been brought off as he felt I had been playing well. But another chance of playing at Wembley had gone.

I apologised to the lads in the changing room, but they were so supportive. I had to live with it, but not before I got some stick that night. Eggy and me were keen to take the wives out that night and we'd planned a night out in Bolton, hopefully to have a celebratory drink and in anticipation of having an FA Cup semi-final to look forward to. I told Eggy that I would get too much stick if we went to Bolton, so we decided to have a meal in Blackburn instead and finish off with a few beers.

I was doing my best to get over it, and the few beers had cheered me up. We'd had a great run and that was that. We were in the Ribblesdale pub in Blackburn when *Match of the Day* came on. I was sat there, thinking: "For fuck's sake. I'm going to be on television cocking up in the next 20 minutes." By the time the corner came I was halfway down my chair, trying to hide behind my pint and hoping the lads watching the game hadn't recognised me. No chance. As Beckford scored, a few of the punters watching the game turned to me. A couple shrugged their shoulders as if to say unlucky but the majority were smirking. One even pointed out that Darren Beckford in fact played for Oldham. Really? You fucking prick.

Luckily for me, at the time, the Bolton fans were more forgiving – even though it turned out that we would have played Man United in the semi-final at Wembley if we had won. It was heartbreaking for the players but also gutting for the fans – that would have been one of the biggest games in Bolton's history, and definitely the biggest since they had played United in the 1958 FA Cup final. We finished 11th in the First Division that season, and I got a load of letters from Bolton supporters the week after the quarter-final.

Most of them were sympathetic. Nowadays I would have probably been slaughtered on social media. To this day, I am often reminded of that assist to Darren Beckford.

21

THE THIGH AND VERY
LOWS OF FOOTBALL

1994/95

The 1994/95 season will go down in history as one of the greatest in Bolton Wanderers' history. Promotion to the Premiership and the club's first appearance in a League Cup final, which in those days still meant a great deal. Even now, I am really proud that I played in over half of the league games that season – despite our strong squad, Bruce Rioch's shrewd transfer dealings and some niggling injuries – and five of the eight games in our Coca-Cola Cup campaign.

One of them was possibly one of the greatest cup nights at Burnden Park, the second leg of our League Cup semi-final against Swindon Town. It was a brilliant season with some real highs, but also two real lows and more missed Wembley opportunities for me. Oh, and I also nearly lost my right leg after the last game of the league season.

We came back for the 1994/95 season fresh and raring to go. Well, apart from probably one of us. Jason McAteer had come back that summer as a fully-fledged Republic of Ireland international, after playing for his country in the World Cup finals in the USA. It was unbelievable to see him come on as a substitute in the 68th minute of their famous 1-0 victory against Italy, in front of 75,000 fans in the Giants Stadium in New York, playing against Roberto Baggio and Paulo Maldini. He then went on to play a major part in Ireland getting to the last 16, only for them to succumb to a 2-0 defeat to a Dennis Bergkamp-inspired Netherlands. It was fairy tale stuff really. It turned out that we were lucky to start the season with Jason and his mate Alan Stubbs, as Bruce had turned down a double transfer offer for them both from Liverpool.

We'd gained some new players and lost a couple. The two that we'd lost are really worth a mention for different reasons. Club captain Phil Brown had signed for Sam Allardyce's Blackpool in the summer. I was sorry to see Phil leave – as well as being a good mate, he had been a brilliant servant to Bolton Wanderers and one of the main stalwarts for six consecutive seasons.

He was a near ever-present in the side at that time and was Mr. Consistency. Phil had already amassed 350 league games at Hartlepool and Halifax, so the experience he brought to Bolton from 1988 to 1994 cannot be underestimated. He was still playing regularly at 35 years old. All the players were sad to see him go.

Andy Walker's move to Celtic was a little more expected; we knew that if his boyhood club came calling again, he would be off. I can honestly say that I played with and against some brilliant strikers, and Andy Walker was easily one of the best. A total of 44 league goals in just 67 games had made him a cult figure with the fans, and understandably they were not happy to see him go.

Bruce was a very shrewd operator in the transfer market and brought in a really experienced defender in the shape of ex-Newcastle and Everton right back Neil McDonald from Oldham. His other three pre-season signings really showed how far Bolton had come and the ambition we were now showing in pursuit of promotion to the elite league.

Bruce had gone Dutch on us, bringing in striker Fabian De Freitas and midfielder Richard Sneekes for £400,000 and £200,000 respectively. It turned out that Sneekes wasn't just clever on the pitch. He could also speak five languages – his native Dutch, English, Italian, German and French. The pre-season foreign invasion finished with the capture of strapping Finnish international centre-forward Mika-Matti Petteri Paatelainen – with a thankfully better-known shortened first name of Mixu – from Aberdeen. All three, in differing ways, would play a crucial part in the success we had during the season.

I started the first four games of the campaign, beginning with a 3-3 thriller away to Grimsby as the Paatelainen and McGinlay partnership started with a double strike for Mixu and a penalty for McGinlay. We then lost what would be our only game in league and cup at home for the rest of the season, a 2-0 defeat against Bristol City – a result made even worse when the unfortunate Neil McDonald broke a leg. We then lost 1-0 at promotion favourites Middlesbrough, before I scored a cracking winner in our next home game against Millwall. It wasn't enough to get me in the team to face Stoke, who we hammered 4-0, and it just showed how competitive it was at the time. Bruce was not afraid to show who was boss, like when he decided that another promotion hero was surplus to requirements and let Tony Kelly, one of the major characters from the dressing room, go. Thanks for the memories, Zico.

The only run-out I had was a three-minute cameo at the end of a second round, second leg Coca-Cola Cup 1-0 home win against Premiership club Ipswich Town, after being an unused sub at Portman Road when we had destroyed them 3-0. Wins against Premiership clubs in cup competitions were fast becoming regular occurrences and we were playing great football as well. I was 29 by now and had matured into a club man, so I didn't spit the dummy out as I might have done in the past. I just cracked on in training and worked hard, hoping for an opportunity.

It eventually came near the end of October when Jason picked up an injury, and I didn't waste it as we went to Sheffield United in the third round of the League Cup. Paatelainen bagged an early goal before Blades centre-forward Nathan Blake scored an equaliser just after half-time. To be fair the game could have gone either way and we ended up scraping through in fortunate circumstances, as Blades defender Andy Scott deflected a cross into his own net.

The fourth round took us to Upton Park to play West Ham, in front of nearly 20,000, and I watched on from the bench as we totally took another Premiership side apart. We were 3-0 up before Tony Cottee scored a consolation in the 80th minute and the footballing world was starting to take notice of our playing style and our wins against Premier League sides. The flipside of that is that our manager and some of the players started getting linked again to Premiership clubs. A home tie against another Premiership club, Ipswich's East Anglian rivals Norwich, meant that we were only one step from the semi-finals.

I then did our play-off chances no harm at all with two goals in two games, netting us six points from two 1-0 wins. The first one was described in the *Bolton Evening News* as a "spectacular strike from 25 yards with 17 minutes to go" in an evening victory against Port Vale. On the following Saturday I managed to score the winner a little bit quicker at Bristol City, after 29 seconds! Fair play to the lads as we played out the next 89-and-a-half minutes for a victory that took us to fourth place.

By the time I played in the 1-0 win against Reading on January 2 1995, I'd played in the last seven home games. We had won six of them and only drawn one, and I was really happy with my form. We were in the top four and getting ready to play Norwich in the quarter-final of the League Cup, so what could possibly go wrong? Yep, you guessed it. I felt an injury as I came off the pitch against Reading and ended up missing the Norwich game, and the five in the league that followed it.

I watched from the stands as another top-flight club was dispatched, a cracking David Lee goal enough to beat Ipswich and book our first League Cup semi-final since 1977. There we would meet Swindon over two legs. Swindon were having a great cup run but were struggling in the First Division. We had already taken them apart at Burnden Park, which buoyed us even more.

The winners of the semi-final would play either Crystal Palace or Liverpool in the final at Wembley, and the prospect of making it onto the teamsheet had everyone playing for their places. We went into the away leg at Swindon in an ultra-confident mood and when Alan Stubbs put us 1-0 up after 10 minutes, I think some of the lads thought that was that. However, Swindon fought back and equalised just before half-time. Then they went ahead with 15 minutes to go, which was definitely not in the script. But with our home record, there was a feeling that we were still favourites to go through in the second leg.

I was desperate to get fit and be in contention for the game and ended up getting my chance, but not in the best circumstances. After another home win in the league, this time a 2-1 win against Barnsley, we played promotion rivals Derby County at the Baseball Ground. We were winning 1-0 with an early goal from Jason McAteer when Simon Coleman, who had been in great form, had a bit of a tussle with Marco Gabbiadini, the Derby centre-forward. Gabbiadini was gesturing angrily that Simon, a former teammate of his, had elbowed him.

Nothing was given but within a minute Gabbiadini went in on a tackle on Coleman and broke a leg. Bruce Rioch had no doubt that he had meant to do it and even marched onto the pitch to remonstrate with Gabbiadini, before being asked to leave by a policeman. I came on as sub and did all right. Even though we were all flat, because we knew it was a bad break, we held on until the 86th minute before disastrously conceding two late goals to dent our automatic promotion push.

However, I'd done enough to get myself back in the team and another thumping win, this time 3-0 over Southend, set us up nicely for the second leg against Swindon. With the firepower we had, we were all confident that we could overturn the first leg score and the atmosphere on the night of the game, on a misty, early-March evening, was unbelievable. For just under an hour we were in the driving seat but couldn't get the elusive first goal, which would have actually put us through on 'away goals'.

David Lee had come closest but surely it was just a matter of time as we put the pressure on, and the Burnden crowd pumped up the volume. Then against the run of play Swindon got a corner. I stood helplessly near the taker as he swung a cross over, there was a flick on and Jan Aage Fjortoft, the Norwegian international, bundled it over. It did cross my mind for a second that mine and the club's Wembley dream was over, but Bruce Rioch had built a side that never gave up. We needed to score two goals to take the tie to extra-time and Rioch pulled what proved to be a masterstroke with a double change, bringing Richard Sneekes and Mixu Paatelainen on for David Lee and Owen Coyle.

Within minutes Paatelainen sent Tommo down the left and he hit the woodwork with a brilliant shot. Fortunately, it fell at the feet of Jason McAteer to slot home. Game on! Less than 10 minutes later, Mixu picked the ball up after a bit of a tussle, got it on his left foot and smashed it in the top corner. The crowd went absolutely mental and so did the players. We knew we could do it now and Swindon looked dead on their feet.

The game was heading for extra-time when a free kick was sort of mishit into the Swindon box. After a bit of a scramble it fell to none other than John McGinlay, who tucked the ball away before he wheeled away to celebrate. Only the young legs of McAteer beat me to McGinlay and we both jumped on him before everyone else piled in as well. We'd done it. We were on our way to Wembley!

The atmosphere at the end of the game was just unbelievable, and the crowd stayed behind for ages as we saluted them. Dave Higson, the legendary Bolton commentator and superfan, is sadly no longer with us, but I think his usual summing up of 'What a ding dong do' at the end of the game could not have been more apt for what was an amazing night.

Burnden Park was packed to its old rafters and I don't think I can beat this Bolton fan's description of the night. "What an advert for the true face of English football... a packed, working-class ground, two teams fighting for a rare trip to Wembley and no signs of sheikhs, billionaires or Sky anywhere."

Bolton were a founder member of the Football League, and Burnden Park had seen the best and worst of what the beautiful game could offer. Including, sadly, the disaster in 1946 when 33 Bolton fans tragically lost their lives. The ground celebrated its centenary year in 1995, making one of the best nights the famous old ground had seen even more special.

Two years later, in 1997, the club moved to their new ground, which makes me feel even more honoured to have played for Bolton and captained them for a short period of time whilst they were still at Burnden Park. During my career I was also lucky enough to play at most, if not all, the football grounds that are no longer with us, including Highbury, the Baseball Ground, Ayresome Park, Filbert Street and many, many more. I know all-seater stadiums have quite rightly made football safer, but I don't think they can match the 'old school' atmosphere.

The announcement that Liverpool had also won at Crystal Palace to take their place in the final was the icing on the cake. The gaffer congratulated us in the changing room afterwards but before we could get ahead of ourselves, he soon brought us back down to earth. We had another massive game against the league leaders Middlesbrough on the Saturday.

We managed to put the excitement of playing Liverpool in a major cup final to the back of our minds and went out and beat Middlesbrough, with Mixu again getting on the scoresheet in a superb 1-0 win. Not having a game until the following Saturday should have been a reason to go out and get absolutely pissed to celebrate two brilliant victories, but for me I knew it was potentially a case of potentially drowning my sorrows. After the Swindon game I could feel I had a bit of a groin strain, but the pressure for places was too much and I stupidly thought that, if I could just get through the Middlesbrough game, I would have a week to recover. Some frozen peas at home over the weekend would sort it out.

By the Tuesday or Wednesday of the following week I couldn't hide it any longer and had to admit defeat. I was absolutely gutted. It was only a few weeks to the final and I knew that being out of the team through injury wasn't going to do me any favours at all. We were actually down to the bare bones in midfield, with right-back Neil McDonald, who hadn't played a game since he broke a leg, playing there in a victory at Millwall. I was nearly back to full fitness but didn't even get a place on the bench in the last game before the Coca-Cola Cup final -a 1-1 draw away at Portsmouth.

The build-up to the final was brilliant and the town of Bolton was absolutely buzzing, but underneath I knew that I was going to miss out. I had David Lee, Jason McAteer and Alan Thompson ahead of me in the pecking order and to be fair to him, Richard Sneekes hadn't just proved himself to be good at languages. He had really settled well into the English game, was a great passer of the ball and had a terrific shot on him. He also had a great punch, too, which he produced during a house party. A guest took it upon himself to take the piss out of Sneekers, until it touched a nerve. I'm not sure what was said but the guest was stood in front of the sofa one minute and was laid behind it the next.

I can look back now with unbelievable pride at being part of the squad that got us to the final. On the day 33,000 Bolton fans, including a number of my family and friends, were in a crowd of over 75,000 and I suppose I should have been happy with being named as one of the two outfield substitutes. The other was another inspired signing by Bruce Rioch. Mark Seagraves had benefitted from the unfortunate Simon Coleman's bad injury and started, but Bruce knew we needed another centre-half. Gundi Bergsson was an Icelandic international who'd been at Tottenham, but had been injured for nearly two years and was training to be a lawyer in between playing part-time football. Bruce could definitely spot a player – ask Arsenal and Dennis Bergkamp – and Bergsson had made it onto the bench, with me and the keeper.

The Liverpool team wasn't too shabby on the day and included David James in the nets, Jamie Redknapp, John Barnes, Ian Rush, Robbie Fowler and another young Scouser, Steve McManaman, to name just a few. Even with so many great players the lads still more than held their own and we had a few half chances. Alan Thompson caught a brilliant half-volley from way out which was arrowing into the top corner, only for James to superbly tip it onto and over the bar.

It was a great game. I just wished I was on the pitch!

Unfortunately, as we were looking like we could go in at half-time on level terms, McManaman went on a mazy run, tricking a few of our players before slotting it past Keith Branagan. We again held our own in the second half until just over 20 minutes to go when McManaman again waltzed past Scott Green and slotted another great goal into the net. Bruce had seen enough; it was substitution time. Just like in the Full Members Cup final I was going to get the last 20 minutes, but this time it was against the mighty Liverpool and not

Charlton. In fact, Bruce had decided to give Scott Green a rest and Gundi Bergsson made his Bolton debut at Wembley Stadium.

It would only be a matter of time before I got on, though – or so I thought, especially if we conceded another. At least I would get a run out on the hallowed turf. Then we went forward and a flick on by Mixu meant the ball dropped to Alan Thompson. Facing away from goal, he chested the ball down, swivelled and scored a magnificent goal for 2-1. I think I fist-pumped and was happy for a few seconds, before I realised that Tommo had probably cost me my run out!

We had a couple of half chances and gave Liverpool a real run for their money, but for me personally it would be like finishing fourth in the Olympic Games. Nobody remembers them. An unused sub in the Coca-Cola Cup final. Wembley jinxed again! We had done ourselves proud – well, the lads who played had – and we still had the league to play for. It was all now about securing promotion to the Premiership.

We had nine league games left and I started in seven of them. We won the next two, away at Swindon and West Brom, but in the next few games it started to get tougher and the wheels came off a bit. We had to win away in the penultimate game at Stoke to still have a chance to get automatic promotion on the last day of the season.

With first choice 'keeper Branagan injured it meant Aidan Davison deputised and, in an emergency, the great Peter Shilton aged 45 years and 239 days took his place on the bench. What a legend Shilton was – 1,378 competitive league games and 125 England caps, sat on Bolton's bench. Not for long, though. He had to come on after less than 10 minutes after Davison conceded a penalty and got sent off. The first thing Shilts had to do was pick the ball out of the net.

He then went on to have a great game and we battled away, with John McGinlay equalising before half-time. We had played brilliantly and come away with a point, but this wasn't good enough and it meant that Middlesbrough were promoted as champions. Gordon Sharrock, the *Bolton Evening News* chief reporter was very complimentary about me in his report of the game. "They were heroes to a man, but one player's performance stood out amongst the rest," he wrote. "Patterson, with his cropped hair and rolled up sleeves, always looked the combative part and the occasion was made for him."

So, instead of having the chance to get promoted on the last game of the season, at Fortress Burnden, it was a dead rubber. With the play-offs to look forward to it should have been played like a friendly, especially as Burnley had already been relegated. But with a huge following and playing one of their local rivals, Burnley were never going to lie down and die.

Richard Sneekes had also been ruled out for the rest of the season some weeks earlier, so it was all hands to the pump. We didn't play well and it took a late equaliser from Mixu Paatelainen to save our amazing home record. Credit to Mixu, who refused to celebrate his goal as he had been booed by some of the crowd. It's really strange and sad, seeing one of your teammates being booed after the season he had helped to give some of those same fans who were now giving him stick. Bruce Rioch wasn't a happy man either, making his feelings known.

After the game a bunch of players and wives had arranged to meet at the Holiday Inn Hotel in the town centre. I was really looking forward to a few beers but as I was getting changed, my right thigh became really sore. After I had put my strides on, I was struggling to walk at all. I had picked up a dead leg in the first half, clashing with my former teammate Gary Parkinson.

His knee smashed into my thigh and as painful as it was, I had managed to run it off. I decided to continue with our plans and headed to the hotel but within a couple of hours, the thigh was swelling up and becoming quite painful. I was beginning to worry so I phoned our physio Ewan to explain. He ordered me to go to the Beaumont hospital immediately.

On arriving I was led to a private room and waited for Banksy, the surgeon, to assess the injury. When he eventually arrived, he was suited and booted. He'd been at a wedding when he got the call from our physio. Fortunately for me, and in an unbelievable coincidence, Banksy and his surgical team had carried out the exact same emergency operation the week before on the Man City keeper, Tony Coton. Tony had gone home following a game, after taking a blow to the thigh. Later in the evening he was rushed to the Beaumont for an operation. Unbelievably, Tony's was the first operation Banksy had done of that type, in 25 years' service.

Bruce came to the hospital to see how I was and brought a bottle of bubbly with him, which was a nice touch. It turned out that I had internal bleeding in my right thigh; when the thigh was lacerated, the muscle jumped on to the table due to the pressure. At least it was only my standing foot. But in all seriousness, if I hadn't gone to the hospital I could have possibly lost my leg. Or at least never played football again.

I ended up having two more operations in the following days and I now have a 16-inch scar down my thigh. A decent war wound. The bad news was I was out of the play-offs, but the good news was my playing career wasn't over. Down the road at Blackburn, my beloved Rovers had just won the Premiership and as I lay on my bed, watching the celebrations, I smiled to myself. If all went well in the play-offs, we'd be playing against them in the Premiership the following season.

The rest, as any Bolton readers know, is history. The boys managed to overcome Wolves over two feisty games, with Neil McDonald sent off near the end of a 2-1 away defeat in the first leg. We'd been a bit lucky to concede only two. Well, it was either luck or the brilliance of our 'keeper, the legendary Peter Shilton, who pulled off some cracking saves. Jason McAteer also scored a brilliant equaliser (and away goal), so it was all to play for in the second leg at Burnden Park.

A full house saw what became the Super John McGinlay show, and not just for the two goals he scored. With the game looking like it was going to go to extra-time, John was then involved in a right tussle with David Kelly. The Wolves forward took exception to McGinlay justifiably putting his foot in as their 'keeper spilled the ball, and Kelly pushed John in the face. I don't think anyone expected John's reaction, as he knocked Kelly down with a cracking left hook!

Going down to 10 men with extra-time to come would have been a disaster, but unbelievably the referee only gave McGinlay a yellow card and even booked Kelly as well. If it was in this day and age, John would have been banned for six games and got a YouTube boxing match out of it! When the game went into extra-time, McGinlay – who else? – scored the winner to cement his place as a Bolton legend for all time. I don't think he's on many Wolves fans' Christmas card list, though!

Bolton had made it to Wembley again, and guess who wouldn't be playing again at the home of football? The ups and downs of life as a professional footballer, all in one season! I could just about walk again by the time the final came around, on the May Bank Holiday Monday against Reading, and I took my place in the Wembley stands with Lindsey.

We were that short of midfielders that day that I still nearly got a game! Right back Neil McDonald was forced to play in the centre of midfield, and Neil must have been the unluckiest, luckiest player ever to play for Bolton! After breaking a leg in only his second league appearance, he played just four more times in the league all season and got sent off in his only Coca-Cola Cup game! Now here he was, playing an unfamiliar position in a play-off final at Wembley.

We'd had a long season, and injuries and tiredness had caught up with us. But I don't think anyone expected us to be 2-0 down in the first 10 minutes. The boys were never going to give up – Bruce's mentality and unshakeable belief ensured that – but with a makeshift side, and in our 58th game of the season, it wasn't looking good. Jason McAteer then conceded a penalty, still before half-time, and it looked all over.

Keith Branagan was having none of it though, and pulled off a great save from Stuart Lovell. It was a bit too close to him, but it was struck well enough and Branny pulled off a superb save before the ball was scrambled away. The noise of the Bolton fans was incredible. It was as if we had scored a goal. Then what followed is written in Bolton folklore.

Neil McDonald was subbed at half-time – at least you got on, Neil! – for another striker, Fabian de Freitas, which meant we started the second half with four forwards on the pitch in John McGinlay, Mixu Paatelainen, Owen Coyle and de Freitas. It was a masterstroke again from Bruce Rioch, even if it took us until the 75th minute to get back into the game when Coyle scored a great far-post header from McGinlay's brilliant cross. Again, game on!

We were actually lucky not to go 3-1 down in the 86th minute before we broke away with a storming run from skipper Alan Stubbs. He passed it to Alan Thompson who put de Freitas through with a sublime pass.

These days VAR might have ruled the goal out, and de Freitas still had a lot to do, but he coolly slotted the ball into the bottom corner. There were absolute scenes on the terraces and the belief that it was Bolton's day seemed to transmit to the players. Reading held on for extra-time but they were out on their feet and we got our just rewards for going for it with a great headed goal by Paatelainen.

Nobody was booing him this time as he wheeled away to celebrate, with the lads chasing him. There was still time for even more drama, too. First, de Freitas made it 4-2 and then my ex-Rovers teammate, veteran Jimmy Quinn, smashed in a consolation deep into added time. What a game. What a season. We'd made it to the Premiership.

On the final whistle me and Didsy 'raced' onto the pitch. On his crutches, Didsy was almost as fast as me limping flat out. We all celebrated a fantastic result with our amazing supporters and I managed to limp my way to the changing room after the game as the champagne and beer continued to flow.

It had been an up and down season for me, but I'd played my part in getting Bolton to a major cup final and we were back at the pinnacle of English football. We celebrated with an open-top bus ride from Burnden Park to the Town Hall. Rovers had won the Premiership, we would be playing them the next season, and Burnley had been relegated as well. Bring it on.

22

A GLIMPSE OF THE PROMISED LAND

August to December 1995

The celebrations at Bolton's Premiership promotion were tempered a little – well, a lot – when we lost our prized asset, who many felt would be our main chance of staying in the top division. It was nothing short of what he deserved, but it was a sad day for us when Bruce Rioch was offered the Arsenal job. It wasn't a real shock when he accepted it but I was gutted.

Bruce had become a massive influence on my career. Yes, he was a tough taskmaster, but me and the other senior pros at Bolton had nothing but good things to say about him. Even now, everyone who was involved in that tumultuous period for the Whites knows it was Bruce's stewardship that sparked the success.

He'd turned me into a seasoned professional and guided me through the most stable and successful period of my football career. I had made it to the promised land – the division I had dreamed about playing in when I was a little lad, banging my ball against that mill wall. Peter Barnes and Colin Bell, my idols, had played in the top-flight. Now I, a lad from Darwen, was going to do the same.

Bolton had acted quickly on Bruce's departure and brought in Roy McFarland, who had not had his contact renewed at Derby County. Strangely, it turned out that he had been sort of made 'joint manager' with Colin Todd. In hindsight it was never going to work, and it didn't. It was clear that our first season in the Premiership would be all about survival, which was reflected in the club's transfer business. Two experienced defenders were brought in, in the shape of Premiership defender Chris Fairclough from Leeds and Gerry Taggart from Championship club Barnsley. A young Andy Todd joined from Middlesbrough. He had a familiar name, as our new joint manager's son!

A particular game had caught my eye when the fixture list had come out. We were paired with my hometown team and current Premiership champions, Blackburn Rovers, at home in the third game of the season. I must admit it had put an extra spring in my step during pre-season training, and I was hopeful that I had done enough to be in the joint managers' minds in Bolton's first-ever fixture in the Premiership.

It was the club's first game back in the top division for 15 years and it would have been great for the fixture gods to have given us a glamour tie, to celebrate Bolton's journey from the old Fourth Division to the Premiership. They gave us Wimbledon away. Known as the 'Crazy Gang', they were led by Vinnie Jones and were a force to be reckoned with, even if they didn't even have their own ground. They had finished ninth in the Premiership the season before and were now seasoned campaigners in the top-flight, so it was never going to be easy.

I was picked to start and made my Premiership debut. I had been a professional for 12 seasons by that point, and was finally kicking a ball as a player at the top of his profession. To be fair, I more than held my own against Vinnie and Co. and although we were 2-0 down within the first 25 minutes, we showed that the fighting spirit that Bruce instilled in us still remained despite his departure. We scored two goals before the break to level, and I was involved in both. For the first I was fouled in the box, Alan Thompson slotting home Bolton's first Premiership goal, before a perfectly-weighted pass sent Fabian de Freitas clear to score, sending the 4,000 travelling Wanderers fans bonkers. We went into half-time with them cheering us on, and we were definitely on the front foot.

Unfortunately, it wasn't to be as Dean Holdsworth scored early in the second half. With the injured duo John McGinlay and Mixu

Paatelainen unavailable we ran out of steam on a boiling day at Selhurst Park. Things didn't get much easier, with our first home game against Kevin Keegan's big-spending Newcastle United next up. They had been installed as some bookies' favourites for the league title, and it was little wonder when you saw how good their forwards were.

Les Ferdinand and the French genius David Ginola were absolutely brilliant on the night. Ferdinand scored a great header to open the scoring but once again for a good hour or so, even with flashes of brilliance from Ginola, we held our own. We even had the audacity to equalise with Gundi Bergsson scoring from one of my corners. Unfortunately, Robert Lee ghosted in to make it 2-1 before Ferdinand waltzed past about three or four of our lads for their third.

Being in the Premiership was great, but in two games we had conceded six goals and our defence came in for a bit of flak from the fans. Skipper Alan Stubbs came in for the most stick and, at the time, it was well known that Arsenal and champions Rovers were interested in signing him. Alan and Jason McAteer had also been linked again with Liverpool. Alan was still a young man, but he was a quality player and deserved the interest he was receiving from the top clubs. He had been a great servant for Bolton and didn't deserve the stick he was getting.

So, with our defence's confidence at rock bottom we could have done with an easy game. But you don't get many of those in the top-flight – and especially against the best strike force in the Premiership at the time. Alan Shearer and Chris Sutton were known as the SAS and a full house at Burnden Park, against the champions, would be enough to get anyone's juices flowing. For me, a game against my hometown team was even more special and I remember the atmosphere was unbelievable. It was a little strange to know that a load of friends and family would be there, wanting me to do well but not wanting my team to win.

They would be disappointed. I had a great game against the likes of England international David Batty and Rovers skipper Tim Sherwood. It was an all-star Rovers cast, with my old mate Colin Hendry playing along with Tim Flowers and Graham Le Saux, but three sides of Burnden Park were rocking when, after a bit of a melee in the Rovers box, Fabian de Freitas scored his second goal in three Premiership games.

Rovers were never going to let us settle and came back strongly but our three central defenders, Chris Fairclough, Alan Stubbs and especially Gundi Bergsson, were immense. Rovers equalised in the 60th minute with a low shot past Branagan but we had got stronger and stronger as the game went on and it had come against the run of play. So, in the 80th minute when I swung over a free kick and skipper Stubbs got on the end of it, outjumping Hendry to direct a superb header past Flowers, it was no more than we deserved. The feeling when the final whistle went, and we had managed to hold on to beat the Premiership champions, was something I will never forget. Just in case though, I decided to go out round Bolton that night to celebrate.

There were some great headlines in the national Press about how newly promoted Bolton had beaten the champions, and the connections between me and my hometown team.

The report in the *Daily Star read*: "Patterson, at five foot six inches, the shortest player on the pitch, had eclipsed the giants of the game like Shearer, Sutton, Batty and Le Saux to help Premiership new boys Bolton to a famous, first Premiership victory." I was a bit gutted really as I'm actually five foot, six and a half inches!

Two losses then followed and one was even more damaging than the others. Aston Villa beat us 1-0 at Villa Park before, at the beginning of September, we lost Jason McAteer to his boyhood club Liverpool. It was always going to be a tough season but not being able to hold on to our best players would make it even harder and after starting my fifth game out of five in a draw with Middlesbrough, I was disappointed to be left on the bench against Manchester United at Old Trafford.

A 3-0 mauling with two goals from Paul Scholes and one from Ryan Giggs and a scoreline that actually flattered us meant that I came back in for the next game; Liverpool at Anfield. I have two statistics from that game that nobody can ever take away from me. Alan Stubbs was injured so the management duo gave me the captain's armband which meant I can proudly say I have captained Bolton Wanderers three times against Liverpool, one of the biggest clubs in the world. I also managed to score against them on the day as well, to record my first Premiership goal. Yes, okay, my only Premiership goal! The fact that we were 4-1 down at the time, with a young Robbie Fowler scoring all four, did put a bit of a dampener on it at the time but it's something that I can look back on now with pride. There was no famous comeback that day, either, as Liverpool scored again to win the game 5-2.

Unfortunately the Rovers and Liverpool games would be the highlight of my season with Bolton as we really struggled to pick up points before my departure in December. There were some great moments for the club, especially with the return of Bruce Rioch and his Arsenal side. Bruce received a tremendous reception from the fans and also all the players and staff at Burnden Park. On the pitch was a different matter, though, as the lads beat Bergkamp, Ian Wright and Co. 1-0, with a John McGinlay goal.

Frustratingly, I had to watch on from the bench and it was around that point that I realised I was starting to get pushed out of the club. I really believe it would have been different if Bruce had still been in charge. Not necessarily that I would have been in the team, but that we would have been picking up more points and everyone would have known where they stood.

The situation was complicated a little more when Bolton brought in another midfielder, Saša Ćurčić from Partizan Belgrade. He had class, and showed it, but he couldn't stop us from losing our next three games on the trot. Saša was great going forward but a fucking liability when we had to defend – and we had to defend a lot! I knew my time was nearly up in early December when I didn't even get on the bench for a home game against Nottingham Forest. And when Bolton signed my own personal Grim Reaper, Scott Sellars, and he went straight into the team for the home game against Liverpool, I knew it was *definitely* up.

At least I managed to score another goal as a Premiership player, albeit in the Coca-Cola Cup against Brentford on our way to the fourth round. After missing out on another Wembley appearance the season before, the competition managed to jinx me again as I missed a penalty in the shoot-out against Norwich which saw us knocked out. Bryan Gunn, the Norwich 'keeper, saved it and looking back on YouTube now, I feel a bit better, even though long-serving Bolton fans always remind me of my last kick of a ball for their club – there were six missed penalties in the shoot-out before mine! Even John McGinlay missed the target and Ćurčić actually had a chance to put us through, but couldn't. For my penalty, I made the fatal mistake of changing my mind at the last second and Gunn guessed the right way.

That was on a Tuesday night and by the Thursday night I was a Sheffield United player. Colin called me into the office on Thursday morning and said that they had put in an offer for Nathan Blake from United – now managed by Howard Kendall – but Howard would only let Blake go if they could have me as part of the deal. Toddy said that it was up to me if I spoke to Howard but with the situation I was in, knowing my time had come to an end at Bolton, I had no hesitation.

Howard was the man who had given me the opportunity to become a pro footballer all those years before and to say I was excited to work with him again was an understatement. We met again in the Premier Inn in Wakefield that afternoon, with another ex-Rover in Viv Busby, Adrian Heath and United's chief executive Charles Green also waiting for me. My first thoughts were: "I'm outnumbered, I need help here" and, just to fuck my head up a bit more as I turned to sit in my chair, I noticed Colin Todd, Roy McFarland and Gordon Hargreaves, the Wanderers chairman, sat across the room with Blake and his agent. It felt like I was being stitched up.

Howard had a big smile on his face. "Paddy, great to see you again son," he said. "It's been a long time." Once the niceties were done with, he was straight to the matter in hand. "Right son, you're on £900 a week and they owe you your £25,000 signing-on fee. They're going to pay you the £25,000. We want to offer you a three-year deal. So, I know what you're currently on. What do you want from us?

Fuck me, I thought. It's getting worse. Howard was putting the ball in my court. *I'm a fucking footballer, not an accountant.* THINK, THINK, THINK.

"Can I make a call, please?" I eventually asked. It felt like a police interview, not a friendly chat about my transfer. I phoned my old Rovers teammate Vince O'Keefe, who was now working for the PFA. "Vinny, it's Paddy," I said. "I'm speaking to Howard Kendall regarding a move up to Sheffield United. Any idea what the wage structure's like?"

"Well Paddy," he said. "If you get a wage rise, you've done well."

"What about £1,200 a week?" I asked.

"That's a good wage Paddy, you should be happy with that."

"Okay Vinny, cheers. See you soon."

I sat down a little more confident and began my negotiations. "I want £1,200 a week," I said.

"Okay," said Howard.

I was getting excited now. "That's just for this season," I said.

"Okay," said Howard again. Shit, I thought. That was too easy.

"Then £1,400 next season, and £1,600 the following season."

Howard agreed again, before asking me about a signing-on fee. I said £30,000 a year.

"So that's £90,000 over three years," Howard said. "Okay, Paddy... let's shake hands. We have a deal."

The look on my face must have told a story. Howard knew he had done me up like a kipper, and so had Vince. We shook hands and Howard looked me in the eye. "Paddy, you won't change your mind, will you son?" he asked. I looked him back in the eye and told him he had my word.

I kicked myself all the way home. If I had an agent, I would have got a much better deal. Someone once said to me, it ain't bad for a lad from Darwen. Fucking bollocks in this case! I'd made it to the Premiership and at that stage of my career, although I was dropping down a division, I thought I could make it back again. I had played over 200 league and cup games for Bolton Wanderers, helping them to get from the old Third Division to the Premiership with two fantastic promotion campaigns.

I played a part in all the FA Cup and Coca-Cola Cup runs, and was the captain on that famous night at Anfield. Many of the characters I met there, players and staff, are still my friends. The four-

and-a half seasons there were definitely my most successful as a footballer.

It wasn't the perfect way to leave Bolton. I had started 12 out of the club's 16 Premiership games and really enjoyed the buzz of the top-flight, with the bigger crowds and the iconic stadiums. But I also wasn't stupid. I had been in football long enough by now to recognise when I was getting pushed out. Strangely, I was once again leaving a club around Christmas time and once again, I managed to get a decent leaving present as Bolton paid me the £25,000 signing-on fee that they still owed me. It was time for another new adventure – this time with the Blades in the steel city of Sheffield.

23

REUNITED IN THE STEEL CITY

December 1995

As good as my word, I returned to Sheffield on the Thursday night, meeting up with Howard Kendall and his staff in a hotel, and the evening went well. Probably a bit too well, actually. They got me as pissed as a fart and the next morning, when I was introduced to my new teammates and trained with them for the first time, the beer was oozing out of my pores. From that day onwards, getting to know my teammates and the staff at Sheffield United was professionally one of the best periods of my life.

I embraced the club right from the start and realised quickly how important the football club was to the red and white half of the city of Sheffield. The Blades fans were both passionate and friendly in equal measure and how brilliant they were with me will stay with me for the rest of my life.

Bruce Rioch had taught me so much as a forward-thinking coach, getting rid of my rough edges and turning me into a professional footballer, but Howard Kendall was my kind of man. I already knew he was the best man-manager and coach in the business, and so I didn't hesitate when the chance came up to work with him for the second time. He had proved himself to be ahead of his time in many ways, going on to manage in Spain after his glorious days of managing Everton to two league titles, an FA Cup and the European Cup Winners' Cup, playing brilliant football. When English clubs had been banned from Europe, Howard showed that he wasn't scared of a challenge by taking up the chance to manage Athletic Bilbao.

While Bruce was a disciplinarian and drilled his players to success, Howard Kendall got players playing for him by different means. He was an absolute genius as a man-manager and bringing in players to do a job for him. Don't get me wrong, he could be ruthless – as I was to find out in my second season at United – but in that first year, it was all about Howard bringing in his players, changing the style and getting a team who were second bottom when I joined, to finish ninth in Division One.

Howard had himself only arrived the week before I did. He had taken up the opportunity to join a club that had recently been in freefall both on the pitch and off. A new chairman, Mike McDonald, had come in and manager Dave Bassett, who was a legend at Bramall Lane after taking the Blades from the third tier into the first, had resigned. Howard quickly made his mark, signing experienced Dutch defender Michael Vonk from Oldham and bringing in David White on a permanent basis, after initially joining the club on loan from Leeds.

I made my debut two days after signing, away at Stoke, on December 23 and I managed to endear myself to the travelling Blades fans by scoring a worldie from outside the box, smashing a 20-yarder in. To make it even more memorable, a Stoke player ripped my shorts during the game and my balls were hanging out. So just like when I played my first-ever game for Howard Kendall, I managed to play well again and get my privates out! David White scored the other in a 2-2 draw, and Howard was really happy with my performance. He waited for me to come off the pitch and shook my hand. "Great debut, Paddy," he said. I knew I'd started too well!

It was great to be playing for him again, the man who had first given me a chance in a senior Rovers shirt. Things in many ways had gone full circle for me. Howard knew my personality. He knew I was a cheeky little bastard, but also that I had matured and was now a leader. I also knew my way round the second tier and had been holding my own in that division for a few years. Howard knew I brought a tenacity to the middle of the park, and that was what the Blades needed at that time to try to steady the ship.

United were also the first club I had played for professionally outside of Lancashire. I had been a pro for 12 years! As such, it was the first time me and the family, Lindsey, Jade and Scott, were potentially going to have to move from Darwen. We didn't move straightaway because the kids were both at school and we needed to think about that. We then looked at moving to Holmfirth, near Huddersfield, so it wouldn't be such a long commute for me, and Lindsey could go back to Darwen at the weekends.

Our marriage wasn't that great at that point and, being honest, I was a bit gutted in the end that we didn't move to Sheffield, because Lindsey didn't want to and also didn't want to move the kids from their schools. Scott and Jade were five and eight and, in my eyes, they were old enough to go to new schools without it affecting them that much. I think this was the beginning of the end. Instead, I ended up commuting to training every day for the next five months until the end of the first season. A typical day saw me get up at six o'clock in the morning for a cold shower, before driving to Bolton and catching the train to Manchester. I'd jump on another to Stockport and change again, before going onto Sheffield.

I got used to the travelling and even enjoyed the daily updates from the other commuters, whether it was about the women going on about their marital problems or husbands shagging about. On one occasion a woman was having an affair with her boss. It made the journey fly by and sometimes Howard and John Bailey would board the train at Liverpool. Howard would always be on a table and save the seats opposite. That was an education it itself; Howard had brought John to United and he was a laugh a minute.

He was bonkers when he was a player when I was a kid at Rovers and hadn't changed. It was a bit surreal; Howard would be sat on the busy train in a polo shirt, boxer shorts and flip flops. I didn't like asking him why, but I think it was just for comfort. I'm not sure what the other commuters thought but Howard wasn't fazed. Why should he be? None of them had won two league titles and a European trophy.

Me, Whitey and Michael Vonk would do the commute from Manchester every day, along with Lee Sandford, who had been signed from Stoke. We'd get to Sheffield by around nine before making our way to the training ground, getting changed and having a bit of breakfast. After training we would get back on the train and get back home late in the afternoon. Timewise, it was like doing a proper job! The atmosphere at the club made up for the pain of travelling, even if it dawned on me after speaking to my train mates that I had been stitched up completely with my contract by not having an agent. Players always end up talking about their salaries and it was obvious that I'd been done.

I definitely wasn't the luckiest bloke when it came to money. I even lost out by not moving to a new house. At that time, when you moved from one club to another you got an £8,000 moving allowance. But because the missus didn't want to, we didn't move, and I didn't have anything in my contract around commuting. So I made an appointment with the chief executive, Charles Green, about getting a rail pass. He wasn't for giving me fuck all; he came across as a tight sod and stubborn to say the least. I ended up having a word with Howard, who sorted it out and I got my pass.

With the £25,000 pay-off from Bolton and a £30,000 signing-on fee from United, my P60 at the end of that season showed income of £151,000 before tax. It took me into the higher bracket, so I got absolutely battered for tax. But this was 1996 and for the next three or four years, my earnings were over £100,000 a year. Back home in Darwen, after the decision not to move, we upgraded from our terraced house on Sandy Lane to a lovely bungalow, which stood in a third of an acre. We invested in it and converted it, so we had four double bedrooms and three en-suite bathrooms. The house was everything we wanted, and we had two nice cars on the drive as well.

Things were so good; I just didn't think it would end. I know it sounds ridiculous to the man in the street, and so naïve, but I think it was because I went from earning decent money to even better money and we just spent more and more. The kids had wanted for nothing and didn't for the next few years. It was a whirlwind time and money seemed to be no concern. But more about that later.

I made my home debut on Boxing Day against top-of-the-table Birmingham City, in front of nearly 18,000 fans. I'll never forget the atmosphere that day, which carried on throughout my time at Sheffield United. The passion of the Blades fans was second to none and they were brilliant to play for. I managed to score a headed equaliser and get man of the match. Two goals in my first two games was not a bad start to my career in Yorkshire and the United supporters must have thought they had signed a goalscoring midfielder. Little did they know!

As well as the goals, I had also picked up a booking that would rule me out of the next two games. The first one was in the third round of the FA Cup, away at Arsenal. Everyone assumed Arsenal would beat us at Highbury and I thought I had missed out on playing against my old manager, Bruce Rioch. But local lad Dane Whitehouse, a huge Blades fan, scored in a morale-boosting 1-1 draw as we earned a replay back at Bramall Lane.

Howard had pulled a masterstroke before the Arsenal game by signing ex-Aston Villa legend Gordon Cowans from Wolves. Known as 'Sid', Cowans was 37 but still looked every bit the top-class player who had won the league title and European Cup for Aston Villa, and been capped by England. I had about 20-odd games with Sid to the end of that season and he turned out to be the best English footballer I ever played with. I would win the ball and give it to him, and he would work his magic. He was like a slim Tony Kelly, only even better.

After the brilliant Arsenal draw, we were brought back down to earth with a point away at Tranmere and by the time we played the Gunners in the replay, we had actually drawn five games on the bounce. However, Howard had brought a different style of play, as well as an infectious belief that we could beat Arsenal, and I went straight back into the team, partnering Sid for the first time.

Arsenal had all their England stars playing – David Seaman, Lee Dixon, Paul Merson, Ian Wright and David Platt – and Bruce had made a major signing to mark the start of his tenure there – the one and only Dennis Bergkamp, who was playing up front with Wright after a £7.5m move from Inter Milan. Bergkamp went on to be one of the best players in the world. But on a cold January night in Sheffield, he and his Arsenal teammates were played off the pitch by us lads in front of 22,000 – mostly Blades fans going ballistic.

We had two local Sheffield lads playing that night, Dane and Mitch

Ward, and I bet they still have a few pints bought for them to this day for their performances that night. We played brilliantly from start to finish, chasing and harrying the Arsenal lads, and I don't think they had a decent chance all the first half. David White hit the crossbar for us and at 0-0 at half-time it was all to play for. We knew before the game that the winners would play Aston Villa in the next round, which would be a big occasion for Sid as his achievements there had rightly earned him legendary status. We came out in the second half like we finished the first.

I then played a hand in the only goal of the game. I sent Dane Whitehouse down the wing with a nice pass, and he crossed for Australian Mark Veart to put his head in where it hurts and score with a brilliant diving header in the 67th minute. Our captain, goalkeeper and superhero Alan Kelly pulled off a fabulous save and Arsenal did have a great chance near the end when David Platt flashed a header past the post, but we were well worth the win at the end. Veart nearly made it 2-0, and but for a world-class save by Seaman he would have. By the end we were passing it around all over the pitch, with the noise level from the home fans at top notch, and Bergkamp and Co. were glad to hear the final whistle. The salute to the fans at the end was something special. And the piss-up after the game, with Howard's permission, was not bad either!

We played Watford at home on the following Saturday, with our new record signing from West Ham, Don Hutchinson, making his debut. With a new signing in the squad and a brilliant FA Cup win, you would think things were looking up. We drew 1-1, and we were certainly looking up... picking up only a point meant we fell to the bottom of the table.

Howard was never one to panic, though. He had seen it and done it all over Europe, so the buzz in training for the next week before the Villa game was superb. Villa were flying high in the Premiership at the time, with a raft of internationals such as Mark Bosnich, Gareth Southgate, Paul McGrath and Dwight Yorke, but we were convinced we could beat them. As an added bonus, the game had been chosen as the live 4pm Sunday game on the BBC, so the nation would be watching.

The plan was to meet at the ground on the Saturday morning, have a light session and brush up on set-pieces. The lads who had travelled would then stay in hotels, the lads within driving distance would go home and we'd all meet on a Sunday morning for a pre-match meal. On Saturday morning, I drove over to Manchester to meet Vonky, who was injured and so the designated driver, and Whitey. It was snowing quite badly as we hit the M62 and then M1, and as we neared Sheffield it was getting heavier. The side streets were particularly bad, and the main roads were getting worse.

When we arrived at the ground it was busy with stewards and helpers clearing the car park. It was already getting to the stage where the game could be in doubt. We got changed and waited for the other lads to arrive, but after a while it was decided to cancel training. Me, Whitey, Sid Cowans, the gaffer and coaching staff had a few games of head tennis in the sports hall instead.

Afterwards, we got changed and then headed to the hotel. Vonky decided to go home. It looked certain that the game would be called off and he didn't want to get stuck in Sheffield if he didn't need to be there. As me, Sid and Whitey sat down for a bit of lunch in the hotel near the ground, the snow was coming down extremely heavily and we assumed there was no way the game was going to be played. We also knew that there was no way that we would be able to get home, either.

We ordered the mandatory bottle of red wine to wash our steaks down, followed by a couple of pints. Nothing that would affect our performance the following day if the game was on. The snow was now inches deep and the roads outside the hotel were absolutely dead. We then made an executive decision, unanimously deciding that the game would be postponed, for sure. "Waiter, more wine!" Before we knew it, it was about five in the afternoon and we were probably a couple of bottles of wine and four pints into our extended lunch when Whitey decided to call it a day.

Don Hutchinson was staying in a hotel not far from ours and knowing that he would be bored on his own, we invited him down. Initially, he wasn't up for it. "Come on, Hutch," we tried to persuade him. "The game's off tomorrow, come and have a few beers with us at our hotel."

To be fair to Hutch, he was a little reluctant after some previous misdemeanours at Liverpool and West Ham had made it into the national Press. On signing him, Howard Kendall had told him to stick to his playing ability, leaving his drinking skills in London. "No, I'm not doing it," Hutch said. "If I have a few beers, someone will find out and it'll all end in tears."

We persuaded him a little more and he managed to walk through the heavy snow to our hotel. We had probably had about half a dozen pints by the time he arrived, and we were absolutely buzzing. The loud cheer that greeted Don as he walked through the door raised a few eyebrows from the few other people in the hotel lounge. What could we do? Sheffield was like a ghost town and if the game hadn't officially been called off yet, it would surely only be a matter of time.

Hutch laughed as he sat down, asking us how many drinks we'd had. He was keen to get on our wavelength as he called a waitress over. "Here, love," he said. "Can I have six double vermouth cocktails?"

In the space of half an hour, Hutch had smashed the lot. He then started on the pints. Me and Sid had been drinking steadily but soon, it became evident that the vermouths were taking effect. In no time, Hutch was absolutely rocking and starting to get a bit noisy. The hotel bar was on a split level; there was a youngish couple about 10 metres from us and further away on the level below was an older couple. The older fella seemed to know who we were, smiling at us and passing a few pleasantries.

When Hutch went to the toilet, I decided to have a quick chat to the older couple and explain that we were just chilling out because the game had been called off. The bloke was as good as gold; he was a United fan and knew who we were. As I was trying to keep the peace with them, Hutch came out of the saloon-style toilet door, ran and did a kneeling down slide across the floor. He came to a stop in front of the young couple at their table and before I could intervene he was already in full flow.

"Now," he asked. "Are you two married or just knocking each other off?"

They were soon out of their seats and heading to the bar, to pay their bill and leave. Back at our table, Hutch was giving them a bit of stick. He picked up a bread bun off the table and, from fully 20 yards, hit the fella on the back of the head with it as he was leaving. It was out of order but a great shot and funny as fuck, to be fair. We were falling off our chairs in stitches.

Hutch by this point was absolutely steaming and we decided it would be best to order him a taxi back to his hotel, so he wouldn't get stuck at ours. It took some doing, with very few taxis running in the snow, but one arrived eventually and we got him packed off to his hotel. We apologised again to the older chap and his wife at the side of us, but they were all smiles and told us not to worry.

Me and Sid carried on having a great chat and by this time, it had become a full-blown drinking session. For all he had achieved in football, Sid was just a great down-to-earth bloke. What you saw was what you got with him. By the time we necked a double malt each, we'd definitely had enough and decided to call it a night. It dawned on us that we hadn't heard anything official from the club about the game being called off. The snow had stopped but we were convinced it would be as we headed to our room.

How far I had come, I thought. From a lad dreaming of playing professional football, to rooming with an ex-England international and European Cup winner!

When I woke up in the morning, I was surprised that I didn't feel too bad – until I flicked on the telly, at least. Sid was in the bathroom, 'freshening up', and Des Lynam was on screen. "Make sure you tune in on BBC One this afternoon for the eagerly anticipated game from Bramall Lane," Des said. "They've had a lot of snow in Sheffield, but what a great effort the groundstaff and the people of Sheffield have done to get the game on. It's the resurgence of Sheffield United under Howard Kendall against Aston Villa, and one of the players, playing for Sheffield United against his old club, is the legend that is Gordon Cowans."

As Des was speaking, there were some strange noises coming from the legend in the bathroom. I started laughing. "Fuck me, Sid," I called out. "We'd better get some water down us…"

Luckily, with the game not being until 4pm, we had some decent time to recover. As a player, I had been naughty before and drank the night before a game, but this was a genuine fuck up. I would never have done it on purpose before a game of this magnitude. And especially with the spotlight of live TV on us! We managed to hide our hangovers when the team and management met for a pre-match meal in our hotel, acting the part of senior players. There was plenty of banter flying around. But after about 15 minutes, we realised there was no Don Hutchinson. Where the fuck was he?

Me, Sid and Whitey started to panic and sent a taxi to his hotel, telling the driver to go inside, get Hutch and bring him to our hotel, but through the back entrance. The taxi driver did a great job and managed to get Don up and out of his hotel, before we snuck him into ours. He was rough as fuck though, and somehow Howard Kendall got wind of something. We managed to convince him that Hutch just wasn't feeling 100 per cent.

Me and Sid took Hutch to our room and ran him a cold bath, to try and bring him round. It worked a little, but he was still looking a bit green around the gills. There was still deep snow on the streets around the ground when we arrived, but it was evident that the groundstaff and volunteers had done an amazing job. The game was definitely going to go ahead.

In the dressing room, Howard named his team. "Paddy in the middle with Sid… Hutch up front… Whitey out on the right-hand side." I sat there, chuckling to myself. Nearly half of the outfield players were worse for wear! It wasn't my first time, though, and I can honestly say I felt great. I was still up for it. I wanted to get out there and make an imprint against a Premiership side, in more ways than one.

I wanted to win the ball and give it to Sid so that he could work his magic. At Bolton, I won it and gave it to Tony Kelly. This was the same. Win the ball and give it to Sid. Get it and give it and get stuck in.

The game kicked off and we were doing okay, except for Hutch. He was not very mobile at all, even though he nearly scored before half-time when Bosnich pulled off a great save. I think that was the only time Hutch got anywhere near the ball in the first half and as we left the pitch, I looked at Sid. He raised his eyebrows at me and was obviously thinking the same. It was still 0-0 and we were more than holding our own, so we thought that may have saved Hutch.

Howard, though, had seen it all before and as we got into the dressing room, he told Hutch to get his kit off and get a shower. Me, Whitey and Sid all looked at each other, knowing that there was trouble ahead. On our way back out for the second half, we passed Hutch coming out of the shower and had a quiet word, about him being on his own the night before. It was a bit naughty, telling him not to drag us down with him, but there was no point four of us getting bollocked when one could just take a bit of shit. Hutch gave us the nod.

We were doing well in the second half as the game really got going, and started to get a bit tasty. I was playing well, Sid was playing well and David White was still doing all right, too. Then Sid got kicked, ending up with a gash on his knee and was stretchered off. As he was passing me, we gave each other a wry smile. "Cheers mate," I said to him, "leaving me on my own."

Savo Milošević, Villa's Serbian centre-forward, was starting to wind up the United fans, and us players, with his theatrics, and he won Villa a penalty with another bit of diving about. Yorke stepped up to take it and despite being pelted with snowballs, chipped the ball, Panenka-style, over our goalkeeper Alan Kelly. Fair play; it was a great penalty, and it proved to be the winner. But we had put in a good performance against a quality side and when I watched it back on TV later, I remember the commentator saying I was having a good game. Not bad for double-figure pints the night before!

As a group we thought we had got away with it, until we went in for the warm down on the Monday and Hutch collared me. He said he thought we had been grassed up by someone. "What do you mean?" I asked him. "You've not dropped us in it, have you?" He said he hadn't and was probably just about to explain, when Howard Kendall came in and gave us the answer.

"Paddy, Sid, Hutch, Whitey," he said. "My fuckin' office, now."

In we trooped.

"Right, Paddy," Howard said. "What the fuck has gone on on Saturday?"

I started to try and blag it. "To be fair, gaffer, we honestly thought the game was going to be called off with the snow and we couldn't get home, so we had a few beers."

"Whoa, whoa, let me stop you there before you go any further," Howard said. He then pulled out a till roll from his desk drawer. As he began to unravel it, I knew this was going to be costly.

"A few beers? A few fuckin' beers? Well, this is your fucking bar bill…"

He started reeling off the drinks. "Lagers, Guinness, wine, meals, cigars and vermouths, vermouths… what the fuck is vermouth?

We didn't dare look at each other but we were all pissing ourselves inside. We were like naughty schoolchildren. Howard seemed to know that we weren't going to say anything.

"Forget it," he said. "I don't want to know."

The bar bill was well over £200. Naughty, but a good effort by just four of us. Then Howard showed his excellent man-management skills. "Right," he said. "I'm not going to take any action today. We are still in a shit position and we need to get away from the bottom of the league, so we need to put a run together. So, I'm going to leave it until later in the season and see where we are. But you four owe me big time!"

To some extent we'd got away with it, but I was still keen to find out how Howard found out. "By the way gaffer," I asked. "How did you know what had happened?"

"Well, Paddy," Howard said. "The couple you were talking to in the restaurant, the bloke is a director of the club…"

I don't think I've covered as many miles on a football pitch as I did for the rest of that season. What a manager Howard Kendall was. The incident was kept in-house and kept out of the Press which stopped it causing friction with the rest of the team and the fans, who we knew we had let down. It really was a genuine mistake, though!

24

CAPTAIN PATTERSON

January to July 1996

From the end of January, after the Villa game until the middle of March, our results meant that we were still very much in a relegation dogfight. The money that was now being thrown around in the Premiership meant that the First Division was such a competitive division and we weren't winning enough games because of our lack of firepower. In the 11 games after the Villa game, we only scored two goals in two winning games and seven in total. Nathan Blake finished as our top scorer that season, and he had moved to Bolton in December.

Howard Kendall described our performance in defeat at Millwall the worst since he had taken over, and to top it off we lost our goalkeeper and skipper Alan Kelly to a serious injury. But on the plus side, one of my old mates had returned to English football. Howard had signed Andy Walker from Celtic in late February and, from our time together at Bolton, I knew that Andy would fit into our style of football. Howard had also signed striker Gareth Taylor from Crystal Palace, so it wasn't as if he wasn't trying to do something about our lack of goals.

The next game was what is commonly known as a relegation six-pointer. We were at home against Luton, who were two places below us and in the third relegation spot, and with Kelly injured, the armband was up for grabs. When Howard told me he was making me skipper before kick-off, I have to admit I was a bit overwhelmed. I couldn't have been any prouder.

I think my performance matched my enthusiasm as I managed to get man of the match in a poor game, which saw Don Hutchinson score from a free-kick from about nine yards out! We hadn't had much luck with refs all season, but for once we got a decision. He gave the free-kick for a backpass, which most of us didn't think it was. But we took it. It was all about results at that stage of the season. The craic in the changing room after the game was great. It got even better when the chairman came in and announced that if we beat Leicester City away, the following Saturday, he was going to make some money available for us to have an end-of-season piss-up in Magaluf.

It would be no mean feat. Leicester were in the play-off hunt and would eventually go up to the Premiership via that route. But it's amazing what the incentive of a free jolly-boys outing to Magaluf can do for team morale. We duly went to Filbert Street and turned them over 2-0! Andy Walker notched and local lad Mitch Ward scored a penalty. This win went a long way to nearly guaranteeing our survival.

On the Monday, Howard then pulled me, Sid Cowans, Don Hutchinson and Whitey into his office and told us it was time to face the fine for our pre-Villa drinking misdemeanours. "Right lads," he began. "You've done ever so well in the last few months, so we are going to take it easy on you. Me and the coaching staff have decided to fine you £300 each."

Fuckin' result, we thought. He then said that we had to tell the lads that we weren't training on the Wednesday, but were instead going to the Norton pub in Meadowhead. And it was compulsory. "And tell them all that every one of them has got to have a joke ready," he added. It was all about team bonding with Howard Kendall. With £1,200 of our money in the kitty, we headed for the Norton for a slap-up meal and a few beers, and a cigar on the side of the plate. Howard loved his cigars.

At the end of the meal we all had to tell a joke, followed by a puff on the big Cuban cigar. The jokes were mostly shit and we then headed for the bar leaving the coaching staff in the dining area. Dougie Hodgson, our big Aussie centre-half whose house I used to stay at if we played in midweek, started being a bit daft. There was an area near the bar, up a couple of steps, where the cutlery was kept and Dougie, drunk by now, started whizzing the knives and forks at us, while we used the large table mats as shields. The more we laughed at him, the harder he threw them.

"Come on you Aussie twat," we goaded him. "You couldn't hit a cow's arse with a banjo."

But Simon Tracey, the goalkeeper who had come in and done a good job in place of the injured Alan Kelly, got a bit pissed off with it. "Fack off Dougie," he said in his southern accent. "Enough is enough."

Dougie had obviously had a few too many by this point and just carried on telling Tracey to fuck off back. Tracey was getting more enraged now. "I'm telling you to pack it in," he said, "or I'm going to do you."

Dougie just gave him the finger, which was probably not the wisest thing to do. A bit stupidly, and in a matching Southern accent, I started to wind Tracey up. "Come on, saan," I said. "Sort him out, get a grip of him."

Tracey got up and started walking up towards the steps. Dougie warned him not to carry on towards him. Tracey asked him why and when he carried on towards Dougie, he soon got his answer. Dougie jumped up and, kickboxer style, kicked Tracey straight in the mush, knocking him down. Unfortunately, Tracey didn't know that Doug had been a kickboxer in Australia before he'd taken up football.

He certainly hadn't lost any of his technique! Tracey got back up and ran from the restaurant, with blood pouring from his mouth. He wasn't doing a runner, though, and returned with a golf club from the boot of his car. Luckily, we managed to get the nine-iron off him before it escalated further. Team building activities sometimes do go wrong!

"Skipper, skipper," came the shout from the management team in the restaurant area. I made my way up a little sheepishly. Howard asked me what was going on and I told him that we were just having a bit of banter which went a little bit too far. Then, Howard asked bluntly: "Did he deserve it?"

I told him he did. "Right, no worries," he said. "Crack on..."

Brilliant, I thought. We did just that. The lads kept Trace and Dougie separated and we carried on having a few more pints. Dougie was some character and was always up to something. We had a great club bus driver, Martin, who was ex-Armed Forces, so he was a bit of a crazy fella himself. But even Martin had to be on his guard when Dougie was about. On one Friday afternoon we were all sat on the team coach ready to travel down to London for an away game.

As we set off some of us noticed Martin stood at the main entrance talking to someone. Who the fuck was driving the bus? It was no surprise to see the mad Aussie at the wheel. He had decided to take us on a circuit of the car park. The look on Martin's face was a picture as he set off on the run trying to stop Dougie, but it was too late as Dougie did a few circuits of the car park with us cheering him on.

On another occasion we were on the bus travelling from Bramall Lane to the training ground. We were travelling at about 30mph when Dougie decided to get a bit of fresh air and pushed open the skylight at the back of the bus. He then pulled himself up and out and then he began walking on top of the bus. Complete madness!

He then dropped down through the skylight at the front of the bus in front of Howard Kendall and the coaching staff. They didn't know whether to laugh or bollock him and Martin was giving him a few swear words. But that was Dougie, a great character. He lives back in Australia now but keeps in touch with a lot of us old Blades from that time. He's suffered a lot of ill health but is still a fighter and a great lad.

Apart from that unfortunate incident, the blow-out did team morale no harm whatsoever and on the following Saturday, we continued our winning streak with a 3-0 demolition of ex-Liverpool player Ronnie Whelan's Southend.

For being made captain I got a profile page in the matchday programme against Southend and in my own words explained what it meant to me to be made captain of Sheffield United in Alan Kelly's absence. "I was just so proud to lead United out against Luton," I said. "It's not just a question of wearing an armband, it's setting an example and driving the players on. That suits me, it doesn't put me off my game and I hope it works for the lads."

We went on to finish the season undefeated, in total winning seven out of the last nine games. Unbelievably we finished ninth in the league, after previously being in relegation trouble, and I had been fully accepted by the Sheffield United fans as one of their own, even though I was a Lancashire lad. The punters were singing: "He's a Blade, he's a Blade" and I earned the nickname of "the Lancashire Terrier."

I gave my complete all for their club, and they gave me respect for that. No matter if it was a good game or a bad game, I always gave 100 per cent, which got me a long way with the man in the street. I had to laugh when I was doing a bit of research around my time at Sheffield United and came across this post on a Blades forum: "Mark Patterson was some player. Covered every blade of grass, fierce in the tackle and intelligent enough when he had the ball to give it to someone with more talent." I'll take that all day, especially when that player was usually Sid Cowans.

I loved playing for Howard Kendall that first season, but also got on with all the coaching staff he'd brought in. As well as Bails, Howard brought in Adrian 'Inchy' Heath, another one of his former Everton players as a player/coach, and Viv Busby brought some great experience. Bails was the joker in the pack, though. Each morning he would come into training like a kid in a sweet shop, happy to say the least, and always made us laugh.

It was no secret that Howard and Bails liked a drink and along with Inchy and Buzzer, they kept their local off-licence, near their digs, ticking over nicely. When they all eventually left the club, the rumour was that takings in the off-licence dropped considerably. But they never came into training looking anything less than immaculate and ready to go.

On one occasion, though, Bails failed to turn up for training. Or at least we thought he did. Whilst we were out training, Mitch Ward stayed behind having some treatment and decided that after a shower he would have a sauna. He switched on the sauna before jumping in the shower and looked over to the sauna as it began to shake. Then the door burst open and out fell Bails, fully clothed! He'd come into training early a little worse for wear and decided to have a nap under the benches in the sauna. Unfortunately, he'd slept longer than he had anticipated…

In the end we had more than earned our end of season piss-up to Magaluf, which was a mecca for a large number of professional football teams by that time. Port Vale and Bury's players and staff were there at the same time as us and we could have played a mini-tournament amongst ourselves, if we weren't all too busy getting hammered.

I remember heading back to the hotel following a 24-hour bender with Whitey, Vonky and another Dutchman, Port Vale's Robin van der Laan. I was passing a bar when I heard someone shout the nickname I had been christened with at Preston. "Gizmo!" It was Sam Ellis, my former manager from Bury and just a top all-round guy.

"Fuckin' get up here and have a beer," he said.

"Fuckin' hell Sam, I'm fucked," I told him. "I've been on the lash non-stop for over a day."

"Come on, have a coffee whiskey… you'll be fine."

Along with Sam there was Stan Ternent, the new Bury manager who I'd never met before, Terry Robinson the chairman and Alan Raw, the physio. Bury were in the Second Division, but would win it the following season. I had about half an hour with them, had a good laugh and then set off again. Little did I know that a couple of seasons later, Stan would sign me for Bury. My drinking stamina must have made an impression on him!

A few bars further on I came across Howard.

"Skipper, you all right son?" he asked. I told him I was great, and he told me to sit and have a cigar with him. I was in a bit of a state by now, but it was an offer I couldn't turn down. Not only was Howard a great man, he was also a great drinker. He would sit in a certain bar, just between Magaluf and Palma Nova, with some of his coaching staff, having beer after beer and also a big bowl of alcoholic punch. All the other football managers would be out with him, no doubt listening to his magnificent football stories. Howard never used to miss Magaluf. The 1980s and 90s were great times for end of season trips. Howard embraced them to the full, and why not? He was a hard-working manager just letting off a bit of steam like the rest of us.

He would run the show. He would get up at half eight for breakfast, before heading down to the bar and finding a spot in the full sunshine until the mid-afternoon. Once he'd had his fill, he would head back to the hotel and would then be back at it by seven or eight o'clock, carrying on into the early hours. We used to ask him how he managed to sober back up. "Cold bath," he replied simply.

The newspapers were always trying to catch footballers and managers out and get a story, but they never caught Howard. He was an expert at keeping his leisurely drinking sessions under wraps. He would be in the bar, wearing sunglasses and a baseball cap and nursing a pint and a bottle of water. He would have spotters on the front looking out for the Press; watching for journalists and anyone looking out of place with a camera.

If he got the nod that someone was about, he'd change from drinking his pint to his bottle of water. He had it off to a tee and was always jovial and happy to speak to the Press lads. Then, once they'd left him alone, he would go back on the session. What a bloke. RIP Howard Kendall. Legend.

25

BORNEO DELICACY
TO BARNSLEY CHOP

July 1996 to March 1997

How times had changed. When we returned to pre-season training, we found out our itinerary of friendlies was a bit different than usual. I think we all had to look it up on a map when it was announced that we would be playing three friendlies in... Borneo. I'd come a long way from playing in the Manx Cup on the Isle of Man in the early 1980s.

Borneo was an island, but a little bigger than the Isle of Man – it was the third largest island in the world, off the coast of Malaysia, over 7,000 miles away from Sheffield. It was bloody massive, and we had to do some internal flights to get to the different games the club had lined up.

It took a little longer than a few hours on a ferry to get there as well. Borneo, we found out, was a country owned by Malaysia and we had to have a stop in Singapore to get there. It was a very unusual place to go, to say the least. Apparently the chief executive, Charles Green, had done some business over there and he'd organised it. Once we landed in Borneo, the reality of the poverty hit us. None of us had been in a third world-type country and it was both sad and amazing to see the conditions that the locals lived in. Just seeing people travelling around on rickety old bikes for transport surprised us all.

I think somebody later found out that around 95 per cent of the people lived in poverty, with five per cent owning all the wealth. And it showed. We stayed in the capital of Sarawak state, a place called Kuching. But we weren't in the middle of the city, we were in the middle of nowhere. I think even Howard Kendall and the coaching staff were gutted when we threw our bags in the rooms. Of course, it was luxury compared to the ramshacks we had seen as we travelled from the airport. But as we got further and further from the city, all the lads just started shaking their heads. It was a very basic hotel, to say the least, and the training facilities consisted of a five-a-side pitch and a swimming pool.

In fairness, the lads were more bothered about the drinking facilities than the training ones. In those days, the first thing any footballers did on a pre-season tour was to find out where the nearest watering holes were – usually more the alcohol ones than the third world ones. Unfortunately for us, a scouting party was sent out and they came back with the news we were all dreading. There was fuck all out there. Intentionally or unintentionally, we had been done.

After settling into our new surroundings and the humidity for a couple of days it was time to get down to some pre-season training, which turned out to be the easiest I had ever been involved in. It was more about the team bonding, the camaraderie and the banter. It definitely worked as you had nowhere to go if you fell out with anyone, and to be fair they were a great bunch of lads anyway. We were split up into two groups, one going in the pool and the others doing some basic drills on the five-a-side pitch before a mini game.

The hotel was basic but half decent, set out over two floors with stairs at either end of the ground and first floor. The food there was fucking awful, and we were never rushing down to meals. But one day, the change in menu was interesting. Me and my roomie Phil Starbuck had just returned to the room after the afternoon training session when we heard a scream and thought a woman was being murdered. I don't think either of us would be classed as heroes, but instinctively we both ran out of the room to see what had happened.

We were met by a five-foot-long Komodo dragon bounding along the corridor. The woman had shit herself, and me and Phil weren't far off. But before we could run back into our room and lock the door a man in a white coat, with a bag and a stick appeared. He expertly manoeuvred the dragon into his massive bag and off he went.

We went back to our room, lay down on our beds, and started laughing. *What the fuck were we doing here?* Fast forward a few hours and we were ambling downstairs for our evening meal, knowing how crap it was going to be. That evening, there was a change to the menu and one of the specials was Komodo dragon! It doesn't get much fresher than that, caught in the hotel grounds a few hours earlier, so we thought we would give it a try. Unfortunately, it was like the rest of the food. Bloody minging! I thought so, anyway. Phil thought it was okay, although neither of us were exactly connoisseurs of the delicacy.

A couple of the single lads got friendly with one of the employees of the hotel, a bit of a Jack-the-lad type character whose job it was to look after the players and the staff. On the fourth day, with not much to do at night, boredom had set in. Unknown to the rest of the team, the two lads arranged a little entertainment for the rest of us. We were informed to be on our balconies at a certain time and wait for it to begin.

Within a few minutes a minibus, with darkened windows, pulled up. Me and Starby looked at each other and both raised our eyebrows in a bit of anticipation. The doors of the minibus slid open and out stepped a very small, scantily-clad woman, followed by another and another, until there were seven very small women in total. It was like a scene from a *Snow White and the Seven Dwarfs* erotic film, and the only thing missing was Snow White.

I know it was before their time, but it was very much a Paddy McGuinness and Peter Kay "How far away are they?" moment from *Phoenix Nights*. Everyone was just shaking their heads, struggling to contain themselves. It certainly did the job that the lads wanted and lightened the mood. Even more so when we found out that the two organisers had paid $800 to secure the entertainment. I think they were hoping that after a successful show there would be a whip round. Instead, as quickly as they had disembarked, the ladies were being ushered back on the bus and off the hotel premises.

Once we were sort of acclimatised, we played our first friendly against Sarawak, who played in the Malaysian Premier League. It was like playing in a sauna and on concrete, but we still managed to take it seriously and came out 2-1 winners in front of 10,000 fans, with both Andy Walker and Don Hutchinson notching.

Between light training for the next game, we played a few rounds of golf. The course went on to the beach and if one of us played a shit shot – which was pretty often – they would be met by a million sand crabs when retrieving the ball. It was amazing and a real education. If we hadn't gone to that place, we would never have seen stuff like it.

It wasn't the usual pre-season tour, and I did wonder what the new lads and the trialists that Howard was having a look at would think. We took an African lad on trial, who I think had been playing in Italy. He put the lads to shame with the fags… he would finish training and go to his room and smoke like a chimney!

Our next game was against Sabah, the Malaysian champions, and getting there was some experience. We flew on a little plane that was like something out of Indiana Jones. It hadn't even been chartered for us but was like a flying bus on an airbus route. We had four stops on the way to the capital and I think a few prayers were said, but eventually we made it. We didn't pick up any goals, in a 0-0 draw, but we picked up plenty of blisters!

We ended up staying in Sabah for a night so at least we managed to get out and let our hair down. We played the game and when we went out straight afterwards in the city, there were rats running across our feet. But it was a great city for a 'few' beers and we ended up in a pub/nightclub which, in the past had been the fuselage of a plane! It was great craic and, for the record, we won the last friendly 3-0 against a Sarawak XI with Andy Walker, Mitch Ward and even big centre-half Dougie Hodgson getting a goal.

On the way back we had three nights in Singapore, which was absolutely amazing. We were walking around at 4am and the place was absolutely jam-packed and buzzing. Everything was open, restaurants and bars. We had a week with our families once we got back home, before rounding off our pre-season travelling with a four-day trip to Northern Ireland. We played out a 0-0 draw with Linfield at Windsor Park and then beat part-timers Glenavon 4-0. After the games, we were treated to some great Irish hospitality. In 1996 the Troubles, unfortunately, were still prevalent and although things had calmed down a bit by then compared to the 1970s, we were still told to get back into our hotel by 11pm and be careful.

We had a few funny looks in the pubs when our English accents were exposed but, overall, it was a great trip to end the pre-season. Even with the 11pm curfew supposedly in place, a few of us carried on in the bar in the hotel and had had a few too many. By around 1.30am, me and Starbs headed back to our rooms and as we passed the gaffer's room, we could hear a conversation going on. Howard's was the first voice we heard,

"So, who are we going to leave out on Saturday, Paddy or Hutch? Who would you rather play in there with, Spackers?"

Nigel Spackman had joined in the summer as a player/coach. "I'd rather have Hutch in there, gaffer," was the reply.

My head went straightaway. *What a twat.* There's only one thing to do when you have your nose pushed out like that... take revenge. And it came like an SAS mission. We waited until Spackman returned to his room, nicked the skeleton key from reception and gave it a while, until we thought he'd be fast asleep. Once in the room, the two of us took hold of the double bed at the bottom and on the nod, we smashed it against the wall.

Spackers was now upside down, pinned against the wall, and was squealing like a baby as we gave him several digs in the ribs. We let the bed drop and made for the door. Mission complete. Ant Middleton would have been proud of us. When we got up for breakfast, he made it clear that he thought we were the culprits. We played dumb whilst he came out with a few expletives. "I don't know if I'll be able to play at the weekend now, Howard..."

***

After the somewhat unconventional trips to Borneo and Northern Ireland, and a great end to the previous campaign, we were more than ready for the new season and a promotion push. After my captain's exploits covering for Alan Kelly, I also now had the proud honour of being made the club captain. Alan showed what a brilliant professional and great man he was by doing a little speech and handing over the captain's armband. What a class act Alan was, and still is.

I was 31 at this point of my career and I knew I was slowing down. If I was going to be able to still compete, I knew I had to do something a bit different. I went to see the sports scientist, Dr. Spence, who was into his rugby and his weights. I told him that I knew I was really slowing down and needed to get stronger for the central midfield battles I was no doubt going to have. Dr. Spence gave me some great advice and said that, until I could master my own body weight there was no point going on weights. He prescribed me a series of press ups, squats and upper body exercises.

I was back to commuting so decided to catch an earlier train and do my own bit of fitness training before the rest of the lads arrived. I'd get to the training ground about 8.45am, have a slice of toast and then do three sets of 30 press ups, three sets of dips and then hundreds of sit-ups. Not being too modest, I'd always had great abdominals. When I was a young lad at Rovers one of the trainers, Jim Walker, used to batter us with sit-ups, especially when I had my serious injury and was out for five months. I ended up doing 800-1,000 sit-ups in a session. Within a few weeks I could feel a massive difference, so I'd always kept them up.

As part of our fitness training, and to keep us fresh, we had two fitness guys who used to come in. We called them 'Chuckle Vision', because they looked like the Chuckle Brothers, but fitness coaches were the in-thing at the time and they had us doing a 'press-up bleep test', as opposed to the running bleep test.

Roger Nilsen, the Norwegian left back who was blond, tanned and looked like a Viking, had a fantastic physique and worked out a lot. On the day of the press-up bleep test, Roger was on one of the mats in front of me. As the bleeps continued, people started dropping out, but me and Roger were both going strong. In the end it was just us and then at level 52, Roger collapsed. I had beaten all the lads and a Viking, so was chuffed to bits.

As much as anything the extra strength training also kept me going psychologically, because it gave me something to believe in. Not only was I stronger, I believed I was getting stronger. Every time I played, I thought that pound for pound I was as strong as anyone. I had definitely matured from that cocky kid at Rovers, now the captain of Sheffield United and even putting in extra training at the age of 31.

We didn't have the best of starts to the season, with an away defeat to Reading, before we were involved in an eight-goal thriller at Bramall Lane. Unfortunately, we threw away a two-goal lead and it finished 4-4 with Gareth Taylor and Andy Walker scoring a pair apiece. Some of the new players were still bedding in, but we began to pick up points. Nigel Spackman came in – luckily, not at the expense of me or Hutch – and we won four of our next five.

In one of them, away at Molineux, Wolves had equalised through an 89th-minute penalty before we went up the other end and scored the winner through another new lad, Petr Katchuro. Petr was a bit pleased to say the least. I'd recently christened him "the Moose from Belarus." He was a big lad but was very quiet, probably because he couldn't speak a word of English when he joined us. But he was a brilliant lad. When he wanted the ball, he just made a weird noise, sort of like a moose. So I christened him the Moose from Belarus, and it stuck.

After a Howard Kendall bollocking for a 3-2 away defeat to Southend, after being 2-1 up, we went on a really decent run of 10 games without defeat, winning five. One of the games I enjoyed during that period was against my old team Bolton Wanderers, who were absolutely flying at the time. I got a great reception from the Bolton travelling support but was a bit gutted when my reason for leaving Bolton, Nathan Blake, scored an early goal. Gareth Taylor made it honours even in a 1-1 draw.

It's amazing how many old friends and teammates you play against during your career and when we played QPR it was great to see my old midfield mate from my Rovers days, Simon Barker. Simon was by then a veteran of the Premiership and then the First Division with QPR who he'd left Rovers for in 1988. Eight years later and he'd played nearly 300 games for the same club whilst I had been travelling around Lancashire, Greater Manchester, and Yorkshire. It was great to see him, and we had a right old tussle, but Barks took the spoils by scoring a penalty as we were beaten 1-0 at Loftus Road. Remembering that I used to score some goals when we were together might have inspired me to get my only one of the season in a 3-1 home win against Yorkshire rivals Huddersfield Town!

By December we were very much in the play-off hunt and the good form carried into January. I was playing well, but we just weren't consistent enough to open up a gap. Only Bolton really started pulling away from the rest of the pack and it was very tight at the top. We were in the top four, but my place was very suddenly in jeopardy when the club signed Nicky Henry from Oldham at the end of February.

I was still the captain and had played in every game, doing okay, but all of a sudden, I knew I might have been in trouble because of the competition in the middle of the park already. Like Bruce Rioch had done with me some years earlier, Howard had started bringing Dane Whitehouse into the middle of the pitch from the left wing and he had been playing well. Add in my old foe and assistant manager Nigel Spackman, and Hutch who could also play in the middle, and you could see we were a bit overloaded.

So, when Nicky Henry came in, I knew I was definitely in trouble. To be fair, in my eyes, Nicky was a better player than me and also had a lot of Premiership experience. I'm always honest about players and Nicky was a genuine central midfield player. It was fair enough that Howard liked him and brought him in but at the time, the way I thought my Sheffield United career was ending was pretty poor. It was how Howard Kendall worked, though. Very matter-of-fact and straight to the point.

We had beaten Port Vale 3-0 on a Tuesday night and were travelling the very short distance to Barnsley for a derby game that was being screened live on Sky Sports' Friday Night Football. I'd played all right against Port Vale and was looking forward to getting stuck in, as Barnsley were having a great season and one point above us in third place. On the team coach driving over to Barnsley, Howard called me to the front of the bus and said, in a very matter-of-fact way: "I'm not playing you tonight, Paddy. I'm playing Nicky Henry, and you can look for another club if you want to, lad."

Just like that.

Fuck me, I thought. I didn't see that coming. There were 12 games to go and if we had beaten Barnsley, we'd have gone above them and been one point off automatic promotion. I sat back down a bit shocked, not saying anything to the rest of the lads. I must admit at the time I was gutted and angry. I just thought: "Fuck it. They still owe me some money. I'll get my signing-on fee and get myself another club."

My kid brother Sean had driven to the game but with me not playing, we fucked it off and went back to Darwen to go on the piss. I didn't take much notice of the game as I drowned my sorrows with a few beers. For the record though, we didn't go above Barnsley, losing 2-0 to end a four-match unbeaten run. I didn't have a clue when I would play another first-team game. And then my phone rang.

DOWN SOUTH AND BACK

April to December 1997

When Sheffield United had beaten Southend United 3-0 at Bramall Lane in January, I had a great game, dominating their midfield. At the time, their manager Ronnie Whelan had told Howard Kendall that he fancied signing me. So, not long after letting me know that I was surplus to requirements, I got a call from Howard saying that Southend wanted me to go down on loan, with a view to signing for them.

It was a long way away from home, but it was also nice to be wanted so I thought, why not? It was also quite flattering that Ronnie Whelan wanted to sign me. Ronnie was not in Phil Neal's league for total trophies won but he didn't have a bad haul – six league titles, two FA Cup winners medals, three League Cups, a Super League Cup and a European Cup winner's medal. Not bad at all!

Being so settled at Sheffield United, I still hadn't got myself an agent so for the first time I thought I'd get myself one. Better later than never, I suppose. Of all people, I called Scott Sellars – the lad who had hounded me out of two clubs! I was just surprised that Howard hadn't signed him to replace me, rather than Nicky Henry.

Scott's agent was Paul Stretford, so he gave me his number. It turned out that Stretford was Ronnie Whelan's agent as well. Football really is a small world! Paul asked me to meet him in a hotel on the East Lancs Road. We met and chatted, and it coincided with Southend playing Tranmere in a Friday night game, so I went and met the lads on the coach. They were a great set, including ex-Liverpool player Mike Marsh. The only problem was they were in trouble in the league, and got tonked 3-0 on the night to make it eight games without a win.

The following week I went to Paul Stretford's office and we talked about a few things because it looked like I was going to go on a permanent transfer. Southend offered me a two-year deal, on the same wages and with the same signing-on fee I had at United. The Blades were going to pay me up as well and Southend said I only had to train three days a week, so I could commute and the kids didn't have to be uprooted.

First, I went on loan as the deal got worked out. The plan was for Lindsey, Jade and Scott to fly down in the school holidays and stay at Orsett Hall, which was to be my digs for a few weeks. It was a 17th century building set in acres of parkland and with a royal suite on the top floor, which I stayed in. I'd stayed there a few times when I'd played for Bolton and we'd played Southend – it was a great set-up.

I played four games on loan for Southend, with a view to signing on a permanent. They had stopped the rot the week before with a 2-1 home win against Portsmouth and the first two games I played in, Swindon away and Bradford City away, finished in draws. Southend were in a desperate position, really needing the points so draws were no good really. Ronnie, knowing I was staying on my own, would make sure I was okay. We would go to training then have a round of golf in the afternoon before meeting for a couple of beers. Ronnie had been a player then the player/manager at Southend for the previous two years and started telling me that he was staying in the royal suite at Orsett Hall when Bolton had come down to play and he and his wife had had to move out of the room.

I nearly spat my beer out laughing! I told Ronnie about the story of Alan Stubbs and Jason McAteer staying in the royal suite, and Aidan Davison jumping out of the wardrobe wearing a nightie. It turned out to be Ronnie's wife's negligee! We pissed ourselves laughing. I don't think she'd have wanted to put it on after a hairy-arsed goal-keeper had worn it, but it was ripped everywhere anyway!

Two things got in the way of me signing on a permanent for

Southend. I started really struggling with an Achilles tendon injury, which I couldn't exactly hide, and the final nail in the coffin, or the deal to be exact, was when I got a call from Ronnie on the way back up north following the last game of the season after Southend had been relegated.

"Patto, I've been binned, pal," Ronnie said, "and you're no longer wanted at the club."

It was no surprise. So I turned my attention to getting fit for the next season. I still had a year to go on my Sheffield United contract, so I thought I'd get myself back to Bolton and have an operation on my Achilles. Once again, I had a short break at the Beaumont Hospital following an Achilles scrape by my old butcher, Banksy. It was obviously agreed with the Sheffield United medical staff so I was a bit surprised when one night, a week or so after I'd had the operation, I got a call out of the blue from Howard Kendall.

"Hello Paddy," he said.

"All right gaffer," I said. He asked how I was, and I thought he was concerned for my welfare after my operation. He asked if I was on holiday. Footballers had the trick of going straight on their holidays as soon as the season finished.

"No, I'm sat in my house watching the telly," I replied.

"Are you fit?" he asked.

"No, I've had my Achilles scraped," I told him. "Surely you know about it?"

"You've had your Achilles scraped?" he barked down the phone. "Why didn't I know about it?"

"Well, I told the physio and he let me go ahead," I said.

"Well, son, I'm in a bit of a spot," Howard admitted. "We've lost Nick for the final and I was going to put you in."

For fuck's sake. Not again, I thought. Not again. *Another* chance of playing at Wembley down the toilet. I was more than a little frustrated. If Howard, or anyone from Sheffield United, had called me before the operation, I could and would have postponed it. I asked the medical staff and they gave it the go-ahead. I would have been fine to play, and would have had the surgery straight after to be ready for the new season.

United ended up losing 1-0 to Palace at Wembley. I sat at home and watched it on TV and their central midfielder Dave Hopkin, a ginger-haired lad with a front tooth missing, had an absolute blinder and scored a worldie in the 90th minute. If I'd have been playing, I'd have been up against him and my job would have been to sort him out. Looking at the team, without Nicky playing, they were definitely lightweight in midfield on the day. The season had started so promisingly, for both me and the club, and had ended terribly for both. And there was more to come for me.

Howard left United after the play-off final defeat, to return to Everton once more, and my rehab was going really well until I was told that Adrian Heath, the Burnley manager, wanted to sign me. I would be allowed to go, and I could meet Inchy that very afternoon at Turf Moor. I have to admit that I went with my eyes completely open and I wasn't being naïve at the time. I knew that I would get caned because of my Blackburn Rovers connections.

I would get slaughtered at every turn: by my mates, by Rovers fans, and quite possibly, especially if things weren't going well on the pitch, by Burnley fans themselves. There is no love lost between Burnley and Rovers, and that's putting it mildly. I supported Blackburn since I was a little kid. I'd played for them and still watched out for their every result. I knew I would get absolutely hammered by Rovers fans, and especially the lads from Darwen!

However, by that point I was 32 and I had realised I was coming to the end of my career. This was just another job, another pay day. Probably ill-advised, but a pay day nonetheless. So, I went to have talks with Inchy and the chairman, Barry Kilby. They were both concerned about my Achilles injury, but I assured them I would be fine as I'd had it done before and come back strong. So, they offered me this, that and the other, I had my photograph taken with them both and I thought that was it. I hadn't signed anything but as far as I was concerned, I was a Burnley player.

I was going to do it and take the chance. I was obviously in the position where I could have got stick from the Burnley fans as well for being an ex-Rovers player, so I knew I would have to pull my tripe out when I played my first game. I would have to win the fans over by smashing a few people, and maybe even get sent off. I know it was a bit of a mad way to think, but I just thought it would show how much I cared. That was my intention, my way of thinking.

Then, the next day, Adrian Heath got a call from Howard Kendall. Howard wanted Inchy back at Everton as his No.2. He agreed, and Kilby then got on the phone to Sheffield United to say that Burnley were not going to sign me. I read in the paper that Kilby and the Burnley secretary, John Howarth, said that my medical with their doctor showed that I wasn't going to be fit until September or October. It was all bullshit. As I had told them, I would be fit in weeks rather than months. I knew my body, knew the injury. It was just their way of getting out of signing me.

That was that and after looking like I could have started the new season playing for either Southend or Burnley, I was still a Sheffield United player. And after Howard's exit, we had a new temporary manager in charge… Nigel Spackman! I didn't really fancy my chances of getting a look in with Spackers as the gaffer, especially following one training ground incident.

I was rehabilitating while the players were warming up, with coach Willie Donachie at the helm and Spackers running behind the pack, making sure no one fell behind him. As they were nearing the pitch outside the pavilion, I stripped off and tied a five-pound weight round my cock and balls and started swinging on the crossbar like a circus chimp. Spackers wasn't too pleased, and fined me a tenner!

In the pre-season, chairman Mike McDonald had really pushed the boat out and brought club legend centre-forward Brian Deane back to the club, for £1.5m from Leeds. Do you remember me telling you that I never got decent wages, compared to those with agents? Brian had an agent, and he was reputed to be on £15,000 a week. You would never have known it though, as he was a great lad.

The Blades also brought in a football legend in the shape of Paul McGrath on a monthly contract, but one of the surprise great signings for me was the Greek lad Vassilios Borbokis. He made an instant impact and stole the show in the first game of the season at home to Sunderland, landing a great free kick on the head of Jan Aage Fjortoft for our first goal before timing a great run and smashing home himself for 2-0.

Deane got a hero's welcome, coming out to the strains of 'Deano, Deano' from the fans, and we really went at Sunderland. Spackers picked me in midfield and Deano's partnership with Norwegian international Fjortoft scared the life out of the Sunderland defence all game. I did enough to keep my place in the team and the United board had seen enough to offer Spackman the manager's job on a permanent basis, so a bit of an uneasy truce began between us.

I respected him for what he had achieved in the game, playing for some huge clubs in Chelsea, Liverpool and Rangers, but I don't think I was one of his favourites. He certainly wasn't my favourite manager to play under, but he had given me a chance, sadly because of a serious injury to Nicky Henry, and I was determined to take it.

We were playing some great football and didn't lose a game in the first 10 matches. We beat the eventual champions Nottingham Forest at home 1-0 with a brilliant goal from Gareth Taylor, but the standout match for me was when we went up to the north east and played Bryan Robson's Middlesbrough, another team that would go up automatically. We went toe-to-toe with them in front of 30,000 fans in their brilliant new stadium, the Riverside, and showed our mettle and our promotion qualities to come from behind and win 2-1.

We equalised with a quality goal from Deano, before Dane Whitehouse sent our fans bonkers with a close-range goal to send us into joint second at the time. My extra strength and training were really helping me and I was showing great form after my Achilles operation. I held my own against the likes of Paul Merson and Andy Townsend, nearly scored a cracker from long range and then missed a great chance from just outside the six-yard box!

Sheffield was a great city and an even better place to be if the Blades were playing well. During my time there, the city was bouncing and when we went out on the lash the atmosphere was fantastic. I remember playing in a live Friday night home game, which we won, and we'd arranged a lads' night out for after the game. After a great night around the buzzing pubs, about half a dozen of us ended up at a house party. It was a mad female United fan's house and I needed the toilet, so when I wandered upstairs to the bathroom and passed a bedroom with the door open I couldn't help but notice a Blades scarf hanging on the wall above the bed. Below it was the current season's team poster. From where I was standing it looked like a couple of the squad had their faces drawn on, so I walked in to take a closer look.

Certain players had their faces circled by a black felt tip pen and even in my drunken state, I realised why. I decided that, after having a piss, I would make a sharp exit. As I walked out of the bedroom I passed a woman on the tight landing and as I tried to squeeze past her, she pinned me against the wall. "I'm just going to the toilet," I mumbled. I made my sharp exit soon after and it's probably one of the only times I have been gutted not to be pencilled in – or in this case, felt tip penned out – on someone's teamsheet!

We kept up the pace through October and November and I even managed to get on the scoresheet with the only goal in an away game at Reading, sneaking in the six-yard box and getting a nosebleed to finish off a great move and win us the game. When we came back from 2-1 down to beat Stoke 3-2 in early December, we hadn't lost for another eight games. The club had made another major signing, bringing in free agent Dean Saunders, and things were looking good.

So, when we went to Norwich and I got substituted, in a game we went on to lose 2-1, I wasn't happy and confronted Spackman. "Why the fuck did you bring me off?"

"I didn't want you to get injured," he said. "I'm selling you... Bury want you."

Well, there is not much you can say to that is there? If one manager doesn't want you and another one does, especially if it's a club you already know and only 20 minutes from your house, you take it. It was the one last pay day and contract I needed. And, in hindsight, a better move than going to Burnley!

27

BACK TO THE OLD SCHOOL

December 1997 to July 1999

I loved my time at Sheffield United and left on really good terms with all the players and the fans. I have absolutely great memories, but it was a bit of a culture shock when I moved back to Bury. It was like going back in time. I had come from playing with Norwegians, Greeks and a Portuguese lad at United and the teamsheet for my first game back at Bury, against Crewe in December 1998, was full of lads from Manchester, Lancashire or Yorkshire.

I must have made a good impression on Stan Ternent when I saw him when I was worse for wear in Magaluf, because Bury paid £125,000 to sign me and I got another decent contract. It obviously helped that by this time the former Bury boss, my former gaffer and all-round top man, Sam Ellis, was Stan's assistant manager. Stan had done an amazing job at Bury since taking over from Mike Walsh in late 1995, and back-to-back promotions had already secured him legendary status at Gigg Lane. But by late December 1998, Bury were struggling at the bottom end of the First Division with more or less the same players that had brought them through the lower divisions.

Stan had put together a group of lads who would fight for each other all over the park and you could see why they had achieved back-to-back promotions straight away. My old teammate from Preston, Tony Ellis, was up front. Lenny Johnrose, who was on Rovers' books just as I was leaving them, was a key member to the success of the club. He was a no-nonsense midfield dynamo with a heart as big as a lion and a genuine tough tackler. Oh, he could jump too. Lenny is still a good friend and has needed all his competitive and will-to-win attributes since he was diagnosed with motor neurone disease in 2017. MND is a horrible, debilitating disease that affects the brain and nerves and since he was diagnosed, Lenny has worked closely with the MND Association to raise funds and awareness of the disease.

Other sportsmen including rugby legends Doddie Weir and Rob Burrow, are fighting it and so is Stephen Darby, a fellow ex-professional footballer. Friends of Lenny set up the Len Johnrose Trust in 2018 to help Len achieve his goal to raise awareness and to help him live as full a life as possible. Look up the definition of bravery and Lenny's name, along with these other sportsmen and anyone fighting MND, should come to mind. It really does put your life into perspective.

Another Bury teammate from that time, defender Andy Woodward, showed bravery of a different kind in 2016 when he went public about being sexually abused when he was a youth footballer at Crewe. By Andy coming forward, it helped many ex-professional footballers to also reveal that they had also been the victims of youth coaches and others involved in the professional game in the 1980s and the 90s. I was shocked when my Sheffield United mate, David White, had the courage to reveal he had been a victim, as had Dave Eatock, the ex-Newcastle United player who I managed when he played for Chorley.

I've also played against most of the lads who have since come forward and I can understand why they didn't feel able to speak to teammates or anyone else during their careers. Football in the 1980s and 1990s was a macho sport and although I'm not a big fan of the academy system nowadays, if there is one good thing that has come out of modern football and the 'new school' it is that safeguarding for children and young people in football has improved dramatically. More clubs also have mental health support in place.

As well as Tony, Lenny and Andy there were also couple of Yorkshire lads in Bury's team, in the shape of striker Tony Battersby from Doncaster and centre-half/forward Peter Swan. Goalkeeper Dean

Kiely was from Salford and this was no international team, but a group who would sweat blood and tears for the cause. Bury had gone nine games without a win when I went back there and without trying to cause any offence, it was a real culture shock at Gigg Lane after the great football I'd got used to playing at Bolton and Sheffield United.

Bruce Rioch showed me what playing football on the floor was all about, and that carried on at Sheffield United. Going back to the long ball game as a central midfielder just didn't fit with me. Stan, just like Bruce, had got his players drilled to play a certain style of football and in Lenny Johnrose and Nicky Daws, had fit lads in the middle of midfield who would just run forever. However, Stan's style wasn't as easy on the eye as Bruce's. The style was to just launch it into the corners, and the midfield lads would chase in behind to support. At that stage of my career, and after playing good football for a few years, I didn't enjoy it. It really was back to old school.

I remember one training session at Gigg Lane. Dean Kiely spotted me free in the middle of the park and threw it out to me. I got hold of it and passed it to someone in midfield. Stan stopped the play and told me not to play it through midfield, but to just 'help it on'.

"So what would happen in a game when I get the ball?" I asked.

"Fuckin' help it on!" he replied. "You don't control it in midfield, you hit the fuckin' corners with it!"

He then even sent me up in the stands to show me how it would work. As soon as the ball got anywhere near midfield, they just humped it on and then Lenny and Nicky would follow up the sides supporting the front men. It just meant that a lot of the time, the ball was either in the air or in the corners. Neck pain soon set in. It was like watching a match at Wimbledon in the late 1980s on Centre Court!

The games mirrored the training, so it really wasn't enjoyable. It had been effective in the lower divisions and had brought the club success, but it certainly wasn't pleasurable to play in, especially when you weren't winning. By the time we played Manchester City at Maine Road on Valentine's Day in 1998, we hadn't won for 14 games and were second from bottom and in real trouble. Unbelievably, City were only three points above us and it was a real relegation six-pointer.

It was the first time that Bury had played at Maine Road since 1966 and it was like the World Cup final for our fans. We sold out our allocation, with over 3,000 Shakers fans in the near-29,000 crowd. We knew that, if we could give them something to shout about, it would put the City players under pressure. Well, we only went and pulled it off! After going in all square at half-time, we scored early in the second half – and I managed to set the goal up with a superb cross. My memory's not that good, I just know it's a great cross because I've watched it back a few times.

We got a corner in the 51st minute and I swung it over. One of their players tried to clear it but it came straight back out to me. I controlled it first time and swung in a looping cross for Paul Butler, a lifelong City fan, to leap like a salmon and head it towards goal. A City player looked like it he'd got a touch on it, but nobody was taking it from Butler. It was as if Bury had scored in the FA Cup final and to be fair, for the fans, it felt like we had in some respects.

We more than deserved to win and didn't really have to hang on. City were really poor, and their fans weren't happy. This was the game when one of their fans ran over from the Kippax End and ripped up his season ticket in front of the home dugout. After the game, as we were still celebrating in the away changing rooms and our fans were setting off back to Bury for probably the best Valentine's night ever, the City fans gathered outside the main gates shouting for the manager's and chairman's head. Frank Clark, the manager, was gone within three days. Joe Royle came in, but even Joe couldn't stop City going down and a result that probably summed up City's season sparked ours into life.

I played in all of the next six games, bringing three wins and three draws, and even managed to score in a magnificent 3-1 away win against Birmingham. Unfortunately our unbeaten run came to an emphatic end when we were hammered 3-0 by leaders Nottingham Forest, but a 1-0 victory at home to Oxford United meant we were homing in on survival.

It was at this point that my relationship with Stan Ternent took a bit of a nose-dive. We played Sunderland up at the Stadium of Light, at that time a brand-new ground that they had moved into at the start of that season. What a stadium, and on that day there was over 37,000, mainly Mackems, in attendance.

Before the day turned sour, there was a funny moment early on in the game when I made a rash challenge on one of the Sunderland players and their fans made their feelings known to me. As I walked over to take a corner, the chant started: "You're just a big eared bastard." Before I could position the ball and get ready to take the corner, the chant was reverberating around what felt like the whole stadium and I just started pissing my sides.

I loved the banter so I tickled both my ears at the same time a couple of times before taking the corner, which got a loud cheer. Unfortunately, before half time I fucked up. We lost the ball in midfield and I didn't chase back, expecting the defence to clear it; they didn't, and Sunderland scored. I was ready to hold my hand up at half time, but Stan didn't give me chance and just ripped into me.

He called me this, that and the other and told me to get a shower as he was bringing me off. Maybe I should have just took it, but I gave him some back as I started to get ready for a shower. He moved on to someone else, but then, as I had just finished getting my strip off, Stan started going at me again.

By this time I'd had enough, so, with just a towel wrapped round me, I told him to fuck off. It was like waving a red flag to a bull. Stan came over to me and started giving me some more verbals; we were nearly nose to nose. Now I knew Stan had a bit of a reputation for sticking the head on people he was arguing with, so I thought about getting the first in. That's how heated the argument had become. Luckily Tony Ellis, who was sat down behind us, had spotted my cocked fist and pulled me down as others also intervened.

We ended up getting beat 2-1 and I must admit I expected to get dropped and fined. But I think the position we were in, and probably my great relationship with Sam Ellis, meant that I stayed in the squad for the next two games, a 2-2 home draw against Huddersfield and then another massive game in the North East against Middlesbrough.

Boro were absolutely flying at the time and it was a game that really amplified the difference in the styles of football.

There were 30,000-plus, in another new, shiny stadium, watching Paul Gascoigne, Paul Merson, Craig Hignett and the Italian forward Mario Branco, who were soon running riot and playing brilliant football. I had played against Middlesbrough earlier in the season for Sheffield United, and we'd beaten them. But that day, Bury were lucky to get nil. Our lads were just humping the ball on and running, and it just wasn't working. I said to Len Johnrose: "Fuckin' hell, Lenny... just stand still and I will give it to you."

"No," was the reply. "Hit the forwards and I'll go and get the ball off them."

I was still turning the air blue when Gazza, still an England international at the time before Glenn Hoddle infamously dropped him from that year's World Cup squad, turned to me. "Fuckin' hell Paddy," he said. "This must be hard work."

I agreed with him, telling him I was too old to be launching the ball into the corner. We both laughed and got on with the game. Boro won 4-0, with Branco scoring a hat-trick.

I think Stan was still fuming about me standing up to him in the changing room at Sunderland, and a 4-0 drubbing was a good excuse to drop me. I couldn't complain that much as we won our next home game against Bradford City, before losing both our next two, to Sheffield United and Ipswich. The table was so tight and we went into the last game of the season, away at QPR, still needing a point to be mathematically safe. Massive clubs such as Stoke, Manchester City and Portsmouth could all be relegated on the final day, which just showed the competitiveness of the division at that time. Stoke had a better goal difference than us so if they'd have won and we lost, we would have been relegated.

I was brought back into the team, but not before Stan pulled me to one side and said that if he felt that I wasn't putting in a shift he wouldn't hesitate to bring me off. That really pissed me off. I had really got on all right with Stan up to our confrontation. Of course I didn't like the style of football, but I understood that was the way he wanted to play and it had worked for Bury in the lower divisions, and to some extent against teams who had far much more money to spend. But me not putting a shift in? That really fucked me off.

Maybe he said it to wind me up, to ensure I played my part in securing the point necessary. Well, I didn't need winding up. As a senior player, I knew it was my responsibility to help ensure Bury stayed up and we duly did the business. Not knowing that results elsewhere would have meant we stayed up anyway, we won 1-0 against a team that boasted Vinnie Jones and an on-loan Neil "Razor" Ruddock in their line-up. Halfway through the first half, I put a corner to the far post, Chris Lucketti headed it back across the face of goal and fellow defender Gordon Armstrong nodded it home.

We ended up dominating the game and even finished above QPR. An article I found in the *Lancashire Telegraph* summed it up. "As more than 1,300 vociferous visiting fans will testify," the report read, "every single player fought like their lives depended on it, controlling the game from start to finish…"

Stan still decided it was time to show me who was boss, bringing me off five minutes from time before we went over to the fantastic travelling support after the full-time whistle. I was pleased for myself, as I'd been brought it to help keep Bury up, but I was even more pleased for the fans and stalwarts such as captain Lucketti, who sounds Italian but is actually from Littleborough near Rochdale, and Lenny Johnrose. Even by that point they had played, between them, more than 400 games for the club.

So, we managed to stay up, which was no mean feat when you consider our position in February, and the clubs and money we were up against. Manchester City and Stoke both ended up going down, along with Reading. Buoyed by survival, and excited to see how England fared in the World Cup in France, we went away for the summer. But before a ball was kicked, Ternent left to join Burnley and Neil Warnock, the ex-Oldham boss, was announced as our new manager.

I had heard a few stories about our new gaffer and returned for pre-season a little apprehensive, although our first meeting was very polite. He pulled me into his office and said: "I'm a Sheffield lad, a big United fan and my family think you are the dog's bollocks. I'm going to play you, not every game, but I'm going to play you in a three in midfield." That's grand, I said. He then told me that, sometime down the line, he was going to manage Sheffield United.

He was true to his word with that one. He just wasn't with his first promise about playing me. He left me on the bench all the fucking time! Warnock went on to become, and still is, without a doubt one of the best managers outside the Premiership, winning a record number promotions at different levels of the Football League. You don't do that without getting your players to buy into how you go about things. But most of the Bury players didn't buy into Warnock and his ways, and for some reason Warnock didn't buy into me.

I really didn't enjoy my time under him and when he kept putting me on the bench, our relationship quickly went downhill. Even then, he was Marmite. Anyone in football either seemed to love him or hate him, and any professional will tell you how it sucks the life out of you when you're taken up and down the country, only to sit on the bench and not play. We went to Norwich in one game, a week after he promised me I would play. I was on the bench again and spent the whole of the game standing against the hoardings away from the dugout. He still didn't put me on!

I'd had enough. To be fair we had a decent squad and the team had started well, but I was desperate to play. I was good mates with Tony Ellis, Andy Preece, Nigel Jemson and Steve Redmond. I told the lads that I was pissed off with the way Warnock was treating me and was going to tell him in no uncertain terms. So on Monday morning, I went to his door. He had two sheepdogs which he used to bring to the club and although one was okay, the other was a horrible bastard. When he was in his office Warnock used to tie the horrible bastard to the other side of his desk and have the nice one next to him. It meant that nobody would ever go in and sit down, as the mad one would be growling at you.

I knew the dog was going to be there so I wouldn't be able to get close to him. But as I went in, I noticed he had tied the bad one next to him and the good one wasn't bothered. So I was able to go right up to his desk and start ranting at him. "You tell me this, you tell me that," I said. "You take me down to Norwich and you put me on the bench and don't even bring me on. You are just taking the piss out of me. All I want you to be is straight with me. I'm fucked off."

"Now then Paddy," he said. "Don't be like that."

As he was trying to argue his corner, four faces popped up in the window behind him, so that only I could see them. I couldn't believe it. I was trying to have a ding-dong with the manager and Jemson, Preece, Ellis and Redmond were pulling faces in the window. I couldn't contain myself and just started laughing. Warnock thought my head had gone.

"Are you stupid or what?" he asked. I told him to fuck off and walked out of his office. Our relationship surprisingly didn't improve and in the few outings I did get, I picked up a few bookings through sheer frustration. Then, for the first time in my career, I tossed a game off. We were playing Stockport at home and during the second half, he put me on the graveyard shift on the left wing. *Fuck this,* I thought. I was that pissed off, I didn't cross the halfway line for the final 15 minutes. That was how pissed off I was with the whole set-up.

I was handed an escape route when I got sent on loan to Blackpool, who were in the Second Division at the time and managed by the future Northern Ireland boss, Nigel Worthington. His assistant was a great bloke called Mike Hennigan, who was proper old school and spoke to me. "Come and play your football," he said. "Get in their faces, you'll enjoy yourself and get a few games under your belt." There was no sign of playing a full game under Warnock, so I thought I might as well add another famous old Lancashire club to my playing CV.

I travelled in with Brett Ormerod and Barry Shuttleworth who both lived in Accrington, and played seven games on loan in all. I even managed a week away in Gran Canaria whilst I was at Bloomfield Road, although it didn't go down too well with my new temporary gaffer. In one of the games, I ended up with a yellow card which took me over the disciplinary threshold of five bookings and resulted in a week's ban. So I thought I'd try my luck with Nigel Worthington and nipped into his office the next day.

"Gaffer, I can't play at the weekend as I'm banned," I said. "I'm going to go away if that's okay?"

He was a bit distracted, and just looked up briefly. "Yeah, yeah, whatever," he said. Result, I thought. I booked a flight and had a lovely week away in the winter sun with the wife and kids. When I got back on the Monday morning, Mick sought me out and looked a bit sheepish. "Paddy, the gaffer wants to see you in his office," he said.

"Where the fuck have you been?" said Worthington, when I walked in.

"I've been to Gran Canaria with the wife and kids," I told him.

"Who the fuck said you could do that?"

"You did, boss. I came in last week and said I had a suspension and you said I could go away."

He knew he'd been had.

"I thought you were joking, taking the piss!" he said.

"Yeah, but I'm ready to go now, gaffer," I said, all suntanned up. "Get me playing Saturday, and I'll do the business for you."

He did, and I did. I played well against Man City in a 0-0 draw, travelling to the game from Darwen in a car full of lads who were City fans. But unfortunately that was my last game for Blackpool. Bury were in free fall by now, dropping down the league rapidly, and recalled me. Then the club held a supporters' question-and-answer session and I approached the end of the road at Bury.

I regret it now, and I know I shouldn't have done it. The Q&A was with the chairman and I questioned Warnock's management in front of the supporters. As a player it wasn't the brightest thing to do, but it did get me a £40,000 pay-off. Warnock pulled me straight in and said he wanted me away. I don't know if he thought I might have been staking a claim for his job, because I was coming to the end of my playing career, but either way my time at Bury was over.

"I want you out of here," he said. "I can't work with you, it's as simple as that." I remember thinking the feeling was very much mutual. "How much do you want? It'll be cash, it won't be all in a lump sum. It'll be weekly for 12 months, or as long as your contract is."

I worked it out and said I'd take £40,000, split up over the length of the contract. He just wanted rid of me and agreed, telling me to see the chairman Terry Robinson. I walked into Greengrass's office and he asked me how much I had settled for. I said £50,000, he said okay, and then I shit it. "No, it was £40,000," I said. No wonder they were in a financial mess.

Then just before deadline day Alvin Martin, the manager of Southend, who had just suffered a double relegation to the Third Division, asked me to come down with a view to signing for them. I met Alvin in the morning, and he resigned in the afternoon! Maybe it was something I said. But I definitely wasn't having much luck with managers.

Alan Little, the brother of ex-Villa boss Brian, took over and asked me to play for him with a view to signing for the next season. I played five games and did okay, but my knee was giving me real grief and had actually been aching for months. I went back up to Bolton to see the specialist at Beaumont Hospital again. I sat down with Mr. Banks, who knew about every single injury and operation I had ever had over the years and said that it was patella tendinitis, or swelling under the kneecap. He said it would clear up but it could potentially take one month, or six.

He asked me my thoughts and I told him I felt I'd done my bit. I was 34 at this point and I had been a professional footballer for 16 years. I was tired, both physically and mentally. He was really good and said that if I wanted his advice, I would be best to get on with my coaching career. And that was it. After one conversation my professional football career, the only thing I had ever wanted to do since I was a little lad, was over.

MEMORY LANE

August 29, 1981

Liverpool (Red Shirts)	Blackburn (Blue and White)
1. Ogrizovic	1. J. Butcher
2. Money	2. P. Greenwood
3. Kennedy A.	3. P. Williamson
4. Harper	4. S. Barker
5. Cohen	5. K. Walters
6. Sheedy	6. D. Byrom
7. Gayle	7. T. Burke
8. Halsall	8. P Comstive
9. Whelan	9. M. Graham
10. Rush	10. S Garner
11. Russell	11. M. Paterson
Sub: Savage	Sub: D. Finch

It's hard to admit to fans sometimes, because so many young lads and now girls dream of it, but in some ways being a professional footballer does end up just being a job. I went on to play well over 500 professional league and cup games in my own career, with many highs and a few lows along the way, and when you are in the middle of it, you often don't really take in who you are playing against. And you never think it will end.

At the end of that 1998/99 season, it did for me. Luckily, my proud parents and grandparents followed my football career right the way through, from when I was a schoolboy, to my first, very memorable taste of senior action for the Rovers in that friendly at 15, right the way through to my retirement all those years later.

They went to as many games as they could, collecting programmes, teamsheets and newspaper clippings from junior football up to the Premiership and then back down again.

They did so to cherish and remember what their son and grandson was achieving, to look back at further down the line. I never ever thought I would be able to use all the memories to get my brain in gear and that it would help me write this book.

The idea to write 'Old School' just came out of the blue. On a night out on the piss a few years ago, the laddish banter was flying and the football stories were in full flow.

There were tales from lads who had played at an amateur level, and my stories from playing right the way through from park football to the Premiership and right the way back down again. It struck me that, whatever level we had all played at, the one thing that bonded you together, through the highs and the lows, was the camaraderie, the banter and the piss-taking.

I can't actually remember which footy story I was telling at the time but, as everybody were laughing, it must have been half-decent. Then one of the lads asked me if I had ever thought about writing a book about my exploits in football. I admitted to him that I had been thinking about it for a little while.

Not to be pretentious, or think it would sell a load of copies and make any money, but because a few people had mentioned it before and I thought it would be good to get something down on paper; for me and my family. It could hopefully be a decent read for anyone who likes football.

So with a bit of prompting from a mate, the next day I decided to collect the boxes of scrapbooks and newspapers and the bin-liners full of programmes and started to have a read through. To see if there was enough interesting material, along with all the stories I had in my head, to put a book together.

The first scrapbook I opened had a number of teamsheets glued in, from the old Central League. One that immediately caught my eye was from a reserve game we played at Anfield. 'Central League Match, LIVERPOOL v BLACKBURN ROVERS, SATURDAY, 29th AUGUST, 1981,' it said at the top.

This reserve match took place just over three months after my 16th birthday, but it wouldn't have been any sweat for me. I had already played a number of games for the reserves at the end of the previous season. But, nearly 40 years later, looking back at the teamsheet really took me by surprise. Back in 1981, at barely 16 years old, did I really play against some of those players at Anfield?

Ignore for the moment that they managed to spell my name wrongly ... the first glance at the Liverpool team got me thinking instantly. Number three, Kennedy A? A few months earlier, Alan Kennedy had scored the winning goal for Liverpool in the European Cup final in Paris, to beat Real Madrid. Google confirmed it was on May 27, 1981 ... three days after my 16th birthday. Unbelievably, he went on to score the winning penalty when Liverpool won the European Cup again in 1984, against Roma.

For the next couple of hours I went barmy on Google, with a smile on my face, and looking through both teams brought back some memories. Anyone else in that Liverpool reserve team worth a mention?

The No.10, Rush? Ian Rush went on to be Liverpool's all-time record scorer, finishing up with five league titles, five League Cup winners' medals, three Charity Shields and two European Cups. Oh, and we may as well throw in the fact that he was the European Golden Boot winner one season as well, and one of Wales' greatest footballers. I was on the same pitch as a future great.

I soon spotted another player who went on to be a Liverpool legend and one of my future managers: No.9, Whelan. The great Ronnie Whelan; in his second season as a Liverpool player, up against a skinny kid from Darwen. This was real 'Old School' football, with the reserves made up of senior players returning from injury and young lads trying to make their way into the first-team professional ranks. I recognised the names of the other 10 players on Liverpool's teamsheet that day but, between them, they only played less than 70 times for the Reds' first-team. A couple never made a first-team appearance at all and their No.6 on the day, Kevin Sheedy, only played three times for Liverpool before going on to be a legend at their biggest rivals, Everton.

Another lad who went on to make his name for the blue side of Merseyside was the No.4 that day, Alan Harper. Two league winners' medals, an FA Cup and a UEFA Cup Winners' Cup proved what a great squad player Harper became for Everton, and what a brilliant and shrewd manager the great Howard Kendall was. A couple of seasons after the Anfield game I came up against Harper in a reserve game at Goodison Park. After a feisty coming-together, he said to me: "When I left my house this morning, I got my Mercedes out of the garage. What do you drive?" I'm sure we'd laugh about it now, but I didn't give him an answer. Mainly because I was driving a Vauxhall Chevette at the time!

I think I could go on and on with the Liverpool team on that day but will finish off with two players; firstly the No.1, Steve Ogrizovic. In five years at Anfield he made only four league appearances but then went on to play against me and at a first team level in a record 601 games in all competitions for Coventry City, helping them win the FA Cup in 1987. And, after almost 40 years, I remember the reserve game against Liverpool because of Howard Gayle, who was the first black player to play for the Reds.

Our right-back Paul Greenwood broke a leg in a tackle with Howard, who became a great teammate of mine at Rovers six years later. In the old school, when the football world was a little smaller, instances such as rival players becoming teammates and older players becoming your manager, such as Ronnie Whelan, happened much more frequently than they do now. In fact, I went on to play against or with all the Liverpool side that day, as a first teamer at different clubs.

I'd love to say that even against such a strong team, with so much experience and young talent at the time in their ranks, that we still gave Liverpool a great game that day. Unfortunately, even with Simon Garner, who would eventually become Rovers' all-time top scorer, and my young midfield mate Simon Barker in the team, we didn't! My Google search showed that the final score was 6-0 to Liverpool, with Rush scoring two and Whelan, Cohen, Gayle and Sheedy bagging a goal each.

As a very young 16-year-old, I also never thought that, just over 11 years later, in January 1993, I'd be playing against Liverpool at Anfield again … and this time as captain of Bolton Wanderers. Liverpool were the FA Cup holders and this was a third-round cup replay, but the outcome was very different result-wise!

The scrapbooks, programmes and newspaper clippings definitely helped me with many more trips down memory lane. But back in 1999, at the end of my professional career, I definitely wasn't prepared for the next phase of my life …

THE REAL WORLD

August 1999 to present day

They say that life is a rollercoaster and for the next 10 years after I hung up my professional boots, it certainly was. I'd like to say I had a plan B for when my football career ended, but like many professional footballers of that era, I didn't. To be fair, probably influenced by how much Bruce Rioch had brought my game on, I had thought about coaching and management during my time at Bolton and also started my landscape gardening business then. I had taken on board Rioch's encouragement to all his players to have something in place following retirement, whether it be in football or not. So, in addition to getting on the wheelbarrow, I had started my coaching courses and took my UEFA B licence. But as my career progressed and I went from earning half decent money to very good money, I put everything on the back burner and just started to enjoy the footballer's lifestyle more and more. You really do think it's never going to end.

But I was in the real world now and the next step, the UEFA A Licence, was the top coaching qualification in Europe. After retiring officially as a player, I was keen to get it. But it could wait. Hanging up my boots also meant that I could go out on the piss with the lads back home in Darwen, and that's exactly what I did. Things had unfortunately not been right with me and Lindsey for a long time, and I probably didn't help to save the marriage too much by going on the lash for the next couple of years.

I spent my first summer without a club at home with Lindsey and the kids and going down the pub more often with the lads. As the new season was approaching I wasn't sure what I was going to do as my appetite for playing full-time had gone. My knee injury had improved and I knew I could still get around the pitch, but only part time. My priority was to pass my UEFA A Licence, but I needed a club who would allow me to take a few coaching sessions. Then I received a phone call from my old Preston teammate David Miller, asking if I fancied playing for Leigh RMI.

Leigh were in the UniBond League at the time but had genuine aspirations to get promoted to the Conference and when I told David I was interested, the manager Steve Waywell called me. We met up at his house and I agreed to sign, but only if I could train when my knee was okay. Steve agreed and my time playing in non-league began. David Felgate, the former Bolton goalkeeper, was in goal and my old adversary Mark Ward, from that famous FA Cup win at Everton, played in midfield with me.

Once the season started, I also decided that instead of just going to watch the same lads I used to play with in the alleys when I was a little kid play Sunday League football, I would get playing with them again! It had been 20 years since I experienced the smell of Deep Heat in the communal changing rooms at Blacksnape, where the Donaldson brothers and Co. threatened to end my career before it started. Now it was me Andy, Howie, Eggy, Matt Atkinson and a few other old timers telling a few tales about the night before. The smell was just the same too. Sweat, farts and, if you weren't looking, the smell of sex wafting under your nose. Ah, the memories just came flooding back.

My football training sessions may have decreased dramatically but the drinking sessions had increased and the ones that followed were even better than the Sunday morning games. On returning to the Alec pub, in Darwen, we would be well fed and watered, the stories began and the session carried on long into the evening. Initially I only intended having a few weeks on the beer with the lads. But the weeks soon became months, and the Sunday sessions became a regular occurrence, leading to bigger and better sessions. Looking back I know now it was wrong, and not fair on Lindsey and the kids. Without realising it, my life was spiralling out of control.

I managed to get some coaching work and practice at Bolton Wanderers' academy before, halfway through the season, I was approached to do some co-commentary games on the Wanderers' games by *Tower FM*, an independent radio station that covered the Bolton and Bury area. It meant the end of my first stint at Leigh RMI. Steve Waywell was great about it, even though I'd been part of a winning team – by the end of a season I was probably a distant memory as Leigh won promotion to the Conference.

I really enjoyed it on the radio, and a lot of people said I was a natural. Well, they said I had a face for radio anyway. The standout game for me as a co-commentator, and no doubt any Bolton fan, was the 2001 play-off final, when Sam Allardyce's Wanderers came out 3-0 winners against Preston and my old PNE teammate David Moyes to land the Whites a promotion said to be worth around £30 million.

It had been great to play with Sam at the back end of his career so I was really pleased for him knowing what it would mean to him – like me, he had played over 200 games for Bolton. What he went on to achieve at the Wanderers in the Premiership years was nothing less than remarkable and I know a few of my Bolton fan mates got a few European trips out of his success. A top manager and top bloke. From my very enjoyable time playing there, I have also got a soft spot for PNE and hope one day to go and watch a game there when they are in the Premiership.

The atmosphere around the Millennium Stadium before kick-off of that play-off final was electric. It was loud, but it was also very friendly with both sets of fans giving each other a bit of stick and the craic was fierce. But opposition fans started to move closer and closer. I thought they were goading each other, and my first thoughts from afar were: "Here we go, it's going to kick off."

However, as they got closer and closer to each other, the chant of: "Oh Frankie, Frankie ... Frankie, Frankie, Frankie, Frankie Worthington," became clearer and clearer and louder and louder. And then there he was, the legend himself, in the middle of thousands of fans chanting his name. I had grown up watching Frank and was lucky enough to play a couple of games with and against him. Frank was in his late thirties by the time I played with him and he wasn't running around that much, but his touch was still first class. RIP Frank – what a player!

Two other legends at that game who are no longer with us were Nat Lofthouse and Tom Finney. Both one-club players and unbelievable ambassadors for two clubs I feel honoured to have played for.

***

The following season, Steve Waywell had seen enough of me in my brief spell to want me to re-sign for Leigh but John Coleman, the manager of Accrington Stanley, approached me to play in the Uni-Bond Premier Division. It was on my doorstep so I thought: "Why not?"

They had just been promoted and my time at Accy was very enjoyable, even if it was also very brief and ended acrimoniously! Coley and Jimmy Bell, his assistant manager, worked well together and still do. When I was there the squad was mainly made up of Scousers. They were a great bunch, and the banter was brilliant.

My initiation was on the team coach on the way home from a game. The coach wasn't cheap so the chairman, Eric Whalley, invited the supporters on board for a few quid. So, with the beer flowing and players, staff and supporters waiting with bated breath, I began to belt out *Bad, Bad Leroy Brown* by Frank Sinatra. Fortunately, it wasn't that bad.

Eric, God rest his soul, was as straight talking as they come, and Stanley was his club. On one frosty Saturday afternoon in February, I arrived at the Crown Ground expecting the game to be called off. I was walking on the pitch, thinking it was dangerous and shouldn't be played, but I was informed it was on. I walked over to the touchline and questioned the decision to a director, before Eric appeared out of nowhere. "Patterson, you little cunt," he said, in his well-known and high-pitched voice. "The game's on. Fuck off out of my club now. Go on, fuck off."

I had a go back and made for my car, but Coley calmed the situation and I played. Nothing more was said, but when I arrived for the home game on the following Tuesday Coley put me on the bench! Enough said. After all, it was Eric's club.

I then signed for Rossendale United. I knew a couple of lads who played for them, Jerome Fitzgerald and Paddy Lauber, great lads, and the manager Jim McCluskie let me take a few training sessions. The Rossendale squad were a great bunch but because of a lack of facilities and the part-time set-up, we only trained one night a week. On one occasion Jim asked me to put on an attack v defence session with the emphasis on attack, and in particular crosses. Everything was going to plan and running smoothly until I asked Paddy to receive the ball, push it out of his feet and whip a ball across the six-yard box taking two touches. He took three touches to deliver the cross.

"Two touches Paddy," I said.

"That's what I did," he replied. I told him he'd taken three. "Did I?" he asked.

"Okay, let's do it again."

Well, he must have had five goes at it but just couldn't do it. I showed him a few times, but it wasn't clicking. Don't get me wrong, Paddy was a talented player but not the brightest. By now the lads were in bits, pissing their pants at Paddy's efforts. This was my first session as a coach where a player couldn't do what I was asking of him. It was a test of my coaching skills. What should I do? Well, on this occasion I told him to go and play centre midfield as he was fucking my session up. Not something I would do on the coaching course, but when you're training and you only have an hour, there's no time!

I really enjoyed my time at Rossendale with Jim and the Rossy lads, but I was looking to get a job coaching. Then, one Sunday morning, I was reading the *Non-League Paper* and came across an article on Scarborough FC. To my surprise the manager was the old Sheffield United youth team and former first-team caretaker boss Russell Slade, and he was looking for an experienced midfield player. After a quick phone call, I was invited to Scarborough to take part in a friendly so he could have a look and see if I could still get about the field. He wasn't disappointed and I was appointed player/ coach.

I was obviously extremely chuffed to be going full-time again in the Conference, but Scarborough was a pain in the arse to get to. The positive far outweighed the negative though, as I was back playing at a decent level and more importantly, coaching. Because of the distance from Darwen to Scarborough, I stayed in digs three nights a week and it was probably the straw that broke the camel's back with my marriage. After training, when the lads had gone home, me and Sladey got a bit bored, so he started taking me to the Laughton's pub in the town centre. Well, it soon became a regular event and before long we became regulars, along with a great bunch of folk that we named "the walk of life".

Teachers, bankers, ground workers, decorators, builders, lawyers… it really was a mix of people from every walk of life. Turbo was nicknamed so because he could knock a gallon back in a matter of minutes. The decorator had a lad working for him that he called "Gimp" and used to throw him around the pub. It was crazy, but fucking funny. Every day there was happy hour, from five o'clock until eight. We couldn't afford not to drink there.

That probably was another factor in the fact that my personal life was suffering. By the start of the second season my dad had passed away, my marriage was over, and I'd moved out of the family home. I know it takes two to tango, but in my head I wrongly blamed Lindsey for the state of our finances when we were both at fault. With me being away during the week and then boozing Saturday night and Sunday, it wasn't good for Jade and Scott to see us arguing all the time. So we called it a day.

To be fair though, I'm not the only professional footballer to go off the rails, get divorced and face bankruptcy, as I soon would. It was rife then and still seems to be now. I've seen some stats saying 75 per cent of ex-professional players are divorced by the time they are 50 and Alan Gernon's 2016 book *Retired: What Happens to Footballers When the Game's Up* revealed that a third of footballers will be divorced within a year of retirement.

Two out of five Premiership footballers face bankruptcy within five years of retiring – even though, at that time, they were earning an average of over £40,000 a week. I'm not after sympathy here, I'm just showing you how it is. Just think about the lads at the bottom end of the professional ladder. It really is no wonder that mental health issues are becoming more and more prevalent in our beautiful game.

On the pitch things were going well and the supporters were coming through the turnstiles in anticipation we would get promotion back to the Football League. But the finances were dire and the chairman Malcolm Reynolds had his hands tied, unable to add that little bit that we needed for the final push.

I only played in emergencies and was really enjoying coaching, getting my A Licence whilst I was at Scarborough following two weeks down at Lilleshall, the old FA headquarters. What a fucking farce that was, by the way. Talk about certain ex-players getting priority. On arrival there I was given a key to my room and asked to meet up with all the attendees in the conference room. There were many ex-pros taking part along with soldiers, teachers, and a Japanese goalkeeper who couldn't speak English!

Over the next two weeks we would prepare our sessions which we would be marked on. For example, one of my sessions was attacking down the flanks. I think you can guess who I got lumbered with, compared to a number of ex-First Division and Premiership players who always seemed to be in the same group? Yes, you guessed it... the school teacher and the Japanese goalkeeper. For the 'attacking down the flanks' session, I would pass it to an opposing player who would take a tame shot at the goalkeeper. The drill was that the goalkeeper would then collect the ball and look to start an attack down the flank by throwing it out to the full-back.

The only problem was that the Japanese 'keeper couldn't understand what I was saying, which really stressed me out. The course had cost £2,000 and I could see it going up in smoke if this carried on. I then put the teacher in goal but he couldn't catch it, letting the first shot go through his hands before a second went under his body and again into the goal. For fuck's sake, I thought. I was struggling to keep calm and smashed a ball off the pitch in frustration. The session eventually got going, but I knew my reaction could have cost me my A Licence.

My tutor/coach was Geoff Pike, the ex-West Ham legend. Geoff was great and took me to one side and gave me a little bit of advice.

Even so, I needed to speak to the course director to let him know my feelings. He reassured me and said he understood how I was feeling. The following days went far better and at the end of the fortnight I passed with distinction. Job done.

Unfortunately, my time at Scarborough came to an abrupt and unexpected end on a Monday morning in November 2002, following a respectable 0-0 draw against Cambridge in the FA Cup. On the Friday before the game, we did our usual morning session, had lunch, went round a few pubs then headed for Laughton's. Normal service resumed and before we knew it, it was 8pm. As per usual Russ took this as home time but I decided to carry on as I was having such a good craic with the 'walk of life' crew.

That night, I did something I had never done before, and will never do again. I was offered some sticky substance wrapped in foil. Turbo told me it would give me a buzz and would wear off within an hour or so. I know it was a stupid thing to do but at the time I thought: "Fuck it." The night was getting better and better, and I felt in full control. It went on until it was coming light, when I was sat in Turbo's flat with Jimmy the ground worker talking shite.

I hadn't had a wink of sleep but I didn't feel tired at all, and I couldn't understand why. I left the flat and set off to my digs, but in my confused state I couldn't find my car. I had no idea where I'd parked it up the day before. The time was now nearing noon and by this point I was feeling completely knackered. I walked to all the pubs that we usually went in until I found my Vauxhall Vectra parked up at the rear of a pub in town. It was about 12.30pm and I decided to have a hair of the dog.

How I got to the ground is beyond me, because I was probably still hammered. I remember falling asleep in the car on the club car park before being woken up by a supporter. I thought I had better nip in the club bar for a slurp before I went to the changing rooms and prepared to take the lads for the warm-up. I can't remember much in the changing rooms, but certain parts of my warm-up I can. According to the lads I was acting like I'd been on whizz all night! I can honestly say I'd never tried it before, and I've never touched it since. Why I took it to this day I'll never know, and I regret it.

I certainly regretted it on the Monday morning when I turned into the car park and the chairman was waiting for me. "Paddy, come in to my office," he said. I thought I might get a fine for being drunk at the game, but I didn't expect to hear what he said next.

"You're fired."

"Why?" I asked, genuinely shocked.

"Because I saw you staggering into the pub at 12.30pm on Saturday and drinking whiskey in the bar before the game. To put the icing on the cake, your warm-up was like nothing I've ever seen in my life. Alternatively, you can resign and we'll leave it at that." So that was that.

I was known as an honest player, so I have to be honest and say my managerial career was average to say the least. But it had its good days. At the end of November 2001, I went straight from Scarborough back to Leigh RMI as Steve Waywell's assistant manager and within two months, I was made manager after Steve resigned. I brought in ex-Bolton legend Peter Nicolson as my unofficial number two as the finances were dire and we couldn't afford an official assistant manager. Peter is a great bloke with so much experience and we've kept in touch, still regularly playing golf together. Against the odds I kept Leigh in the Conference following a tremendous away win at Kettering.

Then for the following season I was not only the football manager, but also the commercial manager to save money. I also had my budget cut in half, to £2,500 a week. I lasted a few games then, after a 4-1 home defeat by Martin Allen's Barnet, I called it a day. The average budget at Conference level was about £10,000. Chorley was next on my managerial list and that didn't end well. Looking back, I know now I was expecting too much from part-time players and found it very frustrating.

Then, in 2006, Scarborough's chairman Malcolm Reynolds handed me an olive branch and the manager's job. However, the club were once again strapped for cash and had been relegated from the Conference to the Conference North. I signed ex-PNE legend Lee Cartwright, who was still phenomenally fit in his mid-thirties and a superb bloke who is liked by everyone. He ended up playing 41 games that season and won the player of the year award.

Jamie Vermiglio was my second acquisition from Lancashire. He played for me when I managed Chorley and wanted to do everyone's job on the park. His enthusiasm and tenacity stood out and I persuaded him to play a holding role in front of the back four, which he did excellently – even if our captain and first team coach, Denny Ingram, had to put the reins on him from time to time. Jamie was another great lad, and what he later achieved at Chorley FC, including that great run to the fourth round of the FA Cup in the 2020/21 season, did not surprise me at all.

I also signed Chris Thompson, who's from Warrington and played for me at Chorley. He was a centre-forward with bags of ability and could have played higher if he could have done the easy stuff well. I was the chauffeur and the provider of chocolate bars for the 90-minute trip to Scarborough, which we did three times a week. On one occasion we were on our way across when we noticed a bloke acting suspiciously. He was carrying a bag but then threw it into the bushes and scarpered. The lads insisted I pulled over so they could retrieve the bag. Once it was in the car, I set off before Jamie began tentatively emptying the contents. The first thing that spilled out was a big dildo, followed by another. There were also loads of porno magazines in the bag. "Fucking hell," I thought. No wonder the bloke scarpered.

Once the lads had read most of the porn mags – just joking – we decided to stitch the rest of the team up. We sneaked the contents of the bag into the changing room and hid the magazines and dildos in all the different team members' bags. I don't remember who got the dildos but they didn't come back and no one owned up to having them. The lads took the prank well even though a couple got a good bollocking from their partners.

We had a great season considering the very limited finances, but had also started the season with a 10-point deduction. Without that we would have finished mid-table, but we were relegated and the following day I got the call. "Paddy, we can't afford your wages next season, so we are letting you go." That's how it went in non-league football. Then my hometown team, Darwen, came knocking. That didn't last long either. I felt the chairman was a clown who was clueless about football. Enough said.

Back in 2007 I became bankrupt and it hit the headlines in the local papers. Ironically, I was taking a few quid out of the cash machine in Darwen town centre after returning from a holiday. There is a hair-dresser's opposite the bank where I knew a couple of the girls. For some reason I turned round to see them looking at me and pointing to the paper shop next door to the bank. I didn't know what they were pointing at until I turned and noticed the billboard about six feet from me. It read: "EX ROVERS PLAYER MARK PATTERSON DECLARED BANKRUPT."

Fuck me, it felt like the eyes were on me from all angles. For about five seconds I didn't know where to turn until I composed myself, turned back round to the girls in the shop, shrugged my shoulders and made for my car. Less than a decade earlier I had been earning over £100,000 a year, and had been for a few seasons on the trot. I was gutted at the situation, but what can you do? Me and Lindsey had unfortunately been living beyond our means for a number of years and it caught up with us.

A big house meant a big mortgage and the interest rates were sky high in the 1990s. Putting an extension on it added to the debt and buying a few properties in that climate hadn't worked as well. I also felt like I had shares in Disneyworld, Florida. Not quite, but when I once said to Jade that I had enjoyed our three visits to see Mickey Mouse, she reminded me that we had actually been at least five times. Perhaps I should have bought a property there. We also paid for Jade to go to a private school in a posh part of Blackburn, Westholme. But luckily, they told us at a parents' evening that Jade was too disruptive and it would be best if we took her out, so that actually saved us a bob or two as the Patterson rebellious streak came out at an early age. Just joking, Jade.

The flash BMW I bought on the never-never didn't help, nor did Lindsey somehow becoming friends with Kenny Dalglish's wife and having shopping trips to Southport every weekend. The kids wore nothing but designer gear and being a boy and a girl, there was no hand-me-downs like I got growing up. Now Kenny's wife could af-ford to do it, but everything we did was going on the credit cards. So once the football contracts finished … so were we. Remember me saying you don't think it will ever end? Well, it has to eventually. That's life and there are no hard feelings. Me and Lindsey got two great kids out of it and still speak now.

A few months after leaving Darwen I headed down at Hednesford, as assistant manager to my old Sheffield United mucker Phil Starbuck, but that didn't last long. On one of the match days, for the craic, I decided to change our pre-match warm-up routine. At 2.15pm the players made their way on to the pitch. I hung back and then ran onto the pitch, with just my boxer shorts and boots on, to a cheer from the crowd and the lads cracking their sides. I then did some press-ups and sit-ups before sprinting back down the tunnel and returning in my kit. Everyone found it funny, except for the chairman and that was the beginning of the end. Some folk just don't have a sense of humour!

I realised I wasn't suited to football management and I decided that if were to get back in the game, it would be as a coach. This will possibly put a few football team supporters' minds at rest, as three of the teams I managed went out of business: Scarborough, Leigh and Darwen! I was at that low point but I decided instead of labouring for mates to earn extra dosh I would concentrate on my landscaping business, which I had recently set up again. I'm as tenacious around grafting with the tools as I was playing football, so I got my head down and soon started to build the business up until I was lured back into the game, when John Coleman and Jimmy Bell took Accrington back into the Football League.

They were on the lookout for a first-team coach, and I was ready to give it a go again and reintroduce myself to the game. As well as continuing with my business I worked with the first team on a voluntary basis and the next 18 months were amazing. The everyday banter amongst the lads took me back to my playing days. A great bunch of lads with a great manager in Coley and coach Jimmy. What a fantastic management team they have been. They would go on to achieve promotion to League One with Stanley and I'm sure they will get an opportunity to manage a big club one day. They definitely deserve it.

Following my time at Stanley, I returned to working full-time on my landscaping business and met Andrea, now my wife, in 2011. Andrea has been with me through thick and thin and we married in 2014. I can honestly say I have no interest in Premier League football but always look out for all the teams I used to play for, especially the Rovers of course. But when Man City are on television, I don't have a choice – my step daughter Lois is City-mad. She knows more Premier League players than I do.

I'm a big Frank Sinatra fan so when I look back over my football career, I think to myself: "Have I got any regrets?" Well yes, but too few to mention. Go on then, I'll mention a few. I wish I could have played at Wembley for more than 20 minutes, and won a few more trophies. But do you know what? I didn't do too badly. I've shared a changing room with Ossie Ardiles and some other brilliant teammates, many who are still friends now. I've played against some football greats including Hagi, Kevin Keegan, Paul Gascoigne, Dennis Bergkamp, Roy Keane, Alan Shearer, David Ginola and many, many more. I played for some of English football's proudest clubs, at the very highest level, and have memories that will last a lifetime.

Off the pitch, I wish I'd have got myself a football agent before it was too late and a financial advisor might have come in handy. But hindsight's a wonderful thing. When I started playing the beautiful game in the back streets of Darwen, practising against that mill wall with the support of my mum and dad, I didn't dream of becoming rich. I dreamt of becoming a professional footballer. So in that respect, job done.

People often say to me: "Just think if you were 10 years younger, you could be a millionaire now." To be fair they might be right, but I wouldn't change a thing. The good times along with the bad. As Ol' Blue Eyes himself said… "That's life."

ACKNOWLEDGEMENTS

To become a professional footballer was my dream from as far back as I can remember. To play for my hometown club, Blackburn Rovers, was the icing on the cake. There were many ups and a few downs over my 19 years and there are a few people I would like to say thank you to.

First and foremost, Mum and Dad. For the support you gave me from being that six-year-old boy, smashing the Striker football against the mill wall. For the encouragement you gave me when standing on the touchline on Avondale footy pitch and driving me all over Lancashire to the games. For the discipline which eventually stood me in good stead. And for allowing me to watch *Sportsnight* whenever there was a midweek game on TV. I love you both.

To Fred O'Donaghue, the scout that gave me the opportunity at Rovers. To Alan Bradshaw, Tommy Haworth and Jim Furnell, thanks for keeping me under control when I tried to go off the rails. Thank you to Bobby Saxton, who gave me my first professional contract and my debut for Rovers. To Don MacKay for selling me to Preston North End, and to John McGrath at Preston for resurrecting my career.

Bruce Rioch and Colin Todd for educating me during the mid-1990s when the game was changing and the opportunity to play in the Premiership. Thanks Bruce, for making me captain of Bolton, and to Howard Kendall for introducing me to red wine and Cuban cigars along with having the privilege of captaining the mighty Blades.

To Kevin O'Hara for encouraging me to do the book. You've done a great job, Kev; thanks mate. Also thanks to Danny Hall and our publisher, Vertical Editions.

To Eggy – no words mate. Thanks!

My lovely wife, Andrea, and stepdaughter Lois. Married for six years, together for 10. I love you both. Finally, to my two children, Jade and Scott. I love you two crazy kids. And I'm proud to be your old man.

ABOUT THE AUTHORS

Mark Patterson is a former professional footballer who made almost 500 league appearances in the 1980s and 1990s. He then had a stint in coaching and management, before taking a break to focus on setting up his landscape gardening business. Mark is married with a football-loving step-daughter, and a grown-up son and daughter.

Co-author Kevin O'Hara is a partnership development manager for the NHS by day, and a writer by night. He wrote a football-based novel in the early 2000s and is happily married with two daughters, aged 16 and 20. A Bolton Wanderers fan, Kevin watched Mark's most successful spell as a player from the stands when Mark helped Bolton rise from the third tier of English football into the Premiership.

Mark was Bolton's captain on a famous night at Anfield when the Second Division side knocked out the FA Cup holders. Kevin was at the game. They met a number of years ago through a mutual friend and Kevin convinced Mark to write his book after hearing a number of very funny stories of Mark's time in football. The rest, as they say, is history...